SAINTS AT WAR IN THE PHILIPPINES

SAINTS AT WAR IN THE PHILIPPINES

Latter-day Saints in WWII Prison Camps

MICHAEL H. HYER

Published by the Religious Studies Center, Brigham Young University, Provo, Utah, in cooperation with Deseret Book Company, Salt Lake City, Utah. Visit us at rsc.byu.edu.

© 2021 by Brigham Young University. All rights reserved.
Printed in the United States of America by Sheridan Books, Inc.

DESERET BOOK is a registered trademark of Deseret Book Company.
Visit us at DeseretBook.com.

Any uses of this material beyond those allowed by the exemptions in US copyright law, such as section 107, "Fair Use," and section 108, "Library Copying," require the written permission of the publisher, Religious Studies Center, 185 HGB, Brigham Young University, Provo, UT 84602. The views expressed herein are the responsibility of the authors and do not necessarily represent the position of Brigham Young University or the Religious Studies Center.

Cover and interior design by Carmen Durland Cole

ISBN: 978-1-9503-0413-4

Library of Congress Cataloging-in-Publication Data
Names: Hyer, Michael H. (Michael Harold), 1950- author.
Title: Saints at war in the Philippines : Latter-day Saints in WWII prison camps / Michael H. Hyer.
Description: Provo, Utah : Religious Studies Center, Brigham Young University, [2021] | Includes bibliographical references and index. | Summary: "Members of The Church of Jesus Christ of Latter-day Saints were among US soldiers in World War II who endured the atrocities of the Bataan Death March in the Philippines and the brutality of Japanese POW camps. This is the story, largely told through their personal accounts, of a group of twenty-nine Latter-day Saint POWs in the Philippines, the events that brought them together to form an informal branch of the Church in an infamous POW camp, a remarkable event in the history of the Church, and the events that would later pull them apart, twelve to their liberation and seventeen to their death"—Provided by publisher.
Identifiers: LCCN 2021015494 | ISBN 9781950304134 (hardcover)
Subjects: LCSH: Prisoners of war—Philippines—Biography. | Church of Jesus Christ of Latter-day Saints—Biography. | Bataan Death March, Philippines, 1942. | World War, 1939-1945—Philippines—Biography. | Mormons—Biography. | Philippines—History—Japanese occupation, 1942–1945—Biography. | LCGFT: Biographies.
Classification: LCC D805.P6 H947 2021 | DDC 940.54/7252092893599—dc23
LC record available at https://lccn.loc.gov/2021015494

TO RUBY SPILSBURY BROWN
AND ALL FAITHFUL RECORDERS OF FAMILY HISTORIES

CONTENTS

ix	Maps
xi	Preface
xiii	Introduction
1	Chapter 1: An Ancestral Gift
5	Chapter 2: You're in the Army Now
21	Chapter 3: What in the World Was Going On?
27	Chapter 4: The Easy Life in the Philippines
35	Chapter 5: Everything Changes
41	Chapter 6: Heroes
45	Chapter 7: The Abandoned Boys of Bataan
51	Chapter 8: The Last Line at Cabcaben
57	Chapter 9: The Captors
63	Chapter 10: The "Hike"
69	Chapter 11: Small Miracles
75	Chapter 12: Death Camps
83	Chapter 13: Del Monte

CONTENTS

91	Chapter 14: Hotel Malaybalay
99	Chapter 15: Back Home
107	Chapter 16: A Place Where a Ranch Boy May Have a Chance
117	Chapter 17: "Where Two or Three Are Gathered Together"
127	Chapter 18: The Unforgettable Christmas of 1942
135	Chapter 19: Escape and Its Consequences
139	Chapter 20: What the World (and George and Ruby) Now Knew
145	Chapter 21: The Scattering
149	Chapter 22: Hell and Magic
155	Chapter 23: Leaving the Philippines
165	Chapter 24: Lasang and the Hope of August 17, 1944
169	Chapter 25: *Shinyo Maru*
181	Chapter 26: Bilibid
189	Chapter 27: The Special Hell of the *Oryoku Maru*
201	Chapter 28: Japan
213	Chapter 29: Liberation
219	Chapter 30: Survivors
231	Epilogue: Those Who Did Not Come Home
245	Afterword: Hate and Forgiveness
251	Acknowledgments
253	Bibliography
263	Index
271	About the Author

MAPS

20   Political Map of the Far East in 1939
25   Luzon and Mindanao Islands in the Philippines
172   Voyage of the *Shinyo Maru*

PREFACE

In 2011 *BYU Studies* published an article by David L. Clark and Bart J. Kowallis entitled "The Fate of the Davao Penal Colony #502 'Branch' of the LDS Church, 1944."[1] It included several references to my uncle First Lieutenant George Robin (Bobby) Brown. I had not known this uncle but had a vague understanding that he had died in World War II. The article also discussed Brown's involvement in a group of members of The Church of Jesus Christ of Latter-day Saints that prisoners of war (POWs) had organized in a Japanese POW camp. When I mentioned the article to my wife, Evie, she suggested a couple of nonfiction books about Allied POWs in the Philippines—*Escape from Davao*, by John D. Lukacs, and *Ghost Soldiers*, by Hampton Sides—that she had recently read. The *BYU Studies* article referenced many of the same places and events described in those books.

With that observation, I undertook to track this uncle's experiences as a soldier and POW by overlaying the few basic facts known from his military records, as well as bits and pieces of information recorded in family histories, over more detailed published accounts of the war. This effort introduced me to the many well-researched books, articles, and websites dedicated to preserving the memories and remarkable stories about World War II

POWs in the Philippines, including first-person accounts by former POWs who had been imprisoned in the same camps as my uncle.

This study then led to another, most rewarding discovery. By combining information from these sources with information from the FamilySearch website, I was able to identify other POWs who were members of the Church and had been imprisoned with my uncle. Many of these other Latter-day Saint POWs had left accounts of their experiences in letters, interviews, talks, and personal histories, all of which had been carefully preserved by their families.[2] Their inspiring stories were largely unknown, however, other than to a few family members. I was able to obtain access to many of those accounts.

Theirs are stories of resilience in the face of adversity, of unwavering faith at times when God may have seemed indifferent and his presence far away, and of goodness and virtue in a world filled with hate and malice. Their stories are the core of this book.

Michael H. Hyer

NOTES

1. David L. Clark and Bart J. Kowallis, "The Fate of the Davao Penal Colony #502 'Branch' of the LDS Church, 1944," *BYU Studies* 50, no. 4 (2011): 109–35.
2. Admittedly, contemporary first-person accounts from a POW camp are scarce. Furthermore, reminiscent accounts omit the experiences of those who did not survive.

INTRODUCTION

Come, come, ye Saints, no toil nor labor fear;
But with joy wend your way.
Though hard to you this journey may appear,
Grace shall be as your day.

—William Clayton, "Come, Come, Ye Saints"

In 1942 Captain Robert G. Davey of Salt Lake City, Utah, then a prisoner of the Imperial Japanese Army, was transferred to the Davao Penal Colony. Also called *Dapecol*, the colony was a notorious Japanese prisoner of war (POW) camp on Mindanao Island in the Philippines. Davey had already survived four months of battle on the front lines in a courageous, but ultimately futile, defense of the Bataan Peninsula. He had also survived recurring bouts of malaria, other diseases, the infamous Bataan Death March, and two other Japanese POW camps where thousands had died of disease, malnutrition, and brutality.

Dapecol was a place of cruelty, starvation, and sickness—a place where the prisoners, seemingly abandoned by their country, were despised, exploited, tortured, and at times savagely murdered by their captors. Oddly, it was also a place that was often quiet. There were no sounds of war—the battles were nowhere near Dapecol—and there were no radios, TVs, or phonographs blaring. Aside from the distant sounds of jungle birds, the most common noises were the quiet conversations of tired and starving POWs, and the low moans and coughs of sick and dying prisoners.

Davey found himself in that camp, sick and starving, on a Sunday. As he lay on his cot in the quiet of the camp, he heard the faint sound of men singing somewhere in the distance. What caught his attention was not so much the singing, but the song. To Davey, a member of The Church of Jesus Christ of Latter-day Saints and the youngest son of the bishop of the Salt Lake City Cannon Ward, the song was familiar but wholly out of place.

Looking "like a human skeleton, literally nothing but skin and bones [and] afflicted with various skin diseases, beriberi, malnutrition [and] malaria," Davey managed to arise from his bed and go looking for the source. He found it. In the balcony of the mess hall were about thirty POWs singing "Come, Come, Ye Saints," the great anthem of the Latter-day Saints, led by First Lieutenant George Robin (Bobby) Brown—not exactly what you would expect in a World War II prison camp in the Pacific; yet there they were, an informal group of brothers in the Davao Penal Colony, a small but bright ray of light in a very dark place.[1]

This is the story of these Latter-day Saint soldiers, who found themselves in wretched circumstances. At particularly challenging times, these POWs found strength in ways unique to their faith. They thought of the Word of Wisdom, the Church's religious health code—especially its promise that they "shall run and not be weary, and shall walk and not faint."[2] They thought of their patriarchal blessings, sacred personal blessings of guidance and admonition, and the counsel and promises in them.[3] In what perhaps may have been homage to the experience of the Prophet Joseph Smith, one soldier, on the eve of his surrender and imprisonment, retreated to the privacy of a jungle clearing to kneel and pray out loud for help; he experienced a powerful and reassuring spiritual manifestation. They thought of the love and faith of their families at home and found strength in the prayers they knew those faithful family members were offering on their behalf. Amidst the suffering of such camps, they considered their blessings.

The religious life of the typical Latter-day Saint soldier in World War II was often a lonely one, especially in the Pacific, where Latter-day Saint servicemen were thinly scattered among a vastly larger number of other soldiers.[4] While some occasionally attended other religious services—usually chaplain-led nondenominational or Protestant services—there were rarely any organized religious services of their own faith.[5] But this was not the case with Latter-day Saint POWs at Dapecol. Although lacking official Church authorization, an informal but functioning group was formed at Dapecol. In light of the circumstances—a Japanese POW camp in the jungles of the Philippines—this was an extraordinary event.[6]

This is the story of the POW members of that group; the forces that brought them together and sustained them; and the events that would later pull them apart, some to their liberation and others to their death. It is an account of survivors—their inspiring stories of how, with faith and by the grace of God, they were able to survive the horrific conditions of their imprisonment to return home to loving families to live full and gratifying lives. This is also a story of Latter-day Saint POWs who did not survive, despite equally faithful prayers. It is a story of faithful families—mothers and fathers, sisters and brothers—who did not see their son or brother return from war. They also have a story to tell and, although it may be different, it also inspires.

Often, stories such as these are presented in a binary fashion: us versus them, good versus evil, nation against nation, and so forth. In reality, everyone is a victim in war, and sometimes forces from each side perpetrate atrocities. Lastly, this book is a lesson about hate, a powerful emotion often exploited for its potent motivating force. But hate is ultimately a destructive emotion whose corrosive effects can linger long after its cause has disappeared. This is a story of how the gospel of Jesus Christ can be its antidote.

NOTES

1. Ruby S. Brown and Nelle B. Zundel, "George Robin Brown . . . His Story" (unpublished manuscript, July 27, 1977); History of George Robin Brown, by his mother and older sister, 18; Spencer W. Kimball, *The Miracle of Forgiveness* (Salt Lake City: Deseret Book, 1969), 288. The accounts in "George Robin Brown . . . His Story," and *The Miracle of Forgiveness* refer to the hymn being "An Angel from on High." This was an error on the part of Ruby Brown in recording the story, and the account in *The Miracle of Forgiveness* was based on Ruby's account. After the war, Davey identified "Come, Come, Ye Saints" as the hymn he heard and that drew him to this assembled group of Latter-day Saint POWs. Robert G. Davey, "Last Talk" (unpublished fireside talk given by Davey, transcript provided to the author by Marilyn Springgay), 3. The quoted physical description of Davey at that time is from a letter Carl D. Rohlfing, a fellow POW and group member, wrote after the war and which is quoted in Marilyn Beth Davey Springgay, "Robert Gray Davey, 2 May 1915–19 July 1968," 31. This is an unfinished draft manuscript of Davey's life history written by his daughter, who graciously shared it with the author.
2. Doctrine and Covenants 89:20.
3. A patriarchal blessing is a blessing a worthy member may receive from a Church patriarch, a Church member specifically empowered to give such blessings. The blessings are transcribed and provided to the recipient to enable the member to later study and reflect on it. They are understood as personal counsel from the Lord to the recipient.
4. Robert C. Freeman and Dennis A. Wright, *Saints at War, Experiences of Latter-day Saints in World War II* (American Fork, UT: Covenant Communications, 2001), 13. Robert Freeman provided an interesting collection of stories about wartime meetings among Latter-day Saint servicemen, including during WWII, under the heading "Worship Meetings and Gatherings." What makes these stories so poignant was the relative rarity of such meetings. Robert C. Freeman, *Saints at War: Inspiring Stories of Courage and Valor* (Springville, UT: Cedar Fort, 2013), 172–222.
5. Indeed, in the absence of a chaplain, Latter-day Saint servicemen would sometimes assist in or lead nondenominational services, reflecting their experience growing up in a church with a lay leadership. See William T. Garner, *Unwavering Valor: A POW's Account of the Bataan Death March*, 2014 ed. (Springville, UT: Plain Sight Publishing, 2014), 89–90.
6. Clark and Kowallis, "Fate of the Davao Penal Colony," 118.

1

AN ANCESTRAL GIFT

Firm as the mountains around us,
Stalwart and brave we stand,
On the rocks our fathers planted,
For us in this goodly land.

—Ruth May Fox, "Carry On"

While not all the Latter-day Saint POWs at Dapecol may have been particularly religious at the time they entered military service, they shared a common heritage. They were from Latter-day Saint families and nearly all from predominately Latter-day Saint communities with their distinctive culture, religion, and pioneer history. To read many of their genealogies is to take a long walk back through Latter day Saint pioneer history.

Peder Niels Hansen, Staff Sergeant Peter (Nels) Hansen's grandfather, joined the Church in Denmark and was among the last of the handcart pioneers to arrive in the Salt Lake Valley. He eventually settled in Sanpete County, Utah, among other Scandinavian Saints.[1]

Isaac Russell, the great-grandfather of Captain Robert G. Davey, was baptized along with the future Church President John Taylor by the early Church Apostle Parley P. Pratt during Pratt's mission to Canada in 1836. Russell later joined Heber C. Kimball in 1837 to open the British Isles Mission. Sarah Ann Butterworth Davey, Captain Davey's grandmother, left her native England and pushed a handcart across the plains to join the fledgling band of Saints in Utah. She lived in the Davey home until her death in 1927.[2] Davey's father, Charles Edmund Davey, served in the bishopric of the Cannon Ward in Salt Lake City, Utah, for more than thirty years, including thirteen years as bishop.[3]

Jacob Hamblin, Private Orland K. Hamblin's grandfather, was the famous Latter-day Saint pioneer, missionary, and diplomat to Native Americans in the West.

One doesn't even have to go back a single generation to find the influence of the early Church. First Lieutenant George Robin (Bobby) Brown was born in Colonia Juárez and raised in the close-knit, isolated Latter-day Saint colonies in northern Mexico.

Brown's ancestors include a New England shoemaker; a rough Kentucky blacksmith; an English bricklayer and his middle-class English wife, who arrived penniless in America; successful southern plantation owners and former enslavers from Tennessee; and Scandinavian emigrants just learning English and the skills needed to survive in the West.

These Latter-day Saint soldiers descended from the resilient pioneer stock that survived persecutions in Ohio, Missouri, and Illinois; went on to colonize the western desert, making it "blossom as the rose" (Isaiah 35:1); and built an ordered religion and society.[4] These differences in national origin, background, occupation, and social status were cast aside in the crucible of the pioneer experience. A new, unique culture and heritage emerged, which became the culture of these POWs and their families.

Leonard J. Arrington, a prominent historian and former official Church historian, made this observation about the Latter-day Saint pioneers: "The resiliency—the rebound power—of the Mormon people was perhaps their greatest asset.... Whether it was a grasshopper plague, prolonged drought, a winter of attrition, an Indian war, or 'invasion' by hostile troops, the Mormons always seemed to rise from their 'bed of affliction' to meet the almost overwhelming challenge."[5]

This resilience, enabled by their religious legacy of sharing one another's burdens, was a defining characteristic of early Latter-day Saints and the culture of these POWs.

These young men grew up during the Great Depression, mostly in rural areas. As unlikely as it may seem, that may have been a blessing. They learned to be resourceful, to make do, to be self-reliant, and to deal with hardship and failure. Staff Sergeant Peter (Nels) Hansen was the second of fourteen children raised on a wheat farm and cattle ranch in Caldwell, an old Latter-day Saint settlement in southern Alberta, Canada.[6] Captain Robert (Bob) Davey's family lost their once-prosperous furniture business in Salt Lake City in the Great Depression.[7] First Lieutenant George Robin (Bobby) Brown learned early in life what it took to survive on a ranch in the remote regions of the Sierra Madre in northern Mexico. Many also learned at an early age to handle firearms and to hunt. Brown was twelve years old when he shot, cleaned, and skinned his first deer. The military was not his first experience with firearms.[8]

From his mother, Brown was also the recipient of an especially comforting gift: the love of music, especially the singing of hymns. His mother, Ruby, taught him and his older sister Nelle to sing duets—tenor and alto. They both had beautiful voices and sang hymns largely because that was all that was available in their remote home in the mountains of northern Mexico. After the family later moved to El Paso, Texas, Brown continued to demonstrate a flair for music and drama, performing in several community theater productions, such as Gilbert and Sullivan's *The Mikado*, and in a radio drama at a local radio station.[9]

All things considered, these Latter-day Saint soldiers and their families seem unremarkable for the time—ordinary families trying to make their way in the depths of the Great Depression. But however unremarkable their Latter-day Saint upbringing and religious faith may have appeared, that upbringing and faith may have been the most important preparation these young men could have received for future events then unimaginable.

NOTES

1. Later Hansen's father, James Hansen, along with some others from Sanpete County, Utah, moved north to settle in Alberta, Canada, in 1887, where Hansen was born and grew up on a cattle ranch. Histories of Hansen and his ancestors may be found at familysearch.org under James Edward Hansen (KWCD-SZK), Peter Nelsen Hansen (KW86-JCJ), and Peder Niels Hansen (KWJ8-XVF).
2. Marilyn Springgay, email message to author, April 23, 2017.
3. "Obituary of Charles Edmund Davey," *Salt Lake Tribune*, September 1, 1941.
4. Early Church members viewed the colonization of the Great Basin in Utah as a modern fulfillment of Isaiah's prophecy that the "desert shall rejoice, and blossom as the rose." Isaiah 35:1.
5. Leonard J. Arrington, *The Great Basin Kingdom: Economic History of the Latter-day Saints, 1830–1900* (Lincoln: University of Nebraska Press, 1966), 161.
6. Wendell J. Ashton, "A Spirit of Love," *Instructor*, April 1947, 175.
7. Springgay, "Robert Gray Davey," 13.
8. Brown and Zundel, "George Robin Brown . . . His Story," 6–7.
9. Brown and Zundel, "George Robin Brown . . . His Story," 12; Nelle B. Zundel, "George Robin Brown," in *The Life and Posterity of Alma Platte Spilsbury*, comp. Viva Skousen Brown (Provo, UT: privately published, 1983), 297–98.

2
YOU'RE IN THE ARMY NOW

Oh, thus be it ever, when free men shall stand,
Between their loved homes and the war's desolation!

—Francis Scott Key, "The Star-Spangled Banner"

We often think of World War II beginning for the United States on December 7, 1941, with the Japanese attack on Pearl Harbor. But for many young men in America, the key life-altering event occurred more than a year earlier with the passage in September 1940 of the Selective Service Act—in other words, the draft. Enlistment was often preferable to being drafted, and at that time it was generally believed you could enlist and be out in one year.[1]

Most of the Latter-day Saint soldiers in this story were drafted into the army or joined to avoid the draft. There were, however, some exceptions. For example, James Patterson of Sunnyside, Utah, who seemed destined to a life as a coal miner in Price, Utah, joined the army looking for something better.[2] Carl D. Rohlfing of Salt Lake City, Utah, had been working the graveyard shift for the D&RGW Railroad at the Salt Lake Depot when, in October 1940, he decided to enlist in the army for one year, both to avoid the coming draft and, ironically, because he did not think his current job was good for his health.³ While a poor, struggling college student, Robert Davey joined the Army Reserve Officer Corps because it provided a free uniform and additional physical education credits.⁴

THE 200TH COAST ARTILLERY REGIMENT

On December 19, 1940, George Robin (Bobby) Brown, along with John A. (Jack) Keeler, his lifelong buddy and a fellow Latter-day Saint, enlisted in the 200th Coast Artillery Regiment of the New Mexico National Guard in Deming, New Mexico, as the preferred option to the draft.⁵ Bobby was twenty-five years old at the time; the oldest son, he was the second oldest of six children of the George and Ruby Brown family in El Paso, Texas.

Bobby was born on August 16, 1915, at the home of Ruby's mother, an experienced midwife, in Colonia Juárez, Chihuahua, Mexico. Shortly before George was to give the child a name and a blessing at a sacrament meeting, George's father handed him a note saying, "It would please me greatly if you would name the baby George Vernon." George ignored the request, held the baby in his hands, and gave him a blessing and the name "George Robin Brown"—George for the child's father and Robin for his mother. "Robin" was Ruby's nickname, given her when she was a young woman growing up in Mexico by some local cowboys, a group that had included George. She was presumably nicknamed after the pretty, but always very busy, bird. The family came to know George Robin Brown as Bobby.

Bobby spent his boyhood growing up on his family's cattle ranch in Chuichupa, a remote mountain Latter-day Saint colony in Chihuahua, Mexico. About ten years before his enlistment, the family left the ranch life in Mexico and moved to El Paso for better educational opportunities for the children. Like most other families at the time, the Browns had been struggling to make it through the Great Depression.

Like Brown, Keeler was also born in Colonia Juárez. At the time of his enlistment, he was living in Deming, New Mexico, and was a close friend of Bobby and his family.⁶ That same month the two

George Robin Brown, United States Army, December 1940. Courtesy of Brown family collection.

young men enlisted, their unit was "inducted into federal service" (activated), meaning it was now part of the United States Army.[7]

Two months later, on February 21, 1941, Orland K. Hamblin from Farmington, New Mexico, was drafted into the army in Santa Fe, New Mexico, and sent to the 200th Regiment of the New Mexico National Guard, followed by training in El Paso.[8] Hamblin was twenty-three years old at the time; before being drafted, he had served in the Texas-Louisiana Mission of the Church.

Shortly after arriving at Fort Bliss, Hamblin found the El Paso Ward, the local Church congregation. An active participant, he became acquainted with the Brown family, also active members of that congregation.[9] Hamblin recruited one of his four tentmates, a soldier from Texas who was not a member of the Church, to attend church meetings and socials with him, earning them the title of "Sunday School Boys" from their commanding sergeant. Hamblin joined the choir and spoke in meetings. Of these experiences, Hamblin wrote years later that the "good people of the El Paso Ward did much to make my stay in Fort Bliss, and army life, bearable," and these experiences were among the "bright spots" he would remember in the following not-so-pleasant years.[10] There were two other Latter-day Saint servicemen in the 200th: William Murle Allred from Artesia, Arizona, who enlisted in March 1941, and Don Charles Bloomfield from Ramah, New Mexico, who enlisted in April 1941. They also may have become acquainted with Hamblin, Brown, and other Church members in El Paso.[11]

Among those with whom Brown also became acquainted in the 200th was Arthur M. Baclawski. A native Ohioan, Baclawski had graduated as a landscape architect from the Ohio State University and was recruited by the Civilian Conservation Corps (CCC)—one of President Franklin D. Roosevelt's "New Deal" natural resource conversation programs—to do landscape architectural planning for various projects in New Mexico. While working for the CCC, he was drafted into the New Mexico National Guard.[12] Baclawski was not a member of the Church, but he and Brown shared a tent and became friends.

The 200th was an old cavalry unit that been consolidated with other units and, reflecting the changing nature of war, converted to the 200th Coast Artillery Regiment with a mission to defend coastal areas from air attacks.[13] It consisted of about nineteen hundred soldiers and its makeup reflected the local population—Anglo-Saxons (like Brown and Hamblin), Mexicans, Navajos, Apaches, and other Native Americans.[14] They trained in the desert around Fort Bliss, just north of El Paso.

Their training centered on firing the army's three-inch and thirty-seven-millimeter antiaircraft guns and fifty-caliber machine guns, as well as operating sixty-inch Sperry searchlights. The guns were old, obsolete, WWI-era equipment. Also, because of a shortage of ammunition, the men were rarely able to fire live rounds. In addition to this artillery training, they received other typical military training, such as marching, close-order drills, and ten-mile hikes in the Texas sun.[15]

Before his enlistment, Brown had been working for El Paso Electric Company in a warehouse, and with that experience he was soon rated as a clerk and placed in headquarters supply. By January 5, 1941, Brown was a private first class and was quickly promoted to a sergeant on March 17, 1941; to a first sergeant on June 18, 1941; and finally to a master sergeant on July 15, 1941, placing him in charge of supplies for the unit.[16] This rapid promotion from a raw recruit in December to a master sergeant by the following July may not have been unusual at this time for the rapidly expanding army. Nevertheless, it is evidence that the army quickly identified Brown as a responsible individual with leadership skills.

Army officials toured the nation to assess the readiness and proficiency of every antiaircraft unit in the country and concluded that the 200th was "the best antiaircraft regiment (regular [army] or otherwise), now available to the United States Armed Forces." For that reason, it was selected for "an overseas assignment of great importance," although the location was not disclosed.[17] The next-ranking unit received the consolation prize—an assignment to Alaska.[18]

In early August 1941, the 200th received orders to prepare to ship out; again, the destination was not disclosed.[19] The local El Paso newspaper carried a nice article about Brown leaving with the 200th for an unknown destination. When asked about being shipped out by the army, Brown, reflecting the practical sense of duty characteristic of this generation of soldiers, simply told the reporter, "This is a job that has to be done, and I am pitching in and doing it." Brown also received a letter from the president of El Paso Electric Company to the effect that a job would be waiting for him when he returned.[20]

Before shipping out, the 200th toured the major towns in New Mexico, parading before thousands who lined the streets to wish them well. Consisting of a 268-truck convoy stretching for miles, the 200th must have been quite a show.[21] Later, with the regimental band playing "O Fair New Mexico," the soldiers of the 200th—including Brown, Keeler, Hamblin, and Baclawski—boarded railcar coaches chalked with *V for Victory* and left Fort Bliss for San Francisco by way of Los Angeles.[22]

The broad smiles in the pictures notwithstanding, this was an emotional parting. Brown's mother gave him a set of scriptures—a triple combination consisting of the Book of Mormon, Doctrine and Covenants, and Pearl of Great Price—and the Church youth group had given him a hymnbook. Just before his departure, Brown also received a special blessing from Church patriarch Harry L. Payne. The blessing included a promise for him "to be preserved to complete a mission on this earth."[23]

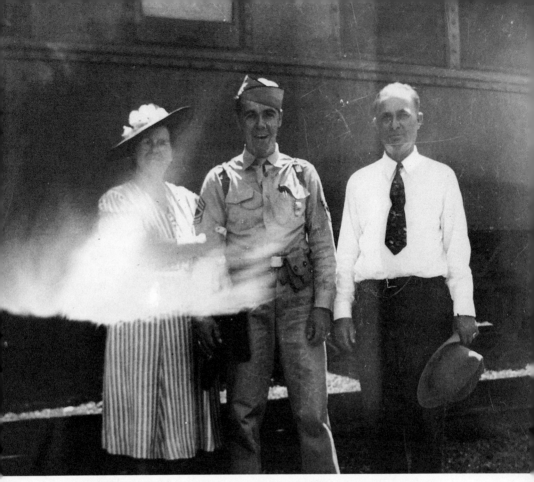

Master Sergeant George Robin (Bobby) Brown with his parents, George and Ruby Brown, before boarding the train for San Francisco, California, August 1941. Courtesy of Brown family collection.

Upon arrival at Fort Mason in San Francisco, the soldiers of the 200th were put on a barge to Fort MacDowell on Angel Island in the San Francisco Bay. At Fort MacDowell, the soldiers received one last physical examination and some vaccinations.[24]

There were a lot of enticing reasons for a young soldier to want to take a ferry over to San Francisco for an evening, and on Brown's last night at Fort MacDowell, he did just that. It was a Sunday, and Brown went to attend church services in San Francisco. He stayed on to attend a Church fireside later that evening.[25]

The next day, September 8, 1941, Brown and others boarded the SS *President Coolidge*, an ocean liner requisitioned by the government for military transport. Passing under the Golden Gate Bridge at sunset, they set out into the Pacific for a six-thousand-mile voyage to a destination still unknown to the soldiers.[26] At the time of this voyage, the *President Coolidge* had not yet been refitted for military transport purposes and was still fitted out as a luxury ocean liner. Although the soldiers were crammed tightly together in the ship's compartments, the voyage was an enjoyable experience for most. The soldiers did not have many duties on the voyage and had time to enjoy pretty sunrises and sunsets, an occasional whale sighting, and other pleasant aspects of an ocean voyage across the Pacific.

The SS *President Coolidge*, an American luxury ocean liner used to transport troops to the Philippines. By J. F. Newman. Public domain.

There was a good chance, however, that some of these soldiers did not especially enjoy the voyage. Unaccustomed to travel on high seas, many were seasick and spent most of their time heaving over the rail, a misery likely aggravated by the high winds and huge waves from a typhoon they may have encountered.[27] All in all, however, the ship's accommodations were comparatively good and the voyage generally pleasant. While they could not have known it at the time, they would later endure other ocean voyages in very different circumstances and conditions.

They stopped in Hawaii for a few days and then sailed out into the Pacific. At that point, the voyage took on a more serious nature as they sailed under blackout conditions. Five days after leaving Hawaii, they were finally told their destination, their assignment of great importance: the Philippines.

THE ARMY AIR CORP, FIFTH AIR BASE SQUADRON

The 200th Coastal Artillery Regiment was only one of many units being mobilized and sent to the Philippines. Among the others was the Fifth Air Base Squadron of the Army Air Corps, based in Fort Douglas, Salt Lake City. This group was responsible for aircraft maintenance and the construction and maintenance of airfields. The Fifth Air Base Squadron left Salt Lake City on October 21, 1941, aboard a troop train for San Francisco. They arrived on October 23, 1941; following the same route as previous soldiers, they were transferred to Fort MacDowell on Angel Island, where they remained for a few days for final physical examinations and processing. On October 27, 1941, the group departed San Francisco aboard the USS *Hugh L. Scott* for a destination that also had not yet been disclosed to them.[28]

Among those in the Fifth Air Base Squadron aboard the USS *Hugh L. Scott* were more than twenty Latter-day Saint soldiers.[29] Similar to the experience of those on the SS *President Coolidge* a month earlier, the voyage was generally pleasant. But they were crowded and some, such as Private Franklin T. East, a Latter-day Saint soldier from Arizona, suffered miserably from seasickness.[30]

Among the airmen in the Fifth Air Base Squadron was Staff Sergeant Ernest R. Parry from Salt Lake City. His father had died in 1935, when he was only thirteen and, as the only son and brother to two sisters, he had a special concern for his widowed mother and sisters. Nevertheless, after high school and with the draft looming, Parry enlisted in the army. Before he left Salt Lake with his squadron, Parry received a patriarchal blessing promising that he would "grow strong in the face of trial and temptation, growing strong in resisting temptation and thereby becoming an example of righteousness." He was also admonished to "be humble and prayerful before the Lord and He will never desert you, for the promise given to the faithful shall be yours, that your yoke shall be made easy and your burden light."[31]

Staff Sergeant Ernest R. Parry, Fifth Air Base Group, United States Army Air Corps, 1941. Courtesy of the Parry family.

The Fifth Air Base also stopped for a few days in Honolulu, Hawaii. For some this stay in Honolulu produced some important, and perhaps unexpected, memories. Private East had married Ione Louise Hatch in the Salt Lake Temple on October 1, 1941, just three weeks before his unit left for San Francisco. In addition to being miserable from constant seasickness, he was also missing his new bride and was apprehensive about the future. He was, in his words, "seasick, homesick and everything else."[32]

Staff Sergeant Ernest Parry came to his aid. They attended Sunday services. It was a special experience, and in a letter home, Parry wrote that he wished the Spirit he felt there could always be with him.³³ With Parry's encouragement, Parry and East also toured the island, went to the Church's mission home in Honolulu, and visited the Church's Laie Hawaii Temple. It was a happy and memorable experience. It was also one that East, in the years and hardships that followed, thought about and in which he found encouragement. Years later when East wrote of his experiences in the war, he wrote in some detail of this time with Parry in Honolulu, concluding, "I was grateful to have a friend like [Parry and] thankful to the Lord that I knew him and what he had done for me."³⁴

East and Parry weren't the only ones to have memorable experiences in Hawaii. While waiting in Hawaii, Staff Sergeant Nels Hansen, a Latter-day Saint soldier from Weiser, Idaho, had his first encounter with the Japanese. He attended a Latter-day Saint Sunday School consisting of about fifteen people, mostly children, all Japanese. While only a brief experience, the sincerity and knowledge of the gospel of these Japanese Saints made a deep impression on Hansen—an impression that, despite all that he would later suffer at the hands of the Japanese, he never forgot nor revised.³⁵

On November 6 the unit left Hawaii in a convoy. The following Sunday, sailing out in the blue Pacific Ocean, Parry and East organized the first meeting of the Latter-day Saint servicemen aboard the ship. Major Ray Elsmore, a member of the Church and commander of the Fifth Air Base group, and Staff Sergeant Nels Hansen were the speakers. Around thirty or so servicemen attended, and it was, according to East, a "very good meeting." At that meeting, they organized themselves, and Hansen was chosen as the group leader. That was the beginning of regular religious services among those servicemen.³⁶

UNITED STATES ARMY INFANTRY

For Robert (Bob) Davey, the events leading to his voyage to the Philippines were different. Davey's father had owned a successful furniture business in Salt Lake City, and Davey grew up in relatively prosperous circumstances in a close and happy family. However, his mother died in 1933 from a prolonged illness, and Davey was deeply affected by her death. Although his father later remarried, the family was never quite the same.

With the Great Depression, the family's furniture business failed. Although Davey once may have looked forward to a substantial inheritance, there was now nothing left. Nevertheless, he enrolled in the University of Utah and, with borrowed money and by working several jobs, managed to graduate with a Bachelor of Science degree in business administration in 1938. During the time he was a student, a friend suggested he join the Army Reserve Officer Corps because it provided a free uniform and additional physical education credits. Davey joined and earned a commission as a second lieutenant in the United States Army.

With the mobilization of forces in anticipation of war, Davey was called into active duty. While Davey was away training at Fort Ord in California, his father died of a heart attack. A month later, in October 1941, having lost both his mother and his father but still with a sister and brothers at home, Davey found himself in the San Francisco Bay aboard the USS *Tasker H. Bliss*, a former luxury liner, as part of the infantry departing for the Philippines. When first notified of the destination, Davey received it as good news. At that time, he had little fear of war in the Pacific; Hitler's war in Europe was the concern. The tour to the Philippines was expected to be short; he expected he would soon be back home.[37]

In addition to their common religion and culture, these Latter-day Saint soldiers would now have this in common: With the voyage to the Philippines, they would all be caught up in a swift and powerful current of world events leading to war and, for them, imprisonment.[38]

NOTES

1. John C. Shively, *Profiles in Survival: The Experiences of American POWs in the Philippines During World War II* (Indianapolis: Indiana Historical Society Press, 2012).
2. James Patterson, "Saving the Legacy: An Oral History of Utah's World War II Veterans," interview by Luke Perry, August 15, 2001, Tape No. SL-283 & 284, Fort Douglas Museum and Marriott Library, Special Collections Department, University of Utah, Salt Lake City, 1.
3. Carl Dennis Rohlfing, "Carl Dennis Rohlfing" (undated manuscript provided to the author by Dennis Autry), 1.
4. Springgay, "Robert Gray Davey," 13.
5. National Guard of New Mexico, Enlistment Record of George Robin Brown, Serial Number 20,842,469, December 19, 1940, National Personnel Records Center, National Archives and Records Administration, 1 Archives Drive, St. Louis, MO 63138 (hereafter "NARA Records").
6. Lowell Eliason Call, "Latter-day Saint Servicemen in the Philippine Islands: A Historical Study of their Religious Activities and Influences Resulting in the Official Organization of The Church of Jesus Christ of Latter-day Saints in the Philippines," *All Theses and Dissertations*, Paper 4579 (Brigham Young University, 1955), 107.
7. Kenneth G. Wickham, Major General, United States Army, The Adjutant General, "Official Statement of Military Service and Death of George R. Brown, 0 890 150," NARA Records.
8. Orland K. Hamblin, "My Experience in the Service and as a Prisoner of War of the Japanese" (unpublished manuscript, June 1956), 1.
9. See also Call, "Latter-day Saint Servicemen," 115 (quoting August 14, 1954, letter from Peter Nelsen Hansen, referring to Hamblin as a close friend of Brown).
10. Hamblin, "My Experience," 1–2. Of Hamblin's four tentmates, only Hamblin survived the war; the other three all died while POWs.
11. The enlistment dates for Allred and Bloomfield are from army enlistment records, and Pacific POW rosters identify them as members of the 200th Coast Artillery. Bloomfield was an active member of the Church, having served a mission in the Northern States Mission before the war, and was likely involved with other Church members. See Freeman and Wright, *Saints at War*, 279–80. Little is known about Allred, although he appears to have come from an active Latter-day Saint family, as his parents were endowed and sealed in the temple.
12. Arthur M. Baclawski, "Personal History" (unpublished manuscript in family records, copy provided to the author by Charles Baclawski).
13. Shively, *Profiles in Survival*, 188.
14. Dorothy Cave, *Beyond Courage: One Regiment Against Japan, 1941–1945*, 2006 ed. (Santa Fe, NM: Sunstone Press, 2006), 25–26.
15. Cave, *Beyond Courage*, 24, 66–68; Shively, *Profiles in Survival*, 188–90.

16. Brown and Zundel, "George Robin Brown . . . His Story," 14; United States Army, "Service Record of George R. Brown, 20842464," NARA Records.
17. Shively, *Profiles in Survival*, 190; Hamblin, "My Experience," 1.
18. The other unit was the 206th Coast Artillery Regiment from Arkansas, which was deployed to the Aleutian Islands in Alaska.
19. Shively, *Profiles in Survival*, 190.
20. Included in Brown's military file is a copy of a newspaper clipping dated August 24, 1941, that contains this quotation and refers to this letter. The name of the newspaper is not indicated. NARA Records.
21. Shively, *Profiles in Survival*, 191; Cave, *Beyond Courage*, 35; Hamblin, "My Experience," 1.
22. The First Battalion, with Hamblin, left on August 22, 1941; the Second Battalion, with Brown, Keeler, and Baclawski, left on August 31, 1941. Cave, *Beyond Courage*, 37–38. An article in the *El Paso Herald-Post*, dated February 11, 1942 (page 2), indicates that Brown left Fort Bliss on August 31, 1941.
23. Nelle B. Zundel, "George Robin (Bobby) Brown," in Brown, *Alma Platte Spilsbury*, 298; Nelle B. Zundel, "Story of the Family of George Andrew and Ruby Vilate Spilsbury Brown," unpublished manuscript prepared for Brown family reunion, June 1961, 5.
24. Cave, *Beyond Courage*, 38; Hamblin, "My Experience," 2. There was also a brawl between the largely Anglo regular army soldiers at Fort MacDowell and the predominately Native American and Mexican-American soldiers of the 200th. There is no indication that Brown or Hamblin were involved, but the event illustrates the racial tensions in the military and the nation at the time. See Cave, *Beyond Courage*, 38; Shively, *Profiles in Survival*, 192. Angel Island had been the "Ellis Island" of the West, where immigrants (largely Chinese) had passed through. At this time, however, it was the depot for processing soldiers who were shipping out overseas. The concrete remnants of buildings of the former Fort Mason still remain.
25. Brown and Zundel, "George Robin Brown . . . His Story," 14–15.
26. Brown and Zundel, "George Robin Brown . . . His Story," 14–15; Cave, *Beyond Courage*, 40–41. Hamblin and those in the First Battalion had left earlier on a different transport ship.
27. Shively, *Profiles in Survival*, 192–94; Cave, *Beyond Courage*, 40–41; Hamblin, "My Experience," 2–3.
28. Allen C. Christensen, "My Life History" (unpublished manuscript, April 1961), 5. A copy of this personal history was provided to the author by Christensen's grandson Cody Christensen.
29. The author has identified the following Latter-day Saint air corpsmen in this Fifth Air Base group: Staff Sergeant Peter (Nels) Hansen from Weiser, Idaho; Private First Class Allen C. Christensen from Tremonton, Utah; Private First Class Charles L. Goodliffe from Park Valley, Utah; Staff Sergeant Ernest R. Parry from Salt Lake City, Utah; Private James Patterson from Sunnyside, Utah; Private Jack W. Bradley from Moroni, Utah; Private Mack K. Davis from Lehi, Utah; Private First Class Woodrow L. Dunkley from Franklin,

Idaho; Second Lieutenant Richard E. Harris from Logan, Utah; Private First Class Ferrin C. Holjeson from Smithfield, Utah; Private Russell Seymore Jensen from Centerfield, Utah; Private First Class Lloyd Parry from Logan, Utah; Private First Class Ronald M. Landon from Kimball, Idaho; Private Harry O. Miller Jr. from Magrath, Alberta, Canada; Private First Class Lamar V. Polve from Kenilworth, Utah; Private Jesse G. Smurthwaite from Baker, Oregon; Private Frederick D. Thomas from St. Johns, Idaho; Private Franklin T. East from Pima, Arizona; Corporal Kenneth B. Larsen from Salt Lake City, Utah; Corporal Carl D. Rohlfing from Salt Lake City, Utah; Corporal Donald L. Vance from Fairview, Utah; and Corporal Raft T. Wilson from Alta, Wyoming. Major Raymond Elsmore, commander of the Fifth Air Base Group at Del Monte Airfield, was also a member of the Church. He survived the war but was never a POW. See note 36. This list is based on the author's research and may not be complete, as there may have been other Latter-day Saint corpsmen in the Fifth Air Base group or in other units on that ship.

30. Franklin T. East, "Army Life of Franklin T. East," November–December 1977, 5, unpublished manuscript accessible at familysearch.org under Franklin Thomas East (KWCR-6W1).
31. Suzanne Julian, "Led by the Spirit" (BYU devotional address, February 11, 2014), https://speeches.byu.edu/talks/suzanne-julian_led-spirit/.
32. East, "Army Life," 6.
33. Crystal Grover, email message to author, April 30, 2017. (Grover is the granddaughter of Parry's sister.)
34. East, "Army Life," 6. East spelled the name *Perry*, but from the context and other information it is evident he was referring to Ernest Parry.
35. Ashton, "Spirit of Love," 174–75.
36. East, "Army Life," 7 (estimating between fifteen and twenty present); Call, "Servicemen in the Philippine Islands," 114 (Call quotes a letter where Hansen estimated that "nearly 40" were present). Elsmore left for Australia before the Philippines fell to the Japanese; in Australia, he was put in charge of military air transport operations in the Pacific. He survived the war and completed a distinguished postwar career in civilian aviation. Trans Ocean Airlines, History, 1946–1960, Airline Officials, http://www.taloa.org/Elsmore.html; Col. Ray T. Elsmore Obituary, "Famed Aviator, Native Utahn, Dies on Coast," *Deseret News*, February 19, 1957, B-9, film #0164622.
37. Springgay, "Robert Gray Davey," 13–14.
38. Another sizable group of Latter-day Saint soldiers came to the Philippines earlier as part of the 20th Pursuit Squadron of the Army Air Corps, based at Nichols Field just south of Manila. Those Latter-day Saint soldiers included Gene Jacobsen, Harold Poole, and Clarence Bramley. They also became POWs when the Philippines fell, but their imprisonment took a different course than the POWs who are the principal subject of this book. For example, the POWs from the 20th Pursuit Squadron were never imprisoned at Dapecol. Nevertheless, the book refers to these three POWs in several

instances to round out our understanding of the POW experience of Latter-day Saints. Their individual stories are well told respectively in Gene S. Jacobsen, *We Refused to Die: My Time as a Prisoner of War in Bataan and Japan, 1942–1945* (Salt Lake City: University of Utah Press, 2004); James W. Parkinson and Lee Benson, *Soldier Slaves* (Annapolis, MD: Naval Institute Press, 2006); and William T. Garner, *Unwavering Valor: A POW's Account of the Bataan Death March* (Springville, UT: Plain Sight Publishing, 2014).

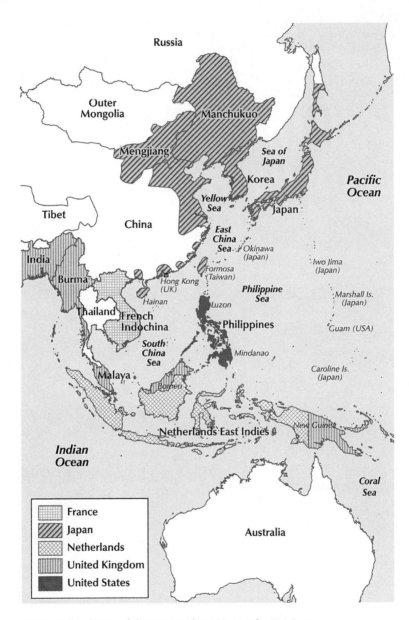

Map 1. Political Map of the Far East in 1939. Map by Nat Case.

3

WHAT IN THE WORLD WAS GOING ON?

> *God moves in a mysterious way*
> *His wonders to perform;*
> *He plants his footsteps in the sea*
> *And rides upon the storm.*
>
> —William Cowper, "God Moves in a Mysterious Way"

What in the world was going on that would make the Philippines, a group of islands in East Asia more than seven thousand miles away, an assignment of great importance to the United States? In a scenario that would seem all too familiar to us in the late twentieth and early twenty-first centuries, it involved oil.

THE OLD COLONIAL ECONOMIC ORDER

In the years preceding WWII, Asia still contained the remnants of the once-great European colonial empires of the eighteenth and nineteenth centuries. There were British colonies in what are now India, Pakistan, Malaysia, Singapore, Myanmar (Burma), and Hong Kong; French colonies (French Indo-China) in Vietnam, Laos, and Cambodia; and Dutch colonies (Netherlands East Indies) in what is now Indonesia. While the United States never developed a colonial system like these European powers, as a result of the Spanish American War in 1898, it came into possession of the Philippines and joined these European colonial powers in having significant economic and political interests in Asia.[1]

THE OIL EMBARGO

In the years leading up to WWII, an emperor ruled Japan, but with an ultranationalistic military becoming increasingly influential. Japanese leaders, and perhaps some elements in the European colonies in East Asia as well, saw Japan as Asia's champion, destined to liberate the Asian colonies from the Westerners and expand Japanese influence through its "Greater East Asia Co-Prosperity Sphere."[2] What the Japanese viewed as liberating Asia from these Western colonial powers, others saw as Japan simply building its own colonial empire following this European model, especially since Japan lacked the natural resources necessary to fuel its growing economy and imperial ambitions.[3]

In 1937 Japan invaded China, a country with which the United States had a longstanding friendship and commercial trading relationship at the time. To pressure Japan to withdraw from China and halt its expansionist actions, on July 26, 1941—just days before the 200th regiment shipped out—the United States imposed a full embargo on trade with Japan, including all oil imports. At that time, most of Japan's oil imports came from the United States. Britain and the Netherlands imposed similar embargos.

The Japanese, however, had no intention of withdrawing from China or halting its drive for a Japanese-led "Greater East Asia Co-Prosperity Sphere." Japan and the United States had been holding diplomatic negotiations to resolve the conflict, but with the full trade embargo, those negotiations deadlocked.[4] While the Latter-day Saint soldiers were enjoying their voyage across the Pacific, Japanese military leaders were planning other, nondiplomatic solutions to their problem.

Geography now became important to the fate of these Latter-day Saint soldiers on their way to the Philippines. The Philippines archipelago comprises almost seventy-one hundred islands. Located more than five thousand miles from Hawaii and seven thousand miles from San Francisco, these islands are situated in the middle of the Far East and lie athwart the trade routes leading from China and Japan to Southeast Asia and the rich supplies of rubber, oil, and minerals in the East Indies.[5] One of the most promising sources of oil for Japan's growing military and industrial appetite was the Dutch East Indies (now Indonesia). However, the Philippine Islands sat between Japan and that source of oil. The US Navy's Pacific Fleet sailed those waters, and any oil-laden Japanese ship going from the Dutch East Indies to Japan would have to pass by the US-controlled Philippines.[6]

WAR PLAN ORANGE

United States military planners for many years had been preparing and revising plans to defend against a potential war with Japan. War plans were color-coded, and Japan was assigned the color orange. War Plan Orange (WPO) was the plan for defense for war with Japan.[7] The Philippines was something of a conundrum for the military planners. The core line of defense of the continental United States was an arc from Panama through Hawaii to the Aleutian Islands off Alaska. The Philippines was thousands of miles west of that defensive line. The problem for defense planners was how to reinforce and supply the military outpost in the Philippines in the face of a Japanese attack and naval blockade.

WPO assumed the Philippines would be able to defend an attack for six months, by which time the US Pacific Fleet would have battled its way across the Pacific to reinforce the troops. However, no one with any authority actually believed that could be done. The navy estimated it would take at least two years for the fleet to fight its way across the Pacific. Although never explicitly stated in the war plans, the implicit conclusion was that the Philippines would have to be abandoned in the event of a war with Japan. In any event, no plans were made to concentrate men or stockpile supplies on the West Coast in preparation for such an attack.[8]

In the summer of 1941, President Franklin D. Roosevelt brought General Douglas MacArthur out of retirement and put him in command of what was then called the United States Army Forces in the Far East (USAFFE), with its command center in Manila. General MacArthur, a charismatic and highly regarded general with unquestioned knowledge of East Asia, was a strong advocate against the defeatist attitude of WPO and a forceful proponent for the reinforcement and defense of the Philippines.[9] A key element of General MacArthur's strategy to defend the Philippines was the use of the then-new ground-based B-17 four-engine, heavy bombers (the Flying Fortress).[10]

General MacArthur's view ultimately prevailed, and WPO was changed. The War Department identified the Philippines as a "strategic opportunity of utmost importance" and contemplated that it would be the key to the US strategic position in the Pacific. The War Department recommended that the Philippines be reinforced by antiaircraft artillery to protect the airfields and bombers that were key to General MacArthur's strategy.[11] The 200th (with Brown and Hamblin) and the Fifth Air Base group (with its group of Latter-day Saint air corpsmen on their way to the Philippines) were tactical pieces in this larger Pacific strategy.[12]

Despite official neutrality (and a general isolationist sentiment among the public), President Roosevelt's administration was nevertheless simultaneously preparing for war with Japan in the Pacific and with Germany in Europe. Yet it is hard to imagine today how unprepared for war the United States truly was, especially for war on two fronts. Although the United States maintained a large and formidable navy, its air and land forces in 1938 ranked nineteenth globally in the size of its total air and land forces, just behind Portugal and slightly ahead of neutral Switzerland.[13]

The accelerated buildup for war on two fronts exceeded the nation's logistical capacity, creating an epidemic of shortages and mistakes. It is not surprising that the intended buildup in the Philippines would turn out to be more of an aspiration than fact. For example,

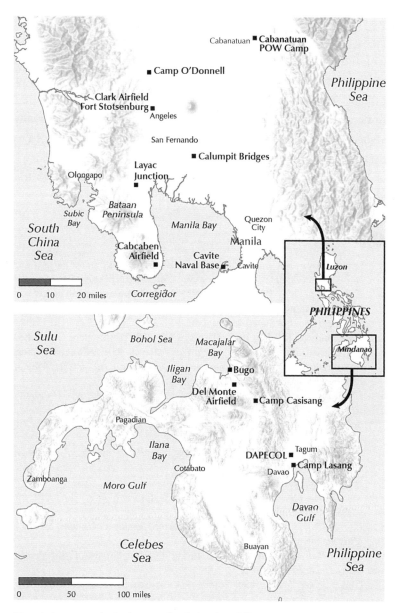

Map 2. Luzon and Mindanao Islands in the Philippines. Map by Nat Case.

pilots would arrive but not their airplanes, and the planes that did arrive often lacked key parts and supplies. Meanwhile, soldiers drilled with the brimmed model M1917A1 doughboy helmets of WWI and old Springfield 1903 and Enfield rifles with suspect WWI-era ammunition.[14] When visualizing these soldiers in the Philippines, do not think of the "steel pot" helmets and the M1 carbines we normally associate with WWII. Those had not yet been developed or issued to these soldiers. Think of WWI doughboys.

In the fall of 1941, these Latter-day Saint soldiers landed in the Philippines and into this political and military muddle.

NOTES

1. Louis Morton, *The United States Army in WWII / The War in the Pacific / The Fall of the Philippines*, commemorative edition (Harrisburg, PA: National Historical Society, 1993), 2–3. In 1935 the Philippines became an autonomous commonwealth of the United States.
2. US Department of State, "Milestones: 1937–1945, Japan, China, the United States and the Road to Pearl Harbor, 1937–41" (Washington, DC: Office of Historian), https://history.state.gov/milestones/1937-1945/pearl-harbor; see John Burton, *Fortnight of Infamy: The Collapse of Allied Airpower West of Pearl Harbor* (Annapolis, MD: Naval Institute Press, 2006), 14.
3. US Department of State, "Milestones: 1937–1945"; Columbia University, "Japan's Quest for Power"; United States Army, *A Brief History of the U.S. Army in World War II* (Washington, DC: Center of Military History, 1992), 3.1, http://www.history.army.mil/html/books/072/72-2/CMH_Pub_72-2.pdf.
4. US Department of State, "Road to Pearl Harbor"; Burton, *Fortnight of Infamy*, 20.
5. Morton, *Fall of the Philippines*, 4.
6. Morton, *Fall of the Philippines*, 52; United States Army, *Brief History*, 31–32.
7. Morton, *Fall of the Philippines*, 61.
8. Morton, *Fall of the Philippines*, 63–64; Burton, *Fortnight of Infamy*, 28–29.
9. Morton, *Fall of the Philippines*, 64.
10. Morton, *Fall of the Philippines*, 64; Shively, *Profiles in Survival*, 12–14; United States Army, *Brief History*, 31–33.
11. United States Army, *Brief History*, 31–33; John D. Lukacs, *Escape from Davao: The Forgotten Story of the Most Daring Prison Break of the Pacific War* (New York: Simon & Schuster, 2010), 10–11.
12. See Morton, *Fall of the Philippines*, 33, 43.
13. Lukacs, *Escape from Davao*, 32.
14. Lukacs, 10–11; see also Morton, *Fall of the Philippines*, 43–45; Burton, *Fortnight of Infamy*, 39; Cave, *Beyond Courage*, 53.

4
THE EASY LIFE IN THE PHILIPPINES

Choose the right! There is peace in righteous doing.
Choose the right! There's safety for the soul.

—Joseph L. Townsend, "Choose the Right"

After sailing some seven thousand miles across the Pacific, the troop transport ships entered the South China Sea, passed by a line of tropical islands making up much of the Philippines archipelago, and finally sailed into Manila Bay. As the ships entered the bay, the soldiers saw to the left the fortress island of Corregidor guarding the entrance to the bay. Beyond Corregidor was the large, green, mountainous landmass of the Bataan peninsula, areas with which many would later become intimately familiar. But as they entered the bay, their focus was on the famous deep-water Manila harbor ahead and to the right, then teeming with ships and boats of every kind.

Many of these Latter-day Saint soldiers had lived relatively isolated lives in small rural communities. The sight of Manila would have been a very new experience—a large, tropical city teeming with people and all else that accompanies a military buildup, and, of course, the oppressive humidity. The Philippines is located just a few degrees above the equator, so the days were invariably the same all year—scorching hot and humid. From here on, everything that happened in their lives in the Philippines happened in this oppressive tropical heat.

After disembarking, Brown and Hamblin and the other soldiers of 200th were loaded into trucks for the trip to Fort Stotsenburg, seventy-five miles north of Manila. From the trucks, these new arrivals saw the wide-eyed stares of curious Filipino children watching the huge American convoy roll north through Manila. Once outside the city, they saw rice paddies and banana trees on each side of the road, green mountains in the distance to the east and west, carabao-drawn carts tended by farmers with strange hats, and bamboo homes built on stilts—all new and curious scenes for these young men. Hamblin described the scene: "Everything was strange—strange sights and strange odors. The [carabao], which is their beast of burden, were everywhere, the little one-horse carts drawn by small horses resembling the Shetland, their carts were called caramotas. . . . We saw many bamboo houses built up off the ground on stilts on account of the water and razor back hogs were seen running around under the houses. These, along with their chickens and other fowls and animals, added to the peculiar odor."[1]

After a few hours, the soldiers arrived at Fort Stotsenburg, an old cavalry post located next to Clark Field. The 200th Coast Artillery Regiment was charged with guarding Clark Field and its fleet of bombers and fighters, which were key to General MacArthur's Pacific strategy. They had some challenges. Much of the WWI-vintage equipment they had trained with at Fort Bliss in Texas was defective and had been abandoned at Fort Bliss. Typical of the snafus in this buildup, the rejected equipment they had abandoned at Fort Bliss had nevertheless been broken down, loaded up, and shipped to the Philippines anyway, and after the ocean voyage, the equipment arrived in the Philippines in even worse condition. Parts were missing or damaged, replacement parts were unusable, and some searchlights were broken and useless.[2] Using the artillery equipment that did work, they practiced ranging, fusing, and loading, but never actually fired the guns because of the shortage of ammunition. They mostly practiced spotting aircraft with the spotlights and radar that weren't broken.

Notwithstanding these mobilization problems, the Philippines was an easy and comfortable post for a young soldier. Days started at 0700 (7 a.m.) and ended with a siesta after lunch. Living costs were cheap, and local domestic help was inexpensive and available. Their barracks would likely have been in a *sawali*, a wooden building on stilts.[3]

These Latter-day Saint soldiers were now thousands of miles away from their families and the religious culture in which they had been raised. They found themselves in a new, exotic location with plenty of bars, clubs, and entertainment of the kind that thrives on soldiers, especially in nearby Manila.[4]

Excursions into Manila, a bustling Asian city teeming with activity and seductive vices, were an exciting event for young soldiers. Gene Jacobsen, a Latter-day Saint soldier from Montpelier, Idaho, came to the Philippines earlier as part of the 20th Pursuit Squadron of the Army Air Corps based at Nichols Field just south of Manila. He later wrote of the abundance of alcohol and prostitutes he encountered on his first trip to Manila and his decision to walk away from it.[5] Private Franklin East from Arizona, who at the time was recovering in a hospital from a surgery and who was part of the Fifth Air Base group, wrote of his disgust with soldiers suffering from venereal disease and his gratitude for his church's standards.[6]

In one of Brown's last letters home, he wrote about his trips into Manila. Through Major Schurtz, Brown's commanding officer and an accomplished musician, Brown and some other soldiers had been invited by the university in Manila to join with the university's chorus in presenting Handel's *Messiah* for Christmas. Brown went to Manila to rehearse with the university choir.[7] While there were no organized church services for Latter-day Saints, Brown, Keeler, and Hamblin, and maybe Allred and Bloomfield as well, attended the religious services conducted by the chaplain and informally met together frequently.

Notwithstanding the generally pleasant circumstances of their posting, it turned out to be a tragic time for Hamblin. On November

15, while sitting in the mess hall after dinner, he was handed a cablegram from his sister that read, "Father not expected to live. Struck by plane at Luke Field." His father, Don Carlos Hamblin, had been working at Luke Air Force Base in Arizona and was accidently struck by the wing of a plane. The following morning, another cable arrived informing him that his father had passed away. Hamblin and his father were close, and the news of his death was painful.

Holding these cablegrams, Hamblin thought back to the day he had left his home for Fort Bliss. Hamblin had been the only son in a family of nine girls until a baby brother was born, and he was the pride of his father's heart. When he had left Farmington on a bus for Fort Bliss, his father had walked with him to the bus depot. It had been a difficult parting, but Hamblin and his father were so close that not a lot needed to be said. His father's parting words had been simply "Be good, son."

Far from home and his family, Hamblin struggled with the loss of his "dear father and counselor." Hamblin later received some letters his father had written to him before he died, which, while gratefully received and treasured, made him feel the loss even more deeply. He "sought comfort and solace through prayer to my Heavenly Father, which gave me strength to carry on."[8] With his father dead and his mother in need of comfort and financial support, Hamblin began arranging for a family hardship discharge.

Circumstances, however, would change. Brown would not sing in Handel's *Messiah* at Christmas that year, and the processing of Hamblin's discharge would never be completed.

The convoy with the Fifth Air Base group from Salt Lake City arrived in Manila a few days later on November 20, 1941, Thanksgiving Day; the men were temporarily bivouacked in tents at nearby Fort McKinley. That afternoon they received a Thanksgiving dinner of wieners and sauerkraut with canned peaches for dessert, a meal that was something of a disappointment at the time. While the soldiers had no reason to do so at that time, many of those soldiers would nevertheless later make such a meal a subject of their dreams.[9]

Luzon, located at the northern end of the Philippine archipelago, is the largest and most populous island in the Philippines. It is home to Manila, the country's largest and most important city and one of Asia's most famous deep-water harbors, as well as Clark Field, then the principal US air base in Asia. Located about forty miles northwest of Manila, Clark Field was originally intended as the principal base for the B-17 heavy bombers that were key to General MacArthur's strategy. General MacArthur later realized that Clark Field was within the reach of Japanese bombers flying from bases in Taiwan (Formosa), and the planes were vulnerable to attack. However, the island of Mindanao, located at the southern end of the archipelago, was beyond the reach of those Japanese bombers. That island was home to a large Del Monte pineapple plantation located next to a large pasture used for cattle grazing. That pasture also happened to be a natural runway for heavy bombers. In November 1941 General MacArthur ordered the construction of a new base for heavy bombers at the Del Monte site.[10] The Fifth Air Base Squadron was assigned the task of constructing this field and preparing to receive these B-17 bombers.[11]

On November 30 the Fifth Air Base group boarded an interisland craft, the *Legaspi*, which took them on an overnight voyage to Bugo, a small port barrio on the Mindanao coast whose principal industry was a large Del Monte cannery. A few miles inland were thousands of acres of pineapple fields and the pasture that would become the Del Monte Airfield.

It was an ideal location. The ground under the sod was hard and would hold up even in wet weather. No grading was required; they just had to cut down the grass. A tractor mower was found, and the farmers in the squadron took over, a group that likely included some of the Latter-day Saint farm boys. There was also all the work of setting up the camp tents, a mess tent, a field kitchen, and then more permanent barracks and all the other facilities needed to sustain a large group of men, as well as the gun emplacements and the structures (*revetments*) to protect the airplanes.[12] The Fifth Air Base group was later joined by 440th and 701st Ordnance Companies of

Del Monte Airfield on Mindanao Island in late 1941. The BenHaven Archives. Courtesy of Walter J. Regehr.

the 19th Bombardment Group at the Del Monte Airfield. This added at least one additional Latter-day Saint soldier, Theodore Hippler, a private in the 440th from Bloomfield, New Mexico, to the group of Latter-day Saint servicemen at Del Monte.[13]

At forty years of age, Staff Sergeant Nels Hansen was older than most of the other Latter-day Saint air corpsmen; before the war, he had served two missions, including one to the Central States Mission. The family had moved around, and when he enlisted, Hansen was living in Weiser, Idaho. He had brought with him copies of the Church's scriptures (the Bible, the Book of Mormon, the Doctrine and Covenants, and the Pearl of Great Price), along with five Deseret Sunday School Song Books and a copy of *Added Upon*, by Nephi Anderson, a then popular novel among Latter-day Saints about our eternal journey based on Church teachings. With this gospel library and Hansen's leadership, these Latter-day Saint soldiers formed a Sunday School at Del Monte with regular meetings each Sunday. They had about twenty participants.[14]

This was a busy time for these air corpsmen, with much to be done to construct the airfield and related facilities. Many of the newest B-17Ds of the Seventh Bombardment Group, which was to be stationed at Del Monte, were already on their way from the mainland. However, the grand plans for Del Monte Airfield and the Seventh Bombardment Group were not to be.

NOTES

1. Hamblin, "My Experience," 3.
2. Cave, *Beyond Courage*, 45, 53–54, 8. See also Morton, *Fall of the Philippines*, 45.
3. Lukacs, *Escape from Davao*, 9; Shively, *Profiles in Survival*, 195–96; Cave, *Beyond Courage*, 45–51; Gene S. Jacobsen, *We Refused to Die: My Time as a Prisoner of War in Bataan and Japan, 1942–1945* (Salt Lake City: University of Utah Press, 2004), 42–51; see also Hamblin, "My Experience," 3.
4. See Shively, *Profiles in Survival*, 195–96; Jacobsen, *We Refused to Die*, 46–47 (regarding the prevalence of prostitutes and alcohol).
5. See Jacobsen, *We Refused to Die*, 46–47. Jacobsen came to the Philippines nearly a year earlier in November 1940. Although Jacobsen was never at Dapecol, his memoir of his POW experiences is a valuable source of additional insight into the experience of a Latter-day Saint POW in the Philippines.
6. East, "Army Life," 8.
7. Nelle B. Zundel, "George Robin (Bobby) Brown," in Brown, *Alma Platte Spilsbury*, 297; Call, "Latter-day Saint Servicemen," 105–7.
8. Hamblin, "My Experience," 3–4.
9. Christensen, "My Life History," 5; Raymond C. Heimbuch, *I'm One of the Lucky Ones: I Came Home Alive* (Crete, NE: Dageforde Printing, 2003), 32; Hayes Bolitho, "The Hayes Bolitho Japanese Story, Parts 1–6," *Hawkins (Texas) Holly Lake Gazette*, a biweekly online newspaper, September 26, 2009–February 13, 2010, Part 1 (accessible at http://www.hlrgazette.com/2009-articles/85-september-26-2009/785-local-ww-ii-herojapanese-pow-1-of-6.html). Heimbuch and Bolitho were members of the Fifth Air Base group that also included some twenty Latter-day Saint soldiers. Carl Nordin was also part of the Fifth Air Base group, and in a memoir of his POW experience he mentions Parry as one of the Latter-day Saints in the group. Carl S. Nordin, *We Were Next to Nothing: An American POW's*

Account of Japanese Prison of War Camps and Deliverance in World War II (Jefferson, NC: McFarland and Company, 1997), 64–65.
10. Morton, *Fall of the Philippines*, 43; Burton, *Fortnight of Infamy*, 63.
11. See Christensen, "My Life Story," 5; Heimbuch, *Lucky Ones*, 26, 33–34.
12. Burton, *Fortnight of Infamy*, 63; Bolitho, "Japanese Story," part 2 (October 10, 2009).
13. Clark and Kowallis, "Fate of the Davao Penal Colony," 120.
14. Ashton, "*Spirit of Love*," 175.

5

EVERYTHING CHANGES

Jesus, Savior, pilot me
Over life's tempestuous sea;
Unknown waves before me roll,
Hiding rock and treach'rous shoal.

—Edward Hopper, "Jesus, Savior, Pilot Me"

On December 7, 1941, the Japanese bombed Pearl Harbor. The attack was swift and brutal. Three hours after the first bomb was dropped, more than two thousand people were dead, and eight battleships and more than 180 planes were destroyed. The attack also cut off supply lines to the Philippines. Across the international date line in the Philippines, it was December 8, and with the news of the attack on Pearl Harbor, the chaos of war soon came to the Philippines.

In response to the Pearl Harbor attack, US military leaders first ordered a bombing attack from the Philippines on Japanese forces in Taiwan. B-17 bombers and P-40 pursuit fighters took to the air from Clark Field. But the attack was delayed, then canceled, then approved again. Consequently, planes that had taken off were left circling over Clark Field while commanders debated what to do. With the bombing run to Taiwan back on, they had to land to refuel. In a case of truly unfortunate timing, Japanese bombers appeared over Clark Field just after the planes had landed; behind the bombers were the fighter planes, the infamous Japanese Zeros.¹

The 200th went into action, frantically firing their antiaircraft guns at the Japanese bombers, but their efforts were largely futile. The 200th had not yet been able to set up all their equipment, and much of what they had was defective or outmoded. The ammunition was WWI surplus, manufactured in 1918, and most shells were duds. The fuses on the antiaircraft shells were badly corroded, and only about one in six actually exploded. Those shells that exploded had fuses that were effective only to about twenty thousand feet, a problem the Japanese bombers avoided by flying at twenty-three thousand feet. With their 37-millimeter guns and .50-caliber machine guns, however, the 200th had a chance at the low-flying Zeros. Even though this was the first time they had actually fired the guns with live ammunition, and despite the fact that only about one in six of the old WWI-era shells actually fired, they managed to down five Japanese aircraft.² The

A B-17 bombed by Japanese in the attack on Clark Field, December 8, 1941. The BenHaven Archives. Courtesy of G. A. von Peterffy.

200th earned the distinction of being the first US unit to fire shots during World War II.[3]

The soldiers of the 200th fought valiantly, and acts of heroism were common. Ground and combat crews manned guns of grounded aircraft, and men dashed into flaming buildings to rescue comrades as well as supplies and equipment. Others braved strafing gunfire to help the wounded. However, the attack was clearly a rout by the Japanese. Japan had largely destroyed America's air force in the Philippines on the ground.[4]

MANILA AND THE 515TH

Realizing that Manila had no antiaircraft protection, commanders in the 200th hastily sent thirty officers and five hundred enlisted men that night—December 8—to Manila to set up an antiaircraft defense. This group would later be formally designated as a separate unit, the 515th Coast Artillery, under the command of Colonel Harry M. Peck, the executive officer of the 200th.[5] While Hamblin and Baclawski remained with the 200th, Brown and Keeler were assigned to the new 515th and deployed to Manila that night with Colonel Peck as commander.[6]

Guns were uncrated, assembled, dug in, and, quite remarkably, ready to shoot in twenty-four hours. About 650 officers and enlisted men from the Philippine Army were hastily recruited, trained, and added to the group. On the morning of December 10, Japanese bombers attacked Manila, including the important Cavite Naval Yard, but this time they met a pattern of antiaircraft fire. The puffs from the antiaircraft guns, however, were again more spectacular than effective, as the Japanese bombers were again flying above the height at which the US antiaircraft shells were set to detonate.[7]

WAR PLAN ORANGE REVISITED—RETREAT TO BATAAN

In the event of a Japanese attack, War Plan Orange called for the Americans to abandon Manila and cross over to the Bataan Peninsula, located on the west side of Manila Bay. The US would retreat from Manila without defending it, leaving it an "open city" and hopefully sparing the civilian population. Surrounded on three sides by water and protected somewhat to the north by mountains, the Bataan peninsula was an ideal place for such a retreat. From Bataan and the island fortress Corregidor, the Americans could still deny the Japanese the use of Manila Bay and its deep-water harbor and could hold out until rescue or reinforcements arrived by sea. Manila Bay was the main prize in the Philippines, and its control was essential to securing the strategic value of the Philippines.[8]

A couple of weeks after the initial attack, the Japanese landed on the island of Luzon, and their air attacks on Clark Field and the Manila area intensified. On Christmas Day, December 25, General MacArthur implemented War Plan Orange.[9] The key to the success of War Plan Orange was a retreat from Manila to the Bataan Peninsula, and the key to a successful retreat lay in the cluster of bridges across the Pampanga River near Calumpit and the bridge over the Culo River at the critical Layac Junction. These bridges connected the roads leading west out of Manila and into the Bataan Peninsula. At Calumpit, the north and south roads met and turned west toward Bataan. Layac Junction was the gateway to Bataan. If those bridges remained intact, the forces could pass safely to the Bataan Peninsula, as the Japanese in the south and east were still some distance away. Without the bridges, however, a long one-hundred-mile detour or crossing a twenty-mile swamp would be required, meaning the retreat would likely fail.[10]

The 200th and the newly christened 515th Coast Artillery were assigned the mission of protecting these critical bridges for the retreat. Hamblin later wrote of traveling through the night to spend Christmas Day digging new positions for their guns to protect the bridges, and from there watching the flames in the night and hearing the explosions from Fort Stotsenburg and Manila as gasoline and other supplies that could not be moved were destroyed.[11]

The antiaircraft guns of the 200th and 515th successfully fought off Japanese bombers targeting the bridges, a fight in which the 515th shot down two Japanese dive-bombers. The American troops were able to cross and move into Bataan. The Americans then destroyed the bridges to prevent the Japanese from following them into Bataan.¹² For this and subsequent actions, these two units would later receive Presidential Distinguished Unit Citations.¹³ This citation may be awarded to units for heroism against an armed enemy from December 7 onward. To receive the citation, the unit must have displayed such gallantry, determination, and esprit de corps in accomplishing its mission under extremely difficult and hazardous conditions as to set it apart and above other units participating in the same campaign.

The evacuation to Bataan, despite the challenges and chaos of the situation, was remarkably successful. General MacArthur's army had been able to slip into Bataan intact, carrying large stores of ammunition, mostly suspect WWI ordnance, but ammunition nonetheless. At the time of the retreat, much of the supplies in Manila, however, were technically within the control of the Filipino government. Due to the tangled bureaucracy of the Filipino government and the Americans' haste, substantial stores of clothing, fuel, and, most importantly, food and medicine were left behind. US troops would later pay dearly for this oversight. In addition to the approximately eighty thousand American and Filipino troops who retreated to Bataan, an estimated twenty-six thousand civilian refugees also fled to the peninsula, compounding the shortages. In one of his first orders on January 5, 1942, General MacArthur put everyone on half rations.¹⁴

NOTES

1. Morton, *Fall of the Philippines*, 85–86; Burton, *Fortnight of Infamy*, chap. 7 (91–110), giving details of the attack from an air force perspective.
2. Stephen M. Mellnik, "The Life and Death of the 200th Coast Artillery (AA)," *Coast Artillery Journal*, March–April 1947, accessible at the Bataan Corregidor Memorial Foundation of New Mexico website, http://www.angelfire.com/nm/bcmfofnm/history/mellnik_history.html.
3. Cave, *Beyond Courage*, 78.
4. Morton, *Fall of the Philippines*, 88.
5. Mellnik, "The Life and Death"; Morton, *Fall of the Philippines*, 92; Shively, *Profiles in Survival*, 199–200; Cave, *Beyond Courage*, 78.
6. See Allan C. McBride, Brigadier General, GSC, Chief of Staff, Headquarters Philippine Department in the Field, United States Army, Special Orders

No. 19, Extract, Paragraph 9, 20 January 1942, NARA Records (the order identifies Brown as a first lieutenant and former master sergeant with the 515th Coast Artillery).
7. Mellnik, "The Life and Death."
8. Shively, *Profiles in Survival*, 17–19; Hampton Sides, *Ghost Soldiers: The Forgotten Epic Story of World War II's Most Dramatic Mission* (New York City: Doubleday/Random House, 2001), 42, 56; Morton, *Fall of the Philippines*, 471.
9. Shively, *Profiles in Survival*, 15–17; Hamblin, "My Experience," 4.
10. Shively, *Profiles in Survival*, 18; Morton, *The Fall of the Philippines*, 203–5. Layac Junction would become the first line of defense against the Japanese invasion of Bataan and a US delaying action at Layac would become the first battle between US and Japanese forces. A memorial at Layac honors the site.
11. Hamblin, "My Experience," 5.
12. Morton, *Fall of the Philippines*, 205–10; Shively, *Profiles in Survival*, 18–21, 201.
13. Cave, *Beyond Courage*, 103.
14. Morton, *Fall of the Philippines*, 256–57; see Hamblin, "My Experience," 5. Some have criticized General MacArthur for wasting time and resources on an ill-advised "defend the beaches" strategy when he could have been better preparing for the move to Bataan, preparation that could have avoided the loss of food supplies. See Burton, *Fortnight of Infamy*, 199–200.

6

HEROES

*Oh, beautiful for heroes proved in liberating strife,
Who more than self their country loved,
And mercy more than life!*

—Katherine Lee Bates, "America the Beautiful"

The Japanese attack on the Philippines was part of a series of carefully planned, coordinated, and nearly simultaneous attacks on the United States at Pearl Harbor and the Philippines, on the British at Singapore and Burma, and on the Dutch at what is now Indonesia. The attacks succeeded beyond Japan's most ambitious expectations—except in the Philippines. The synchronized attacks crippled the US Navy in the Pacific and the British in Singapore, and the Dutch in Dutch East Asia quickly fell to Japanese attacks, but the Philippines did not fall as the Japanese had planned. The Japanese had not anticipated the retreat to Bataan and were unable to quickly defeat the Americans. In what would become known as the Battle of Bataan, the Americans had temporarily halted the Japanese advance.

As part of the buildup of forces in the Philippines, US Army officers, including Captain Robert G. Davey, were embedded with the Philippine Army. With the outbreak of war and the retreat to Bataan,

Davey was transferred back to a regular US Army division. On Bataan, he was assigned to the front line and was among those responsible for halting the initial Japanese invasion. For the next four months, Davey was never more than a thousand yards from the Japanese lines and was consistently under small arms fire.

While commanding an infantry unit, Davey had moved the unit into a densely covered thicket of trees where they would be hidden from the Japanese. They had just dug into their foxholes when Davey felt a strong impression to leave that area. He ignored it. His platoon was tired and hungry, and now, after much effort, it was firmly entrenched and safely hidden in the thicket; no one wanted to leave. The feeling persisted, however, and Davey eventually ordered them to move. The next morning, they marched back through that area and found that it had been heavily shelled. Apparently, the Japanese had seen them move into that thicket. Surveying their former position, Davey stared down at the large shrapnel lying in what would have been his foxhole. He realized, "Had I been there, I would still have been there."[1]

On January 20, 1942, in connection with the formation of the 515th and the retreat to Bataan, Master Sergeant George Robin (Bobby) Brown was given a battlefield commission as a first lieutenant and put in charge of munitions.[2] At this time in WWII, the army allowed the promotion of a soldier to a commissioned officer on the battlefield in exceptional circumstances. A battlefield commission is granted apart from the regular commission sources, such as graduation from the United States Military Academy at West Point, a Reserve Officers' Training Corps, or the army's Officer Candidate School. They are predicated on extraordinary performance of duties while serving in combat and are based on the commander's assessment of the soldier's actual performance in combat conditions in the field. Another officer who knew Brown referred to this battlefield commission as evidence of his "resourcefulness and intelligence."[3]

What little was left of the US Air Force, a few battered P-40s, was based at the Bataan and Cabcaben Airfields at the southern end of the peninsula.⁴ The 515th was assigned the mission of protecting the Cabcaben Airfield, where Brown was the munitions officer. On March 14, 1942, the Japanese again bombed the Cabcaben Airfield. But this time, the Japanese bombers successfully targeted the unit's only ammunition dump.

The explosive and incendiary bombs started fires, which were surrounded by highly combustible dry grass and bamboo, and fires started in some of the ammunition piles. Despite the personal danger, Brown and his friend Staff Sergeant Jack Keeler rushed to extinguish the fires and saved the unit's only ammunition supply. For this act of bravery, Brown would receive a Bronze Star.⁵

These were heroic and brilliant triumphs for the Filipino and American forces, and we should not fail to appreciate what these Americans and their Filipino allies, as poorly equipped as they were, had managed to accomplish. While the Japanese had achieved phenomenal success, sweeping away all resistance in front of them, only in the Philippines had they been halted. The Filipino and American forces had successfully guarded the bridges at Calumpit and Layac Junction and had kept open the strategic points of retreat into Bataan. They had defended the airstrips on Bataan; not one of the precious few remaining P-40s on Bataan had been lost to Japanese bombing.⁶ On the front lines to the north, the soldiers had managed to halt the Japanese invasion.

These US soldiers had demonstrated that the Japanese were not invincible and that they could be stopped by determined soldiers ably led, even though poorly equipped and with the odds heavily against them. In the end, the Philippines would fall, and Bataan would ultimately possess no great strategic importance in the global war. But at a time when the Allies were in full, humiliating retreat throughout the world and the United States was largely consumed by despair and defeat, their courageous stand at Bataan was an important symbol of hope.⁷

NOTES

1. Springgay, "Robert Gray Davey," 15–18: Davey, "Last Talk," 1.
2. Army of the United States, "Oath of Office (Temporary)," of George Robin Brown, January 20, 1942, NARA Records. See also Allan C. McBride, Brigadier General, GSC, Chief of Staff, Headquarters Philippine Department in the Field, United States Army, Special Orders No. 19, Extract, Paragraph 9, January 20, 1942, NARA Records (order identifies Brown as a first lieutenant and former master sergeant with the 515th Coast Artillery).
3. Major Shoss specifically referred to Brown's field commission as evidence of Brown's intelligence and resourcefulness. "LDS Group in Jap Prison Described," *Deseret News*, January 20, 1945, 11.
4. Lt. Col. William E. Dyess, *The Dyess Story: The Eye-Witness Account of the Death March from Bataan, Japanese Prison Camps and Escape* (New York City: G. P. Putnam's Sons, 1944), 35.
5. Harry M. Peck, Col. CAC, to General Jonathan M. Wainwright, Headquarters Fourth Army, March 7, 1946, NARA Records (recommending a Silver Star). Army officials later determined to award a Bronze Star. Report of Decorations Board, War Department, May 21, 1946 (approving citation and award of Bronze Star Medal "V" to George R. Brown, NARA Records).
6. Dyess, *Dyess Story*, 35–36; Cave, *Beyond Courage*, 152.
7. Morton, *Fall of the Philippines*, 584.

7

THE ABANDONED BOYS OF BATAAN

*Cast thy burden upon the Lord,
And he shall sustain thee.*

—Julius Schubring, "Cast Thy Burden upon the Lord"

Behind the military successes described in the previous chapter were some serious problems for the American troops. For the defenders on Bataan, tropical diseases and poor nutrition—not the Japanese—were now the immediate threats.[1] Bataan was an area highly infested with malaria, and the rate of malaria and other diseases climbed as limited supplies of medicine were exhausted.[2]

Food likewise became a serious problem. Rice fields, abandoned by the native Filipinos at the beginning of the war, were taken over by the troops and combed for anything edible. By February 1942, rations were limited to one-half pound of rice per man per day. This was a time when the army was still using horses and pack mules, which were now being slaughtered and eaten by the starving soldiers. Hunting for monkeys, iguanas, and carabao became a necessity rather than a sport, although Hamblin and many others could never bring themselves to eat a monkey. After being skinned, they resembled a newborn baby and, to Hamblin and others, weren't all that appetizing. In a short time, these edible animals became scarce, and snake hunting was the next thing to become popular.[3] Notwithstanding resourcefulness and survival skills, the defenders on Bataan were sick and starving. Now was the time for rescue.

George Brown, Lieutenant Bobby Brown's father, pleaded for help in a February 15, 1942, letter to Congressman R. E. Thomason:

> We have not heard of any effort or influence on your part to have some relief sent to the Philippines Islands [other Congressmen had been publicly calling on the Roosevelt Administration to do something in that regard]. No doubt you are doing all you can, but may I remind you that there are a number of people in this district who are full of anxiety over the Filipino situation.
>
> You know how we westerners feel about a buddy in a jam. Our policy is to get him out or die in the attempt. Anyhow, I don't believe that those American boys should be left to their doom, and I don't suppose they will be.[4]

It is probably just as well that George did not know that leaving "those American boys . . . to their doom" was exactly what the Roosevelt administration planned to do. The cold, hard truth was that there would be no new supplies, no reinforcements, and no rescue. This time, the cavalry was not coming.

With the outbreak of war in Europe, War Plan Orange was scrapped and replaced with plans known as "Rainbow" to deal with a worldwide war involving multiple enemies. Working with the British, US war planners secretly developed a strategy to confront Germany first, as Germany was considered the greater threat. Europe was to receive priority in terms of resources. Thus, those on Bataan would receive no reinforcements.[5]

A convoy of ships with badly needed supplies and reinforcements already en route to the Philippines was redirected and then recalled by Washington—actions that led to heated debates within the War Department and between navy and army commanders.[6]

Everyone wanted to rescue the troops in the Philippines. No one wanted to abandon them. But the cruel fact was that the program to make the Philippines an "impregnable fortress" had not proceeded far enough for the soldiers in the Philippines to be able to defend themselves without assistance, and the United States had made no contingency plans or preparations to provide that assistance. With the Japanese having complete air and naval supremacy in the Philippines, no such rescue attempt was likely to succeed.[7]

The press and, as George Brown had alluded to in his letter, some members of Congress were critical of President Roosevelt and the War Department for failing to aid General MacArthur and the troops on Bataan. But they were at odds with the master strategy for winning the war, and the criticisms were ignored. By late December 1941, President Roosevelt had "regrettably written off" the Philippines.[8]

Nevertheless, relying on misleading messages from President Roosevelt and others in Washington, General MacArthur assured his troops that help was on the way and that thousands of troops and hundreds of planes were being dispatched.[9] While General MacArthur received messages informing him relief shipments were being dispatched, he was not told the convoys were intended for strategic destinations other than the Philippines. President Roosevelt insisted the navy was "following an intensive and well-planned campaign which will result in positive assistance to the defense of the Philippine Islands," but there was no such campaign and there never was a serious plan to rescue them. Henry Stimson, the secretary of war, coldly wrote in his diary with respect to those fighting on Bataan, "there are times when men have to die."[10] Although he hid it from the lower levels of his command and his troops, General MacArthur understood the truth that there would be no help.[11]

The troops on Bataan, believing implicitly that help was on the way, fought with surprising effectiveness while awaiting their expected rescue. The 515th at the Cabcaben airfield and the 200th at the Bataan airfield battled daily not only to protect what was left of their air force, but also to keep the airfields open for hoped-for US planes with supplies and reinforcements from Australia.[12] At the Cabcaben airfield, the soldiers constructed revetments, largely using picks and shovels, to protect the hoped-for arrival of B-17s from Australia.[13]

After a while, the troops wondered about the promised reinforcements. They thought America seemed apathetic. Although the troops never really gave up, morale plummeted as they felt abandoned. In addition to President Roosevelt and Secretary Stimson, the troops began to resent General MacArthur.[14] Views were mixed among the Latter-day Saint soldiers. Rex Bray and Gene Jacobsen detested General MacArthur, while Orland Hamblin considered him a great general and American.[15]

Despite plunging morale, American soldiers maintained a resilient sense of humor. When a baby was born at a field hospital, one soldier quipped that "if FDR won't send reinforcements, we'll make our own." Some soldiers attempted to raise a fund to buy a bomber from their own government—the "Bomber for Bataan Fund." A journalist penned the following doggerel that became the theme of the abandoned defenders of Bataan:

> *We're the Battling Bastards of Bataan*
> *No Mama, No Papa, No Uncle Sam,*
> *No aunts, no uncles, no cousins, no nieces.*
> *No pills, no planes, no artillery pieces*
> *And nobody gives a damn.*[16]

NOTES

1. Morton, *Fall of the Philippines*, 367, 384.
2. Shively, *Profiles in Survival*, 38; Morton, *Fall of the Philippines*, 377–79.
3. Hamblin, "My Experience," 5; Jacobsen, *We Refused to Die*, 65–66; Mellnik, "The Life and Death"; Cave, *Beyond Courage*, 125.
4. George A. Brown to Honorable R. E. Thomason, February 15, 1942, NARA Records.
5. Shively, *Profiles in Survival*, 11–12; Burton, *Fortnight of Infamy*, 39–40. While the original Rainbow plan assumed the abandonment of the Philippines, General MacArthur was able to persuade the War Department to expand the role of his Far East command and, in view of the existing forces and planned reinforcements (the aircraft in particular), to change the Rainbow plan to include a defense of the Philippines. However, such defense would be conducted entirely by the forces on the Philippines, as the revised plan—similar to the previous War Plan Orange—did not provide for any reinforcements to the Philippines. Morton, *Fall of the Philippines*, 65.
6. Shively, *Profiles in Survival*, 22–23; Morton, *Fall of the Philippines*, 145–48.

7. Morton, *Fall of the Philippines*, 152. There were later some efforts to supply the Philippines with additional food and medicine by submarines, but those failed to provide such aid in any significant quantities. Morton, *Fall of the Philippines*, 391–404.
8. Sides, *Ghost Soldiers*, 43; Lukacs, *Escape from Davao*, 34.
9. Morton, *Fall of the Philippines*, 387.
10. Sides, *Ghost Soldiers*, 43, Lukacs, *Escape from Davao*, 32–33.
11. Burton, *Fortnight of Infamy*, 199–200; Morton, *Fall of the Philippines*, 242.
12. Shively, *Profiles in Survival*, 206. At Bataan, Hamlin was assigned the task of keeping telephone lines open through the repeated bombings of their positions by the Japanese; "My Experience," 5.
13. Garner, *Unwavering Valor*, 54–55.
14. Morton, *Fall of the Philippines*, 387–89; see Hamblin, "My Experience," 5;
15. Lukacs, *Escape from Davao*, 37–38. Jacobsen, *We Refused to Die*, 24, 73–74; Kurtis R. Bray, email message to author, February 22, 2017; Hamblin, "My Experience," 6.
16. Lukacs, *Escape from Davao*, 37–38.

8
THE LAST LINE AT CABCABEN

As he died to make men holy,
let us live to make men free,
While God is marching on.

—Julia Ward Howe, "Battle Hymn of the Republic"

Although no American reinforcements arrived, reinforcements did come to the Japanese. By early 1942, the Japanese reinforced their hold in the Philippines with some of their most experienced troops. In April the Japanese launched a drive south down the peninsula. On April 7, after two days and nights of continuous shelling and air attacks, the Japanese infantry units broke through Filipino and American lines in the north and poured south.[1] One soldier described the retreating army as a "tired mob trying to keep out of the way of an annihilating steamroller."[2]

With the front lines broken and the Japanese heading south, the 200th and the 515th were ordered to destroy their antiaircraft guns and take up rifles as infantrymen and defend the line south of Cabcaben Airfield, the last line of defense. Officially, the units were combined and reconstituted as the Provisional Coast Artillery Brigade.[3]

On April 7, 1942, a heavy Japanese armored attack broke through the American-Filipino defenses. Courtesy of United States Air Force National Museum.

Hamblin was among those of the 200th now headed to the front as part of the infantry. He handed his rifle to a friend on a truck about to depart for the front only to have the truck leave while he turned around to get his pack. He nevertheless started marching toward the front without a rifle and against a tide of fleeing civilians and soldiers "staggering from wounds, exhaustion, and lost hope." Hamblin managed to "liberate" a rifle from a Filipino, "moving so fast in the other direction, I figured he wouldn't have any use for it."[4] Despite the Japanese onslaught and the chaos of the retreat, the combined 200th/515th force held their position and managed to force the Japanese attackers streaming south to temporarily stop and deploy.[5]

Hamblin later wrote of his thoughts that last evening. A captain had assigned him as his "runner" to take messages to his command post. Returning to the command post, Hamblin came across a spot where the air corps had just abandoned their own command post. A radio was tuned to a Manila station, then under Japanese control, playing a Japanese propaganda program dedicated to the "Americans on Bataan." The songs included "Waiting for Ships that Never Come In," and "Aloha Oe," among other appropriate tunes. Hamblin wrote of that moment, "I thought of home and it was hard to realize that I was seven thousand miles away, and these things were happening to me. I was brought back to reality by the sound of motors and I realized it was our few remaining aircraft . . . preparing to fly south and escape the advancing army. . . . I strained my ears to hear the sound as long as I could, because I knew it would be the last friendly planes I would hear for a long time, then there was silence, broken by the sound of the jungle night."[6]

He also heard the sound of ammunition dumps being blown up—the tremendous rumbling of the detonation of TNT and hundreds of thousands of rounds of ammunition to prevent their capture by the Japanese. It was the end. Ironically, and perhaps as an omen, this same night a strong earthquake struck the Philippines with its epicenter in Bataan.[7]

SURRENDER

On President Roosevelt's order, General MacArthur secretly left for Australia on March 12, 1942. Along with his family and some staff officers, General MacArthur departed Corregidor on four PT boats for the island of Mindanao in the south. From there, they were taken to the Del Monte Airfield, where the Fifth Air Base group was stationed. Around 2 a.m. on March 16, the group left in two planes for Australia. Private James Patterson, a Latter-day Saint soldier in the Fifth Air Base, was at Del Monte at the time and near the general when he boarded the plane. He heard General MacArthur promise, "I shall return." As one who was staying, Patterson was not particularly impressed. On arriving in Australia, General MacArthur again made his famous pledge, "I shall return," which was largely met with derision among the American troops on Bataan.[8]

With General MacArthur gone, General Jonathan Wainwright crossed over from Bataan to Corregidor to assume command of the Philippines; General Edward King took General Wainwright's place as commander on Bataan.[9] With more provisions and protection within the tunnels, those on Corregidor could hold out a while longer, possibly a month or more. But on Bataan General King knew that it was over. With his troops simply unable to defend against the Japanese attacks, he would be the one to have to surrender. As General King put it in a memo, "The physical condition of the command due to the long siege, during which they have been on short rations, will make it very difficult to move them a great distance on foot."[10] That was a gross understatement. Unit commanders were estimating their combat efficiency, the percentage of soldiers able to perform minimal combat functions, at 25 percent and declining.[11]

General King's surrender was complicated by the fact that President Roosevelt, General George Marshall, General MacArthur, and General Wainwright had all given orders not to surrender under any circumstances. General King assumed he would be court-martialed after the war for his actions, and he insisted on acting alone so that no one else—including General Wainwright, General MacArthur, or General Marshall—would be "saddled [with] any part of the responsibility."[12]

Normally, before surrender, the surrendering troops would destroy anything of potential value to the enemy, such as weapons, ammunition, vehicles, and fuel. When General King ordered such destruction in anticipation of the surrender, however, he reserved a significant number of vehicles and gasoline for the purpose of transporting US troops. He hoped the Japanese would accept his proposal to transport his own debilitated troops to whatever destination the Japanese would designate, as he (quite correctly) believed the Japanese did not have sufficient vehicles to transport such a large number of prisoners—and if they did, they would not use them for that purpose.[13] General King's decision to reserve some transport vehicles from destruction would turn out to have important consequences for Lieutenant Bobby Brown, as he was in charge of some transport vehicles at the time of the surrender.

General King surrendered on April 9, 1942. The surrender ceremony did not go well. The Japanese officer accepting the surrender on behalf of General Masuharu Homma, the commander of the Japanese 14th Army, was angered that General King did not have authority to surrender all of the Filipino and American forces (in other words, those on the key island of Corregidor as well). General King asked that his troops be permitted to march out of Bataan under their own officers to whatever location the Japanese designated and that the sick, wounded, and exhausted men be allowed to ride in vehicles he had saved for that purpose.[14] In answer to that request, the officer simply replied, "The Imperial Japanese Army are not barbarians."[15] With no alternatives left, General King agreed to an unconditional surrender. Brown, Hamblin, Davey, and the others became prisoners of the Imperial Japanese Army on April 9.

NOTES

1. Shively, *Profiles in Survival*, 40–46; Morton, *Fall of the Philippines*, 442–48.
2. Stephen M. Mellnik, *Philippines War Diary, 1939–1945*, revised edition (New York City: Van Nostrand Reinhold, 1969), 111.
3. Morton, *Fall of the Philippines*, 451, 454; Shively, *Profiles in Survival*, 46.
4. Cave, *Beyond Courage*, 103, 146–47.
5. Mellnik, "The Life and Death of the 200th Coast Artillery."
6. Hamblin, "My Experience," 7.
7. Morton, *Fall of the Philippines*, 459–60.
8. *Fall of the Philippines*, 359; Lukacs, *Escape from Davao*, 54; Patterson, interview, 13–14. Allen C. Christensen also notes in his history that he was on machine gun duty the night General MacArthur left; see Christensen, "My Life History," 7.
9. Morton, *Fall of the Philippines*, 365.
10. Sides, *Ghost Soldiers*, 46.
11. Shively, *Profiles in Survival*, 38; Morton, *Fall of the Philippines*, 384.
12. Shively, *Profiles in Survival*, 47.
13. Morton, *Fall of the Philippines*, 457, 466; Hamblin, "My Experience," 8.
14. Morton, *Fall of the Philippines*, 465–66.
15. Lukacs, *Escape from Davao*, 56.

9

THE CAPTORS

*Thru the valley and shadow of death though I stray,
Since thou art my Guardian, no evil I fear.*

—James Montgomery, "The Lord Is My Shepherd"

Japan was seeking to establish itself as the dominant force in East Asia. Predictably, these Japanese ambitions were the source of tension and hostility between Japan and the western powers. But there was also another powerful source of hostility: prejudice. The Japanese deeply resented that the western powers, at least in the Japanese view, treated Japan as an inferior country and race. They were similarly offended by the discrimination Japanese frequently encountered in the western countries. The 1924 Immigration Act, which had the effect of excluding Japanese from immigrating to the United States while permitting western Europeans immigrants, was especially insulting to Japan.

The Japanese military, a highly nationalistic organization and an influential political force, was particularly strident in its hostility to the United States and its European allies. As part of wartime indoctrination, Japanese soldiers were taught to hate Westerners. And the Americans were now surrendering to this Japanese military.[1]

In the period leading up to the war, there was a strain of ethnic arrogance and racism among many in America with respect to the Japanese. Some Americans had scoffed at the Japanese as people who were neither sufficiently clever nor equipped to withstand a modern Western army.[2] The decisive Japanese military victories had erased these prewar myths. The surrendering soldiers were about to receive some sharp lessons on the nature of this Japanese enemy.

The Japanese Army was not heavily mechanized. Fuel was a scarce commodity. Japanese troops generally traveled long distances on foot, twenty to thirty miles a day. The Japanese Army expected the surrendering American forces to do the same, disregarding General King's plan to use American vehicles to transport his sick and malnourished troops.[3] In fact, the American soldiers were not used to marching on foot such distances and were too famished and sick to do so in any event—and certainly not at the pace the Japanese demanded. The Japanese seriously misjudged the health and stamina of the Filipino and American forces and the adequacy of their provisions.[4]

In addition, attitudes about military discipline were very different between the opposing armies. Beatings had long been a routine method of discipline in the Japanese Army, and soldiers could essentially strike subordinates at will.[5] The distinction between ranks was of critical importance. It meant the difference between who could inflict blows and who could expect to receive them. This policy of brutality flowed down the ranks to the lowest private. When an enlisted man, hardened by this policy of top-down violence, found himself suddenly thrown into a situation in which he is the superior and in charge of a group of helpless and hated prisoners, the temptation to beat the powerless often became irresistible.

The Japanese soldiers were also unlikely to feel magnanimous toward their American enemy. The Japanese had not conquered Bataan easily. The American and Filipino defense of Bataan had cost the Japanese five months of combat and ten thousand casualties.[6] When Gene Jacobsen, a Latter-day Saint soldier from Montpelier, Idaho, surrendered, an English-speaking Japanese officer told him, "But, on Bataan you have killed many Japanese soldiers, and for that each of you will have to pay."[7] A few days after the surrender, a Japanese newspaper ran an editorial stating, "To show [the surrendering US forces] mercy is to prolong the war, . . . an eye for an eye, a tooth for a tooth."[8]

Ironically, however, the greater problem for these Americans in the eyes of the Japanese was not their tenacious defense but that they had surrendered at all. According to the Japanese code of Bushido—the Way of the Warrior—in which the Japanese soldiers had been indoctrinated, the goal of life was death in glorious fealty. Surrender to the enemy was beneath the dignity of a true soldier and a betrayal of his emperor, country, family, and comrades.

Rex Bray, a Latter-day Saint soldier who was wounded in the leg in a firefight with the Japanese and captured a few days later, observed, "For the most part, the Japanese treated me much better than the other prisoners who surrendered. My wound caused my capture. The Japanese did not respect those who surrendered without a fight. They would rather die than surrender."[9] In the view of many of their captors, the prisoners were not only hated enemies but also pathetic objects to be despised and loathed.

Soldiers, of course, vary in their competency, temperament, and morality. Soldiers in the Japanese Army were no different. Some were humane and professional in their treatment of the surrendering soldiers, but others were not.[10] Nonetheless, this was war, and the Japanese wanted their best commanders and soldiers on the all-important offensive campaigns, not tending prisoners. Guarding prisoners was not an honorable or coveted duty. Letting this natural selection process run its predictable course, the Japanese Army ended up putting some of its most incompetent, sadistic, and xenophobic soldiers in command of the prisoners.[11]

All these factors came together in a perfect storm of evil for the soldiers surrendering on Bataan. Some of the difficulties they would later face, unfortunately, were not just from their captors. While there were many incidents of great kindness, unwavering support, and personal sacrifice among prisoners, that, sadly, was not always the case. In the deprivations of the prison camp, some would retreat to their

American servicemen being searched by Japanese soldiers upon their surrender on Bataan. Courtesy of United States Navy, Naval History and Heritage Command.

most primitive survival instincts, where the jungle rule of "each man for himself" governed.[12] With their surrender, these soldiers fell into a hellish abyss run by a brutal captor with, on occasion, less-than-trustworthy companions.

The brutality began almost immediately. Upon an American soldier's surrender, the Japanese thoroughly searched him—purportedly for weapons and military intelligence, but the real purpose was simply to loot. Wristwatches seemed to be the favorite, with many Japanese guards strutting around with multiple Timex and Elgin watches on their arms. Parker ballpoint pens, Zippo lighters, and American cigarettes were also popular. For no reason other than malice, guards often shredded pictures of loved ones found on a surrendering soldier. One guard seized a pair of eyeglasses from a prisoner and, after inspecting them, smashed them on the ground with his boot and left the prisoner groping around.

Sometimes the malice was deeper. One guard took a fancy to a prisoner's gold filling, which, with the smack of a rifle butt to the prisoner's mouth, became more readily available for his taking. Another guard, growing frustrated trying to remove a coveted West Point ring from an officer's hand, swollen from beriberi, separated both the ring and the finger from the prisoner with the slice of a machete.[13]

There were innumerable ways an American soldier in the Philippines could end up with a Japanese-made item in his pocket. Japanese logic, however, dictated that a prisoner in possession of any such item—including Japanese currency, Rising Sun flags, or even a small pocket mirror purchased in the United States but made in Japan—must have taken the item from the body of a dead Japanese soldier. This was considered dishonorable behavior with a steep cost, often beheading.[14]

The Japanese guards commonly beheaded prisoners for trivial offenses. As Franklin East put it, "They took you out of the group and you weren't seen again."[15] Major William Dyess, who later escaped and wrote an exposé of the Japanese atrocities, wrote that the first murder he observed was the summary beheading of an air force captain by a Japanese private after discovering a few Japanese yen in the officer's pockets.[16]

For the surrendering POWs, however, these initial searches were just an introduction to the brutality of their imprisonment.

NOTES

1. Holmes, *Unjust Enrichment*, 8–9; see also Manny Lawton, *Some Survived: An Eyewitness Account of the Bataan Death March and the Men Who Lived through It* (Chapel Hill, NC: Algonquin Books of Chapel Hill, 1984), 26.

2. Sides, *Ghost Soldiers*, 51. Not all soldiers, however, carried this racist view. See text accompanying chapter 2, note 35 regarding Hansen's experience in Hawaii.
3. Daws, *Prisoners of the Japanese*, 73–74.
4. Sides, *Ghost Soldiers*, 91–93.
5. Lukacs, *Escape from Davao*, 69.
6. Holmes, *Unjust Enrichment*, 17.
7. Jacobsen, *We Refused to Die*, 91.
8. Holmes, *Unjust Enrichment*, 17 (quoting part of an April 14, 1942, editorial in the *Japan Times and Advertiser*, a minor English-language newspaper published in Japan).
9. Bray, "War Memories," 14.
10. The Japanese Navy may have been more humane and professional, at least initially, in its treatment of POWs than the Japanese Army. A POW's initial treatment upon surrender may have depended on which group he surrendered to. The Japanese Army, however, was responsible for the POW camps. A frustration for the POWs was the unpredictability of their treatment by the Japanese at any particular time. Soldiers surrendering in the southern islands were held for a time at Malabalay in central Mindanao, where they "fared royally" and the Japanese were particularly solicitous of their welfare. Alan McCracken, *Very Soon Now, Joe* (New York City: Hobson Book Press, 1947), 1–6, 39–45; Lukacs, *Escape from Davao*, 113.
11. Sides, *Ghost Soldiers*, 106; Lukacs, *Escape from Davao*, 102. See also McCracken, *Very Soon Now*, 4.
12. Sneddon, *Zero Ward*, 35; Daws, *Prisoners of the Japanese*, 134–35. See also Jacobsen, *We Refused to Die*, 189, 199 (regarding a cruel, vindictive US commander). Many POW camps, especially in Japan in the later months of the war, included POWs from other Allied countries, such as England, Australia, and the Dutch East Indies, some of whom were Black. The relationships among these Allied groups were usually good, but not always, and sometimes the rivalries undermined unity in the camps and resulted in mistrust and wariness between these groups. See Daws, *Prisoners of the Japanese*, 23–24, 135–37.
13. Lukacs, *Escape from Davao*, 62; Sides, *Ghost Soldiers*, 82; Cave, *Beyond Courage*, 166.
14. Cave, *Beyond Courage*, 188–89; Shively, *Profiles in Survival*, 59; Lukacs, *Escape from Davao*, 61.
15. East, "Army Life," 11.
16. Dyess, *Dyess Story*, 54–55.

10

THE "HIKE"

Fear not, I am with thee; oh, be not dismayed,
For I am thy God and will still give thee aid.

—Robert Keen, "How Firm a Foundation"

The geography of the Manila Bay is important to understanding our unfolding story. About three miles off the tip of the Bataan Peninsula is the small island of Corregidor, a heavily fortified island with guns that guarded access to Manila Bay. It was also the location of the bombproof Malinta Tunnel with its honeycombed maze of reinforced concrete laterals and cavernous ventilated shafts used for hospital wards, offices, and storage. With the retreat from Manila, Corregidor had become the command center for General MacArthur and, following his departure, General Wainwright.

Corregidor's strategic significance was that its guns blocked free access to Manila Bay. For safe access to Manila Bay, the Japanese needed to control Corregidor. Corregidor was best captured from the southern tip of the Bataan Peninsula, which was exactly where Hamblin, Brown, Davey, and the other surrendering US troops were now clustered.[1]

A few weeks before the US troops surrendered, Japanese general Homma and his staff had developed a plan to evacuate the prisoners they expected to capture on the Bataan Peninsula. The plan provided for the prisoners to be moved from Bataan to a prison camp some seventy miles north in central Luzon. The plan grossly underestimated the number of surrendering soldiers, the soldiers' health, and the complications of moving the prisoners north to camps at the same time the Japanese infantry was moving south for an assault on Corregidor.

Upon the surrender of the Filipino and American forces, it became obvious that the evacuation plan was wildly out of touch with the reality. While the Japanese had expected about forty thousand prisoners, the actual number was closer to a hundred thousand, including civilians.[2] Moreover, the troops surrendering were concentrated in southern Bataan, exactly where General Homma needed to move his troops to launch the final assault on Corregidor.

General Homma's initial attacks on Bataan had not been successful, and he was now months behind schedule, throwing off Japan's overall timetable for its Far East campaign and putting him under growing criticism in Tokyo. Consequently, General Homma's paramount objective was to get the surrendering troops out of the way of his 14th Army, which was marching south.[3] He would take no time to adjust the flawed evacuation plan to actual circumstances; instead, he ordered commanders and soldiers to do the impossible. The result was a catastrophe of torture, murder, sickness, suffering, and the unnecessary deaths of thousands of surrendering soldiers.[4]

Soldiers surrendered in various locations in Bataan and, after being searched, were organized in groups and marched north. The forced march on foot northward along the East Road to San Fernando became known as the "Bataan Death March." However, with characteristic understatement, the prisoners often simply called it the "hike."[5] Depending on where they surrendered, prisoners walked for five to twelve days—a distance of a few miles to as many as sixty miles—in the tropical sun with little or no food or water.[6]

The guards knew they could be punished or severely reprimanded if a POW escaped or if they did not arrive at the appointed place on time. However, there was no punishment or reprimand for a dead POW. Accordingly, the guards were merciless in prodding the prisoners with their bayonets to speed up the pace. By relieving and replacing the guards at short intervals, the Japanese always had rested guards to step up the pace of the weary, sick, and starving POWs.[7]

POWs who could not keep pace were killed. If a prisoner fell down or fell behind, sometimes the guards would shoot them, but to save bullets often used their bayonets, driving the blade deep into the abdomen and making three twists in the shape of a *Z* to scramble the bowels, leaving the prisoner to die.[8] The Japanese guards were practiced and proficient in the use of their bayonets. Davey wryly noted, "It is amazing how much strength you get to carry on when suddenly someone in front of you falls out and pulls over to the side and the Jap just shoots him and he falls to the side of the road. I think about every hundred feet there was at least one Filipino or American soldier that had been killed in this manner."[9]

When the beleaguered prisoners stopped for what they hoped would be a rest or water break, what they often found was only more torture. The Japanese guards commonly made prisoners stand or sit for hours at a time in the hot sun (the "sun treatment") or had them rest near pools of clean artesian water but killed anyone who broke ranks to drink.[10]

Of his experience on the Bataan Death March, Orland Hamblin wrote, "Many were already weak from sickness and hunger. Some had been on the front lines with very little relief for four months, so it was inevitable that many would fall by the roadside from exhaustion. We were marched out in groups of a few hundred each. Before the last group had arrived at the prison camp, . . . several thousand had died, either shot or bayoneted by the impatient and cruel [Japanese guards]. The civilians who had followed us onto the peninsula were herded out with the rest like cattle; old and young alike, making a scene not soon to be forgotten."[11]

American POWs on the Bataan Death March. Courtesy of United States Air Force National Museum.

For many Filipino civilians, most of whom were Catholics, the march must have seemed a horrifically real passion play. Hamblin records that when they passed through towns, Filipino civilians lined the sides of the road, many hoping to get word of their own sons and husbands who were in Bataan, but also helping the prisoners along the march. They hid cans of water in bushes and threw rice balls and cookies into the columns. Children ran along handing fruit and cassava cakes to the prisoners. The good deeds, however, came with consequences. The Japanese guards often beat or took shots at the local Filipinos. A farmer and his wife were burned at the stake for aiding the prisoners. Further, a young, pregnant Filipino woman who had thrown cassava cakes to the prisoners was bayoneted through her womb.[12]

Eventually, those who survived the hike to San Fernando were then packed into cramped and poorly ventilated boxcars and taken by train about twenty miles north to Capas. By this time, many of the prisoners suffered from dysentery and other diseases. The result was an overpowering stench in the cars, which had temperatures exceeding 100 degrees. Weak from the march and the lack of food and water, as well as suffering various diseases, some died standing up in the boxcars. Survivors were then marched from the rail terminal another ten miles to Camp O'Donnell.[13]

The exact number who took part in or who died on the death march is impossible to know, but about twelve thousand Americans and as many as sixty-five thousand Filipinos began the sixty-five-mile march from the Bataan Peninsula to San Fernando. Estimates vary widely, but a median guess is that around 750 Americans and more than five thousand Filipinos died on the march.[14] The Japanese guards were even more vicious in their treatment of the Filipinos than the Americans. The causes of death were many, from malaria and dysentery to starvation to sheer exhaustion and what can only be described as torture and murder. Sadly, Brown and Hamblin's units, the 515th and the 200th, were well represented on the Death March.[15]

Despite the cruelty and suffering—and with luck, courage, and an occasional miracle—Brown, Hamblin, Davey, and other Latter-day Saint POWs survived the ordeal.

NOTES

1. Morton, *Fall of the Philippines*, 471; Shively, *Profiles in Survival*, 1, 50–51.
2. Shively, *Profiles in Survival*, 53–54.
3. Hamblin, "My Experience," 8; Shively, *Profiles in Survival*, 50–51.
4. After the war, General Homma was tried, convicted, and executed for war crimes related to the Bataan Death March and the treatment of prisoners at the Camp O'Donnell and Cabanatuan camps in the Philippines. Daws, *Prisoners of the Japanese*, 365.
5. Sides, *Ghost Soldiers*, 91.
6. Clark and Kowallis, "Fate of the Davao Penal Colony," 114; see Garner, *Unwavering Valor*, 71–72 (estimates fifty-five miles). Other POWs estimate the distance as about one hundred miles, but those estimates likely include

the twenty-five-mile train ride. Hamblin, "My Experience," 8; Robert G. Davey, "Last Talk," 1.
7. Jacobsen, *We Refused to Die*, 89; Hamblin, "My Experience," 8.
8. Sides, *Ghost Soldiers*, 89; Shively, *Profiles in Survival*, 56–70; Davey, "Last Talk," 2.
9. Davey, "Last Talk," 1–2; "Faith Sustains Interned Mormon Captain," *Deseret News*, March 24, 1945, 7 and 16.
10. Lukacs, *Escape from Davao*, 63–65.
11. Hamblin, "My Experience," 8.
12. Hamblin, 9; Lukacs, *Escape from Davao*, 67; Shively, *Profiles in Survival*, 63.
13. Shively, *Profiles in Survival*, 70–71.
14. Shively, 51; Sides, *Ghost Soldiers,* 90; Lukacs, *Escape from Davao,* 73; see also Daws, *Prisoners of the Japanese*, 80 (no one really knows how many).
15. The New Mexico National Guard maintains a memorial and museum for the Bataan Death March in Santa Fe, New Mexico. There is also a Bataan Memorial Park in Albuquerque, New Mexico, and a Bataan Death March Statue and Walkway at the Veterans Memorial Park in Las Cruces, New Mexico.

11

SMALL MIRACLES

Where can I turn for peace?
Where is my solace
When other sources cease to make me whole?

—Emma Lou Thayne, "Where Can I Turn for Peace?"

When the 515th surrendered on Bataan, Brown was in charge of some trucks. The trucks had likely been spared destruction in the hope that they would be used by the Japanese to transport the surrendering soldiers.[1] The Japanese commandeered the vehicles and ordered Brown and his drivers to drive to Camp O'Donnell. Consequently, Brown arrived at Camp O'Donnell with two other Americans, ahead of the other prisoners, who were forced to walk the same distance.[2] While Brown would endure the horrific conditions of the prison camps, he was spared the horrors of the hike—the Bataan Death March.

When Brown surrendered, he had with him the triple combination set of scriptures his mother had given him when he left El Paso and the hymnbook given him by the Church youth group; he somehow managed to keep them.[3] That these materials escaped Japanese confiscation is surprising, as the Japanese typically confiscated Bibles from the POWs.[4] However it happened, Brown entered captivity with his scriptures and a hymnbook. In an otherwise horrible situation, this was a fortunate turn of events that would help him and others endure the ordeals to come.

Over the next ten days or so, Brown would see others he knew from the 200th and 515th struggle into the camp, including Baclawski, Brown's friend and tentmate from Fort Bliss, along with Hamblin, Allred, and Bloomfield, the few other Latter-day Saints in Brown's unit. At one point during the march, Hamblin had become dizzy and his legs had given way. Falling down or falling behind the group usually meant death by a bayonet from a Japanese guard. When he fell, Hamblin "offered a simple but very sincere prayer asking [his] Heavenly Father to help [him, and he] immediately felt strength coming into [his] body." He recovered and made the rest of the march without further signs of weakness. Indeed, he was also able to help those who were marching with him. Later he wrote that he had always tried to live the Church's health law, the Word of Wisdom, and had been taught since his childhood the scriptural promise that the obedient will "receive health in their navel and marrow to their bones . . . and shall run and not be weary, and shall walk and not faint" (Doctrine and Covenants 89:18–20). He concluded that it "seems to me that I had received a fulfillment of that promise."[5]

If Brown had been scanning the POWs slowly walking into the camp, among those he would have certainly been looking for was his closest friend, Jack Keeler. However, Brown's friend would not join him in the camp. When the POWs, including Keeler, arrived at Camp O'Donnell, the Japanese guards searched them again before sending them into the camp. Keeler, along with several others in his unit, was searched and found with something that appeared to be of Japanese origin. Keeler and the others were summarily taken away and executed.[6] For Brown, this was a heartbreaking loss.

Other sick and exhausted Latter-day Saint POWs who Brown did not then know struggled into camp. Among them was Private Franklin East, the homesick soldier from Arizona who came to the Philippines as part of the Fifth Air Base, a group that was then building an airfield on the relatively safe southern island of Mindanao. Shortly after the Fifth Air Base group arrived in Manila, East underwent a hernia operation and had been recovering in the hospital at the time his unit was sent to Mindanao. As a result, he remained in Manila and ended up on the Bataan Death March.

But on the other hand, East was fortunate to be alive and part of that march. After being released from the hospital, East had been assigned to a unit guarding ration trucks going to the front lines on Bataan. While waiting to get fuel at the assigned fuel depot, he had been impressed to go farther up the road to another depot. On his return, he saw that the trucks that had been lined up at the first depot had been bombed by the Japanese; the men were still in the trucks, burned to death.[7]

Captain Robert G. Davey also staggered into camp. Before the surrender, Davey contracted malaria, and, with persistent symptoms, he checked himself into the field hospital. Two days earlier, the hospital had been bombed, killing two hundred. Concluding that the hospital was not a particularly safe place, he grabbed some quinine and went back to his infantry unit shortly before it surrendered. He became part of the Bataan Death March.[8]

Davey started on the march at Mariveles at the far southern end of the Bataan Peninsula. He survived the march, a distance he estimated at about one hundred miles in ten days, without any medical care and without any food for the first six days. Like the others, he endured the harassing searches by the Japanese—during which he lost his scriptures—and he witnessed the Japanese soldiers shoot or bayonet many Americans and Filipinos who were too weak to continue.

When Davey started the hike, he had a temperature of 104 degrees and was suffering from malaria.[9] Malaria, however, was not his only health problem. The unfortunate fact of war is that in a time of a shortage, those farthest away from the supply depots—such as those fighting on the front lines—tend to receive the least; there was typically a significant "shrinkage" between the time a shipment of rations leaves the supply depot and its arrival at the front.[10] Not only were those on the front lines, like Davey, malnourished, they were also exhausted, having spent nearly four months without relief and with nearly constant engagement with the enemy.

Davey—malnourished, exhausted, sick from malaria, and perhaps beginning to exhibit the symptoms of various other diseases—frankly would not have been a likely candidate to survive the Bataan Death March. But Davey got a lucky break: he had a friend. When Davey left the hospital and rejoined his unit just before the surrender, he met up with his best friend, Russell Sparks, from Las Cruces, New Mexico. Russell quickly figured out that Davey was too ill to survive this march alone. Allowing Davey to lean on him and at times dragging Davey so he would not fall, which they both knew would likely mean death by a bayonet, Russell helped Davey along on the march. They both struggled into Camp O'Donnell on April 22, 1942.[11]

NOTES

1. Shively, *Profiles in Survival*, 48.
2. The accounts in *Miracle of Forgiveness* by Spencer W. Kimball and the *BYU Studies* article (which account was based on Kimball's book) state that Brown drove to Cabanatuan, not Camp O'Donnell, as this is what Ruby Brown had stated in a letter to Kimball and which was the basis for the account in the book. However, a more detailed account prepared by Ruby and her oldest daughter, Nelle, states that he drove to Camp O'Donnell. Brown and Zundel, "George Robin Brown . . . His Story," 16. This family history account is likely the more accurate and it is easy to appreciate how Ruby could have confused the two locations in her letter to Kimball. Some sources indicate that approximately 375 men and officers were loaded into trucks and sent ahead to ready Camp O'Donnell. See Cave, *Beyond Courage*, 177.
3. Clark and Kowallis, "Fate of the Davao Penal Colony," 117; Brown and Zundel, "George Robin Brown . . . His Story," 18.
4. Carl S. Nordin, *We Were Next to Nothing: An American POW's Account of Japanese Prison of War Camps and Deliverance in World War II* (Jefferson, NC: McFarland and Company, 1997), 79. For example, Davey's scriptures were confiscated upon his surrender. In general, Japanese attitude toward religion seemed to have varied among the camps, and for the POWs it was somewhat unpredictable. See Cave, *Beyond Courage*, 234.
5. Hamblin, "My Experience," 9. The Word of Wisdom, or the religious health law practiced by Latter-day Saints and the promises quoted are found in section 89 of the Doctrine and Covenants. The prohibitions against smoking and drinking alcoholic beverages are the most obvious and best-known

tenets of this law, but there are also other healthful admonitions contained in that scripture.

6. Cave, *Beyond Courage*, 188; Brown and Zundel, "George Robin Brown . . . His Story," 16.
7. East, "Army Life," 9–10.
8. Springgay, "Robert Gray Davey," 19–20.
9. Springgay, "Robert Gray Davey," 19–20.
10. Morton, *Fall of the Philippines*, 371, 374.
11. Springgay, "Robert Gray Davey," 23.

12

DEATH CAMPS

Other refuge have I none;
Hangs my helpless soul on thee.
Leave, oh, leave me not alone;
Still support and comfort me.

—Charles Wesley, "Jesus, Lover of My Soul"

Although weak, sick, emotionally drained, and physically exhausted from the Bataan Death March, these surviving prisoners of war found no relief upon their arrival at Camp O'Donnell, a miserable place located on a flat, bleak, treeless expanse of cogon grass. The Japanese attempted to cram about fifty thousand diseased and starved American and Filipino prisoners of war into a half-finished Philippine Army training facility originally intended for no more than nine thousand men; the facility lacked even the basic sanitation facilities.[1] Open-slit trenches overflowed with excrement. The stench was so overwhelming that the Japanese rarely entered the camp; when they did, they wore surgical masks.

The "welcome" speech by the camp's commander, Captain Tsuneyoshi, was a hate-filled diatribe that few would ever forget. As POWs later recalled that speech, Captain Tsuneyoshi made clear that the prisoners, whom he referred to as dogs, were not considered prisoners of war but members of an inferior race and that we "will treat you as we see fit. Whether you live or die is of no concern to us."[2]

Many of the POW soldiers on Bataan had been suffering from malnutrition and various diseases, most often malaria and dysentery, but they had largely kept their conditions under control. However, with the ordeal of the Bataan Death March, a starvation diet, and lacking the most basic sanitation and medical supplies, prisoners began dying of these diseases. For example, with proper diet and medication, dysentery can be simply a case of mild diarrhea that goes away in a few days. For these POWs, on a starvation diet and lacking any medication, dysentery was deadly.

To the tragedy of these deaths from disease, the Japanese added additional deaths through abuse, torture, and executions—the beatings and beheadings continued. In two months, of the estimated nine thousand American POWs who entered that camp, more than fifteen hundred died and were buried in mass graves. The death rate among the Filipino captives was even greater, approximately twenty thousand, or about half of the Filipino contingent.[3]

After a few months, the Japanese realized that they needed a better place to serve as a prison. They chose Cabanatuan, an old Philippine Army base, located about sixty miles east of Camp O'Donnell. Camp O'Donnell was closed, and most prisoners were moved to Cabanatuan. The troops on Corregidor had surrendered about a month after the surrender on Bataan. They were taken directly to Cabanatuan and were already there when the Bataan prisoners arrived from Camp O'Donnell.[4] Not having endured the hike and having been better provisioned than those on Bataan, the Corregidor prisoners were in noticeably better condition.

Even though it was a larger facility, Cabanatuan was no better than Camp O'Donnell. Both were essentially extermination camps through Japanese neglect.[5] Camp O'Donnell and Cabanatuan were homes of the infamous Zero Wards, where thousands of prisoners with zero chance of survival were sent to suffer mind-numbingly painful deaths from beriberi, dysentery, and starvation. Hamblin described the scene at what was termed a hospital at Camp O'Donnell:

It is impossible to paint the picture with mere words. . . . There was no glass or screens at all in the openings [of the hospital building]. Flies few in and out at will, men were lying flat on their backs, tropical sores had set in, eating away at the flesh. Many with dysentery had soiled their clothes to the extent that they were unfit to wear and no way to wash them. So the clothing was thrown away, leaving the men naked and some without blankets. The filth and waste on the floor were cleaned out as best we could with shovels. Flies swarming around the filth would fly directly to the mess hall nearby. We carried bodies out and laid them on the bare ground in full view of the kitchen. They were stripped of all clothing and the clothing thrown in a pile to be burned. The bodies were then placed on bamboo stretchers and carried out of camp where they were put in shallow graves, their last resting place until Resurrection Day.[6]

East described a similar condition at Cabanatuan: "If you were sent to the hospital side of camp [the Zero Ward], you were sent there to die. Because your next move was to boot hill. I've been on burial details where we carried from fifty to seventy-five men a day out to boot hill and dumped them in a hole half full of water and very little dirt put over the bodies and the wild dogs would dig into the grave."[7]

While death was common in these camps, it was not necessarily indiscriminate. Despair, discouragement, and loss of hope, especially when coupled with sickness, often led to death in those camps. Those, especially the youngest, without strong family connections at home, religious convictions, sense of purpose, or other reasons to survive lost hope, fell into a deep melancholy, and quickly slid into death by what the camp doctors called "inanition" (simply giving up).[8] In many cases, the question of whether you had a strong religious belief was a quite literal question of life or death. According to Davey, "Religion became a sustaining factor in the Japanese prison camps. There was never an idle Bible, and men often communed silently with their Maker."[9]

As Davey explained after the war, "Many people died, literally lay down and died because they had nothing to cling to. They had no goals, no reason to put up with the suffering they were going through."[10] Allen C. "Ace" Christensen, a Latter-day Saint soldier from Tremonton, Utah, wrote how they could always recognize those who had lost hope: "Those who gave up weren't necessarily the sickest among us, but their lack of hope was invariably fatal. We could always recognize them. They would lay in their beds in a semi-fetal position and stare at nothing. By morning they would be dead—starved of hope."[11] East recalled, "There were many times it would have been easier to lay down and die than live and many did just that. . . . I will always be grateful that I had been taught the gospel."[12]

It seems that most POWs faced a time in their captivity when they found themselves discouraged, hopeless, and at risk of death—not from sickness, but from the lack of any reason to continue living. Christensen wrote of that moment, which came later in his captivity. Exhausted and discouraged, he had simply given up and quit working. Not unexpectedly, he was severely beaten by the guards. While lying in bed that evening, waiting for death to come and release him from this perdition, he picked up two pieces of paper he had managed to keep concealed. One was a picture of his parents, and the other was a copy of his patriarchal blessing. Christensen later recalled,

> As I read the blessing, I thought of my grandfather, the patriarch who had given me the blessing, and my dear mother who had patiently taken down every word. The words softened me. Maybe there was a future for me. Then I studied my parents' faces. . . . I'm sure they were praying for me. . . . I started to pray. [My mother] made us [he and his brother] promise that we would always live the Word of Wisdom. She told us that if we did, the Lord would bless us. . . . I did not feel like I could run and not be weary. As a matter of fact, my feet felt as though they were encased in very large cement blocks. But maybe I could walk and not faint. That day my spirits lifted. I determined that I would hang on. I had beaten my enemy.[13]

Christensen did not surrender to death. With renewed hope and faith in the promises made to him, he survived.

For Davey, this perilous time came in Camp O'Donnell with the death of his closest friend, Russell Sparks, whom he had come to love as a brother and who had saved his life on the Death March. Sparks slowly died in Davey's arms from dysentery, with Davey helpless to do anything to save him. With Sparks's death, Davey wanted to die too; his will to live was slipping away. Davey later wrote in a letter to Sparks's parents, "When he died it seemed that half of my desire to return home died with him. We had planned so many things that

American servicemen carrying two of their dead for burial at Camp O'Donnell. Courtesy of United States Air Force National Museum.

we were going to do when we returned."[14] This was the low point for Davey—and for his survival, it was a dangerous moment.

At this precarious time came another small but lifesaving miracle for Davey: a personal revelation. After praying one night, he fell asleep and had a dream. In the dream, he was in his parents' home in Salt Lake City watching a lovely girl go in and out of his house. There was, of course, nothing unusual about seeing the old family house in a dream, but what made this scene peculiar to Davey was that he could not understand why this strange girl, whom he did not know, would be living in that house. The peculiarity of the scene was quickly replaced by a calm assurance that he would marry this girl. At that point, he knew that he could survive, marry, and have a family.[15] What Davey could not have known at that time was that the Jacobs family had recently purchased his family's house in Salt Lake City. Dorothy Elizabeth Jacobs was the third oldest of the seven children and, while Davey was suffering in captivity in the Philippines, she was indeed walking in and out of that house as she lived there, just as Davey saw her in his dream.[16]

There was also something else that Davey could not have known at that time. As bad as things were for him then, the worst was yet to come. He would be a POW much longer than he would have then believed. Although he was then sick, he would become much sicker. Not only would he suffer from near starvation, he would also suffer from nearly every disease associated with malnutrition and almost every tropical disease imaginable, including beriberi (both wet and dry symptoms), malaria, pellagra, dengue fever, jaundice, and a variety of skin sores and infections.[17] He would also face more horrors, even greater than those of the Bataan Death March. But he would now face them all armed with the confidence that he would survive to marry and have a family.

Unlike these other POWs, we know little about Brown's experience at Camp O'Donnell and Cabanatuan. However, after the war, Lieutenant Colonel Harry M. Peck, Brown's commander, shared with Brown's parents some thoughts. As later recounted by Ruby and her daughter Nelle, the colonel recalled, "Due to the extreme hardships, physical and mental and spiritual suffering they went through, . . . at times some of the boys acted more like animals than men. And he [Peck] found that difficult to cope with. Finally, when he had exhausted all his own resources, he would go to Lt. Brown and ask if he thought he could help. Bobby would take them off to one side, during the night . . . and talk with them."[18]

"I do not know what power it was that he had," the colonel said, "nor what it was he said to them, but I do know that [when] morning came these troubled ones had become men again, and were back in the human race and ready to face whatever lay ahead."[19]

While brief, these comments from his commander are nevertheless revealing about Brown and his influence on others in those difficult times. We also know of one other incident involving Brown at Cabanatuan, as told to Ruby after the war by "one of the Baldonado boys" (likely either Private First Class José M. [Pepe] Baldonado or his brother Staff Sergeant Juan T. Baldonado), revealing another, more mischievous side of Brown. They were working in the kitchen preparing food for the Japanese officers. They were barely surviving on a half cup of rice per day, and the temptation to steal some of the food was almost irresistible. If caught, however, the punishment would be severe. After preparing the food for the officers' supper in a large kettle boiling on a makeshift stove on the floor, Brown suggested that if they couldn't have any, perhaps they should at least "season it up a little for them." After posting a lookout, they surrounded the kettle and used it as a urinal.[20]

For both very practical and emotional purposes, to survive in that camp, a prisoner needed someone else he could trust and with whom he could share the burdens of daily prison life. Small support groups began to form: army/navy, Texans/New Mexicans, and religious groups. At Cabanatuan, there were several religious "subtribes," and one author noted that "Catholics, Protestants and Mormons were particularly strong."[21] Although there were no organized services, some of the Latter-day Saint POWs were able to find each other and enjoy some "good gospel discussions."[22]

For the relatively healthy prisoners, Cabanatuan was essentially a human warehouse to be held in until they were sent off as slave labor to toil for the benefit of Japan's "Greater East Asia Co-Prosperity Sphere." For the others, it was a place to wait, suffer, and likely die.

Now we turn to what had been going on in the meantime with the Fifth Air Base group at Del Monte Airfield on the southern island of Mindanao.

NOTES

1. Sides, *Ghost Soldiers*, 105; Lukacs, *Escape from Davao*, 77; Davey, "Last Talk," 2. Davey states there were forty thousand Filipinos and approximately seven thousand Americans.
2. Sides, *Ghost Soldiers*, 106 (recollection of POW Abie Abraham); Shively, *Profiles in Survival*, 72.

3. Lukacs, *Escape from Davao*, 79; Sides, *Ghost Soldiers*, 107; Davey, "Last Talk," 2 (Davey attributes the greater death rate among Filipinos to their drinking contaminated water).
4. Shively, *Profiles in Survival*, 79–81. Among the POWs from Corregidor was James Arlo Nuttall, a Latter-day Saint army private from Provo, Utah. He had been serving a mission in Germany when the war in Europe broke out and was transferred back to the United States to complete his mission in the Northern States Mission. After his mission, Nuttall joined the army to avoid the coming draft with the expectation that he would be out in a year, as so many others expected. Instead, soon after enlistment, he found himself in the Philippines among those making the last stand at Corregidor. Call, "Latter-day Saint Servicemen in the Philippine Islands," 113–14. Nuttall was a POW on the *Taikoku Maru*, a hell ship from the Philippines to Japan. West-Point.Org., "Taikoku Maru Roster," http://www.west-point.org/family/japanese-pow/TaikokuMaru/Taikoku-Index.htm. Nuttall survived the war and imprisonment. After the war he married, graduated from Medical School in Chicago, and set up a medical practice in Kamas, Utah. Sadly, he died of a heart attack at the early age of 33. "Kamas Doctor Dies at 33 of Heart Ills," *Salt Lake Tribune*, December 25, 1952.
5. Sides, Ghost Soldiers, 134; Daws, *Prisoners of the Japanese*, 18.
6. Hamblin, "My Experience," 12.
7. East, "Army Life," 13.
8. Lukacs, *Escape from Davao*, 80; see also Daws, *Prisoners of the Japanese*, 270.
9. Springgay, "Robert Gray Davey," 30.
10. Davey, "Last Talk," 6. Similarly, Lt. Col. William Dyess wrote that "during the entire time I was in Japanese prisons I never saw an idle Bible." Dyess, *Dyess Story*, 83.
11. Allen C. Christensen, in Freeman and Wright, *Saints at War*, 300.
12. East, "Army Life," 15.
13. Christensen, in *Saints at War*, 300–1. This story also appears in the March 1991 issue of the *Ensign*. Allen C. Christensen (as told to Renee Homer), "Two Pieces of Paper Saved Me," *Ensign*, February 1991.
14. Springgay, "Robert Gray Davey," 30.
15. Springgay, 30–31.
16. Springgay, 63.
17. Springgay, 19, 31–33, 63–64.
18. Brown and Zundel, "George Robin Brown . . . His Story," 24.
19. Brown and Zundel, "George Robin Brown . . . His Story," 24.
20. Brown and Zundel, "George Robin Brown . . . His Story," 19–20.
21. Daws, *Prisoners of the Japanese*, 136.
22. East, "Army Life," 14.

13

DEL MONTE

Though deep'ning trials throng your way,
Press on, press on, ye Saints of God!

—Eliza R. Snow, "Though Deepening Trials"

Although war had reached the Philippines on December 8, 1941, it did not arrive at Del Monte until sometime later. The Japanese landed a small force at Davao on the southern island of Mindanao in late December, but the decisive battles for the Philippines were fought farther north on Luzon. The immediate capture of the southern island of Mindanao was not part of the Japanese plans and, with the Japanese lacking the troops to conduct operations simultaneously in both areas, Mindanao was largely safe from any large invasion force in the early months of the conflict.

Nevertheless, it was a very busy time for the Fifth Air Base group. With the destruction of Clark Airfield on Luzon, Del Monte Airfield on Mindanao became the center of what remained of US air power in the Philippines. Like those on Luzon, these air corpsmen found themselves at war without adequate equipment, spare parts, weapons, and ammunition, but they resourcefully made the best of what they had.[1]

In addition to maintaining aircraft that continued to fly missions from Del Monte, the corpsmen set about to improve their defenses. Although lacking effective antiaircraft guns, the airfield had machine guns placed at its corners. Private Allen C. Christensen and his Latter-day Saint friend Private Woodrow Dunkley from Franklin, Idaho, were members of a crew assigned to these guns.[2]

While the Japanese had not yet invaded the island in force, small contingents of Japanese troops had landed on the island, and American soldiers conducted reconnaissance patrols to identify the Japanese positions. Private First Class Rex D. Bray, a Latter-day Saint air corpsman from Provo, Utah, led patrols of Filipino and Moro soldiers on two-week long reconnaissance missions into the jungle, searching out Japanese.[3]

Following the outbreak of war on Luzon, those on Mindanao were left without a source of food supplies. Private First Class Charles L. Goodliffe, a Latter-day Saint soldier from Box Elder County, Utah, together with others in the quartermaster group, implemented a system to buy eggs, poultry, vegetables, and other foods from the local Filipinos. The best source of food was in Moro country. The locals, however, advised the corpsmen against going there because the Moros were reportedly headhunters who would "just lop off their head with a bolo knife." Goodliffe and two others went anyway, although not without some trepidation. They managed to gain the trust of the Moros, and the Moros became the army's largest supplier of foodstuffs.[4]

Since the bombers based at Clark Airfield on the island of Luzon were within reach of Japanese bombers in Taiwan, General MacArthur's plan had been to move all the bombers at Clark Airfield to Del Monte. However, only a few bombers made it to Del Monte, because the rest were destroyed in the bombing of Clark Airfield.[5] The few bombers moved to Del Monte continued to fly combat missions, but they mostly just flew from one base to another to avoid being bombed on the ground by the Japanese. Without any replacement parts and with the aircraft mechanics having only limited tools, the corpsmen struggled to keep the bombers operational.[6] Moreover, Del Monte did

B-17D Flying Fortress being loaded with 100- and 500-pound bombs at Del Monte Field, Mindanao, Philippines, where the Fifth Air Base group from Utah was based in 1942. Courtesy of United States Air Force. USAF Historical Research Agency.

not have adequate defenses, and it was only a matter of time before the base would be discovered and bombed by the Japanese.[7]

On December 15, 1942, the bombers were moved to Australia. It was none too soon. On December 19, Del Monte was bombed by planes from the Japanese aircraft carrier *Ryujo*.[8] Two Americans were killed from shrapnel, including Major Chauncey B. Whitney, a forty six-year-old Latter-day Saint from Salt Lake City. Services for him were held on Christmas Day.[9]

With bombings and artillery attacks from ships anchored offshore increasing and Japanese troops having landed in force at several locations on the island, Del Monte was evacuated. In March and April 1943, the air corpsmen moved to the Maramag Forest about fifty miles south of Del Monte near the town of Malaybalay. There, a small, secret runway had been built in the forest and was being used by a single P-40 for reconnaissance. The soldiers were to keep the airstrip open and maintain the P-40. Private Christensen was among those assigned to guard the carefully hidden plane.[10]

Eventually, the Japanese invasion of Mindanao began, and Rex Bray of the Fifth Air Base group found himself on the frontlines in a courageous but futile defense. Bray's unit had set up two lines of defense. Bray was in the second, or rear, line. From this vantage point he could see the Japanese overwhelm the frontline with a Banzai charge. What made a clear and lasting impression on Bray was seeing a Japanese officer leap onto an American machine gun as the gunner was swinging the gun around to shoot the attacking Japanese officer. The officer sliced through the machine gun barrel with his samurai sword and, with the next stroke of his sword, killed the American gunner. Bray was astonished and awed by this display of swordsmanship, particularly watching the water flow from the machine gun's steel cooling jacket as the Japanese blade sliced through it.

Rex Bray. Courtesy of Bray family.

With the frontline collapsing and bullets flying at them, Bray and others in the rear retreated across a swamp to escape the Japanese assault. Bray was shot in the leg during the retreat. Although bleeding profusely from the wound, he managed to hide against a tree while the Japanese soldiers, who had seen him and knew he was wounded but not dead, methodically searched for him. Not finding him, the Japanese moved on. Bray was eventually rescued by a Filipino army unit and taken to an American field hospital.

A few days later, the Japanese captured that field hospital. The wounded soldiers in the hospital were well aware of the Japanese atrocities and how the Japanese had slaughtered captured enemy soldiers at other facilities. As they heard the Japanese approach the hospital, they said their final goodbyes to each other. When Bray heard the hobnailed boots of the Japanese officer hit the wooden floor of the hospital ward, he was certain he had only seconds to live. But the officer came in and addressed them politely in good English. Apparently, the officer had attended college in the United States before the war. He introduced himself and announced that they were all now prisoners of Japan and promised they would be well cared for. And they were, for the brief time they were in his custody.[11]

The departure of the bombers to Australia left the Fifth Air Base squadron without much of an air force to support. With the Japanese invasions of the island, their commander, General William F. Sharp, set upon a strategy to transform this air base group into guerilla soldiers. They were to move to the interior of the island, train the local Filipino soldiers, and conduct guerilla operations. The terrain and conditions of Mindanao, with mountains and dense jungles, were certainly favorable for guerrilla operations. Patterson thought they potentially could have gone "out in the hills and lived . . . until liberated."[12] This fit with General MacArthur's plan to maintain a presence on Mindanao that the United States could later use to establish a base to launch a recovery of the Philippines.[13] Bray and others had been stockpiling supplies at hidden locations for later use in these guerilla operations.[14]

Nevertheless, these air corpsmen had had no significant combat training; besides, they didn't have much in the way of weapons. They were mostly armed with old WWI-era rifles and a few machine guns, many of which were defective, and little ammunition, much of which was also defective.[15] Corporal Carl Rohlfing, a Latter-day Saint air corpsman from Salt Lake City, observed that "very few of us even had side arms, let alone other weapons to defend us."[16] Whether General Sharp's planned guerrilla operation would have been successful will never be known; the fate of these air corpsmen on Mindanao was being determined by an unfortunate set of events unfolding elsewhere.

When Bataan fell and General King surrendered, those in Luzon generally believed Corregidor would not be able to hold out much longer either. That proved to be the case. After a month of intensive bombardment, Japanese troops successfully landed on Corregidor. US casualties were high and, without effective weapons to defend themselves, those troops were facing the likelihood of wholesale slaughter. On May 6, 1942, about a month after Bataan had surrendered, General Wainwright concluded that there was nothing to be gained by further resistance and decided to surrender.[17]

The problem, however, was in getting the Japanese to accept that surrender. The Japanese were still angered that General King had surrendered only those troops on Bataan and not those on Corregidor as well. When General Wainwright announced his surrender to the Japanese, he was told they would accept only the surrender of all US forces in the Philippines, including those in Mindanao. General Wainwright answered that he could not do that; the troops in the southern islands were not under his command. The nub of the problem was that last statement.

When General MacArthur left the Philippines, he put General Wainwright in command of the forces on Bataan and Corregidor, but General Sharp in Mindanao continued to report directly to General MacArthur in Australia. However, this command arrangement had never been clearly explained to President Roosevelt and General Marshall in Washington. In the absence of contrary information from General MacArthur, President Roosevelt and General Marshall considered General Wainwright the commander of all forces in the Philippines and so informed General Wainwright. With these instructions from Washington, General Wainwright felt obliged to assume command of all forces in the Philippines, which he did.

Now, however, in an effort to minimize the effect of the surrender on Corregidor, he was trying to unwind the command structure Washington had put in place and revert to what General MacArthur had originally ordered. While General Wainwright was announcing over a US "Radio Freedom" broadcast his decision to surrender to the Japanese, he was simultaneously sending General Sharp in Mindanao a coded message releasing to Sharp command of all forces in the Philippines other than those in Manila Bay.

The Japanese did not believe General Wainwright and firmly refused to accept anything other than a surrender of all troops in the Philippines. They had monitored American radio broadcasts naming General Wainwright as commander of all troops in the Philippines and claimed to have actually seen the general order announcing Wainwright's assumption of command. General Wainwright was given two days to fly a staff officer to Mindanao to deliver this surrender order to General Sharp. Although the Japanese denied it after the war, General Wainwright and others believed the troops were hostages and that if Sharp and his forces failed to accept that surrender order and carry it out as instructed, the Japanese would open fire on all the men on Corregidor. A temporary suspension of hostilities was agreed to, and Colonel Traywick, General Wainwright's emissary, flew with a Japanese colonel to Mindanao. They met with General Sharp on May 10, 1942. With the benefit of Traywick's explanation of the situation on Corregidor, General Sharp agreed to surrender and ordered his forces to do so.

Ralf T. Wilson, a Latter-day Saint corporal from Alta, Wyoming, in the Fifth Air Base group, explained their dilemma this way: "The major told us, 'We've got two options. You can either go into prison camp with me, or you can take to the hills. But there are consequences if you go into the hills. If we don't turn in all the men on this island the Japanese will execute 750 men captured on Corregidor. They are being held hostage. Their lives depend on our surrender.' What a terrible burden. To a man we agreed to the surrender."[18]

The small group of Latter-day Saint air corpsmen of the Fifth Air Base squadron would not become guerilla fighters in the Philippine jungles but prisoners of the Imperial Japanese Army.

NOTES

1. Morton, *Fall of the Philippines*, 238, 498–501, 950.
2. Christensen, "My Life Story," 5, 8.

3. Rex D. Bray, "War Memories, 1941–1945" (unpublished manuscript, 1998), 6–7, 11–13.
4. Charles LaFount Goodliffe, "Recollections of Charles LaFount Goodliffe," transcript of interview by David Morrell with Charles Goodliffe, October 23, 2003, 6–7 (unpublished copy of transcript was provided to author by Bonnie Goodliffe). While the Moros were then fighting with the Americans against the Japanese, during an earlier insurrection against the Americans in the Philippines, the Moros never surrendered and had inflicted heavy losses on American troops. Bray, "War Memories," 10–11 (an interesting account of the Moros and their bravery as soldiers).
5. Heimbuch, *Lucky Ones*, 34.
6. Morton, *Fall of the Philippines*, 97.
7. Morton, *Fall of the Philippines*, 97.
8. Morton, *Fall of the Philippines*, 97; Burton, *Fortnight of Infamy*, 79–80.
9. Heimbuch, *Lucky Ones*, 38; Ashton, *"Spirit of Love,"* 175; "Graveside Service Announcement for Major Chauncey B. Whitney," *Salt Lake Telegram*, July 18, 1949.
10. Bolitho, "Japanese Story," part 2; Heimbuch, *Lucky Ones*, 40–41; Christensen, "My Life Story," 8.
11. Bray, "War Memories," 11–13; Kurtis R. Bray, email message to author, February 21, 2017.
12. See Patterson, "Interview," 33.
13. Morton, *Fall of the Philippines*, 356–57, 500.
14. Bray, "War Memories," 11.
15. Morton, *Fall of the Philippines*, 499; Patterson, "Interview," 15; Christensen, "My Life Story," 5.
16. Carl Dennis Rohlfing, "Carl Dennis Rohlfing" (undated manuscript provided to the author by Rohlfing's son-in-law, Dennis Autry, 1).
17. The circumstances of the surrender of the forces on Corregidor and Mindanao are recounted in Morton, *Fall of the Philippines*, 521, 562–82.
18. Ralf T. Wilson, in *Courage in a Season of War: Latter-day Saints Experience World War II*, ed. Paul H. Kelly and Lin H. Johnson (privately published, 2002), 323.

14

HOTEL MALAYBALAY

Be still, my soul: The Lord is on thy side;
With patience bear thy cross of grief or pain.
Leave to thy God to order and provide;
In ev'ry change he faithful will remain.

—Katharina von Schlegel, "Be Still, My Soul"

The Fifth Air Base group was ordered by General Sharp to proceed to Camp Casisang near the town of Malaybalay to surrender to the Japanese. By now these soldiers, soon to be POWs, understood the savage reputation of the Japanese Army to whom they were ordered to surrender.

Corporal Ralf Wilson later wrote of this time when he was fearfully anticipating surrender: "Anxiety struck in my throat. I needed help beyond myself. Then I remembered my parents' teachings and determined to go off by myself and pray. In the jungle I came upon an old quarry. It was a beautiful little place. I knelt and opened my heart to the Lord and pleaded for His help. After a time, I heard a very clear and distinct voice say, 'It's okay, Ralf, you're going to be all right.' Immediately a sense of peace washed over me. The sun was shining down through the trees, the birds were singing, and I felt a quiet reassurance." With that, Wilson surrendered, believing he had the Lord's promise that he would return home.[1]

The Japanese did not place many restrictions on what these surrendering soldiers could bring into the camp; in fact, they actually directed the soldiers to bring in all remaining food supplies. Goodliffe and his Latter-day Saint friend, Christensen, were among those tasked with gathering up all the supplies they could in the two days allotted. They were mostly able to load up canned pineapple from Del Monte.[2] The surrendering soldiers loaded trucks with the food and other supplies they had collected and began the slow journey north toward Malaybalay.

A few miles south of Malaybalay, the Japanese had set up a checkpoint, and it was there that the soldiers of the Fifth Air Base group had their first encounter with their captors. Waving their bayoneted rifles, the Japanese soldiers signaled the Americans off their trucks and ordered them to raise their hands. The Japanese then searched each American; because there were more than five hundred American captives, that took a while.[3]

In terms of the discipline and treatment of the prisoners, this was a very different Japanese Army from the one to which those on Bataan had surrendered. Some of the Japanese soldiers took fountain pens and pencils, watches, rings, and similar personal items from the surrendering soldiers. When an armed guard searched Christensen, he pointed his bayonet at Christensen's watch, and Christensen wisely decided to just give it to him.[4] However, there were also accounts of Japanese soldiers, after carefully searching and seizing such personal items, returning them.[5]

Patterson related that with a quick movement of his bayonet, a Japanese soldier took from his wrist the Bulova watch his mother had given him. However, the next day, a Japanese commander lined up his troops, and those who were found with stolen items were severely punished. As for the Japanese soldier who had taken Patterson's watch, "they just beat him practically to death because he wasn't supposed to do that."[6] There was none of the malicious brutality toward the surrendering prisoners that had been so prevalent at Bataan. After the

US troops massing for surrender to the Japanese at Camp Casisang on Mindanao Island. Courtesy of The BenHaven Archives. Courtesy Walter Regehr.

search, the captives were ordered back into their trucks and driven to Camp Casisang.

Camp Casisang had been a training camp for the Philippine Constabulary, a military police force. It was located at the edge of some rolling plains and consisted of several rather crude barracks with walls rising three or four feet, leaving an open space of about three feet below the roofline. The roofs were covered with thatch made from leaves of nipa palm trees. The barracks surrounded a kitchen and dining building with a metal roof, and there were a few crude latrines.[7] Within a week, there were about eleven hundred American soldiers in the camp. While the influx of prisoners put some strain on the camp resources, especially on water, these POWs did not experience the same level of starvation and sickness as those on Bataan. In addition to their own remaining food supplies, they had been able to bring into the camp such luxuries as stoves and refrigerators.[8] Consequently, these captives were given adequate amounts of food and, for a while at least, they were able to continue eating the same kind of food to which they were accustomed. Compared to others, Patterson said they "ate like kings."⁹

Added to their relatively good fortune was the fact that their guards did not exhibit the spiteful and vicious behavior of those on Bataan. Rather, the Japanese for the most part left the prisoners alone. Christensen later wrote that the Japanese commander had attended college in the United States with General Sharp, so the prisoners received "a few unexpected liberties and quite good treatment."¹⁰ There were no work details other than to secure wood for the cooking fires. The captives organized baseball teams, set up a recreation hall, and started a library, among other things.¹¹ In this more easygoing prison environment, the Latter-day Saint soldiers were able to continue the regular Sunday School classes led by Staff Sergeant Hansen that they had begun at Del Monte.

Even in this more favorable prison environment, there were limits to what the Japanese would tolerate, and there were brutal consequences for breaching those limits. Camp Casisang was by no means a maximum-security prison, and it was not difficult to get through the single fence surrounding the camp. A couple of Filipino POWs slipped out one night to visit their wives, who were living nearby, and were caught trying to sneak back into the camp before roll call the next morning. They were summarily tried, sentenced to death, and made to dig their own graves along with the postholes for their execution posts. They were lashed to the posts, shot by a firing squad, and then cut loose and rolled into the graves they had dug. All the POWs were required to watch the executions. It took several rounds for the executioners to kill the two Filipino POWs. The Japanese were not bad shots but wanted to make them suffer and wanted all the other prisoners to see that suffering.¹² The Japanese had made a point that all understood. As Christensen later recorded, "This made us get any such similar notions out of our heads right away."¹³

Although the atmosphere in the camp was more subdued after these executions, Camp Casisang was comparatively still a very good place for these soldiers to be. Their good fortune was not to last, however. In the first part of October 1942, the Japanese asked for men with technical skills to volunteer to work in Japan. Believing that this would lead to a more comfortable place, many claimed to have skills such as driving a truck or other training from civilian life. About two hundred volunteered to go. It was a ruse to bring a labor force to Japan—not for any technical work, but for hard, miserable, non-technical slave labor in the cold and wretched mines and factories of Japan.[14] It does not appear any of the Latter-day Saint soldiers in the Fifth Air Base volunteered for the technical positions.

Two weeks later Camp Casisang was closed. Tied together with loops around the waist of each POW and guarded by soldiers with machines guns, the Americans were loaded onto flatbed trucks and taken to Bugo, the small port barrio on the coast. The POWs were immediately loaded on Japanese Troop Ship #760; they sailed for two days along the northern and eastern shores of Mindanao to Davao. Although crowded into the holds of the ship, the POWs were allowed to spend time on the deck, which relieved the crowding in the holds. For the most part, this was not an especially unpleasant voyage, compared to those that would come later, and these POWs were likely treated as well as Japanese soldiers on troop transports. It was also a relatively short trip. Two days later, on October 20, 1942, they arrived near Lasang on the Davao Gulf. Here things changed, and not for the better.

At noon, in the heat of the day, they disembarked and found themselves with a different breed of guards. These were occupation troops, made up of Japanese as well as some Taiwanese conscripts. They were young and mean. The POWs were marched through the streets and about twenty miles up a narrow road in the hot sun toward the Davao Penal Colony, which was often called *Dapecol*. As the afternoon wore on and the tropical sun took its toll, men began to reel, catch themselves from falling, continue for a distance, and then just collapse. The march did not stop for those who collapsed. However, unlike at Bataan, where those who fell behind were killed, these collapsed POWs were simply thrown in the back of the trucks hauling their gear to the prison camp.

The road narrowed and they entered a thick and impenetrable jungle; the only way through was on the narrow track they traversed.

Using bayonets and rifle butts, the guards stepped up the pace. Finally, at around midnight, dehydrated and exhausted, they walked into a clearing and through the camp gates; to boost their morale, they sang "God Bless America."[15] Each then found a spot and collapsed for the night.[16]

When this group from Camp Casisang arrived, there were already around one hundred POWs in the camp. These POWs had come from Cabanatuan about ten days earlier to prepare the camp; Hamblin was in that group. Those from Cabanatuan had endured the siege and battle of Bataan, the Bataan Death March, and the hellish conditions of Camp O'Donnell and Cabanatuan. They were emaciated, suffering from a variety of tropical diseases and nutritional deficiencies, and had little in the way of possessions, most likely just some sort of cup for eating.

In contrast, the units from Camp Casisang had surrendered intact and had been relatively well fed. Since the Japanese had not put any limit on what they could take, they arrived at Davao with barrack bags and footlockers. The Japanese interpreter at the camp mocked them, saying that with their barrack bags they looked like Santa Claus. The other POWs nicknamed them the "Foot Locker Fifth."[17] With Latter-day Saint POWs from Camp Casisang and Cabanatuan moving to Davao, Dapecol became the focus of their imprisonment.

NOTES

1. Wilson, in *Courage in a Season of War*, 323. An account of this incident is also included in the transcript of a talk Wilson gave in 1998, which can be found at familysearch.org in the documents page of Ralf Thomas Wilson (KWZC-S4H).
2. Goodliffe, "Recollections," 9.
3. Bolitho, "Japanese Story," part 3 (October 24, 2009), 1; Heimbuch, *Lucky Ones*, 42–43; Patterson, "Interview," 29–31.
4. Christensen, "My Life Story," 9–10.
5. Heimbuch, *Lucky Ones*, 43.
6. Patterson, "Interview," 29, 32.
7. Bolitho, "Japanese Story," part 3, 1.
8. Ibid.; Heimbuch, *Lucky Ones*, 44–45.
9. Patterson, "Interview," 31–32.
10. Christensen, "My Life Story," 10.

11. Heimbuch, *Lucky Ones*, 44–45; Bolitho, "Japanese Story," part 3 (October 24, 2009), 2.
12. After the first round, the then-wounded men slouched down. Immediately, a strong voice from the Filipino side of the compound shouted, "You are in the American Army—die like Americans. Attn-Hutt." They then jerked their heads up in an effort to come to attention, as they were killed by succeeding rounds. Bolitho, "Japanese Story," part 3, 2.
13. Christensen, "My Life Story," 10. See also Patterson, "Interview," 31–32; Heimbuch, *Lucky Ones*, 48–49; Bolitho, "Japanese Story," part 3, 2.
14. Bolitho, "Japanese Story," part 3, 2; Heimbuch, *Lucky Ones*, 47–48.
15. Christensen, "My Life Story," 10.
16. Bolitho, "Japanese Story," part 3, 3; Heimbuch, *Lucky Ones*, 50–51.
17. Christensen, "My Life Story," 11; Hamblin, "My Experience," 15.

15

BACK HOME

The world has need of willing men
Who wear the worker's seal.
Come, help the good work move along;
Put your shoulder to the wheel.

—Will L. Thompson, "Put Your Shoulder to the Wheel"

Back in the United States, the families of these soldiers had settled into life on the home front. The Brown family in El Paso was typical. Ruby, Lieutenant Brown's mother, threw herself into various kinds of volunteer work in support of the war effort, including acting as a volunteer Red Cross worker, an air raid warden, and a member of the Bundles for Britain project, as well as serving in the rail station canteen for servicemen.[1]

Brown's father, George, was busy as a US marshal, transporting prisoners to various federal institutions.[2] During this time, he was also a witness in a high-profile trial involving a Nazi spy ring based in El Paso.[3] Other siblings were also involved in the war effort at home. Brown's youngest sister, Fern, volunteered as a nurse's aide at the Masonic hospital and also kept busy dating Latter-day Saint servicemen training at Fort Bliss or Briggs Field in El Paso.[4]

The Brown Family in El Paso, Texas, in 1936 before the war. Back row, left to right: Fern, Nelle, Bobby, and Jane. Front row, left to right: Ruby, Rulon, George, and Paul. Courtesy of Brown family collection.

Rulon, Brown's youngest brother, was unable to serve in the military for physical reasons and instead served the war effort in another way. He became a captain in the Briggs Field Fire Department.

Briggs Field, which was located near El Paso, became a major training facility for B-17 bomber pilots. One of the often-overlooked tragedies of the war was the number of accidents and fatalities in flight training: some fifty-three thousand accidents in the continental United States resulted in the loss of approximately fifteen thousand pilots and other crew members.[5] A number of those accidents involved those training at Briggs Field and typically involved a deadly encounter with Mount Franklin near El Paso. The principal activity of the Briggs Field Fire Department was rescuing the downed flight crew members—or, more often, recovering their charred remains.

These rescues were neither easy nor safe, but Rulon became an innovative and distinguished rescuer.[6]

During WWII, government censorship of war news was strict and pervasive. The public saw only carefully screened information about the war. Details of casualty statistics, strategic failures, or any visual proof of dead or maimed soldiers were censored.[7] The author has a copy of a stack of newspaper clippings of stories on the war in the Pacific, and the Philippines in particular, that Ruby carefully clipped and saved. With respect to this period on Bataan prior to surrender, these newspaper articles all evince a positive sentiment about the Americans bravely defending Bataan and Corregidor with headlines such as "Battered Yanks Exact Heavy Tool for Nippon Gains," "Smashing Air Blow Downs Thousands of Japanese," and "American Troops on Bataan Beat Back Japanese Patrols."

While a few of the stories acknowledged the difficulty in supplying the troops on Bataan, they gave few hints to the desperate condition of the Bataan troops. In a later story about the surrender in Bataan, the local El Paso paper quoted Ruby as saying, "I trust President Roosevelt and I trust the Lord, but I can't help asking, why didn't they take them to Corregidor yesterday?"[8] Cleary, Ruby had no appreciation for the desperate state of affairs in the Philippines—Corregidor was as doomed as Bataan—and, although it may have been for the best, Ruby did not understand that President Roosevelt had already "regrettably written off" the Philippines back in December.

A month or so after the surrender on Bataan, some of the families of the surrendering soldiers began receiving notices from the government. On May 16, 1942, the Browns received a letter from the army adjutant general, informing them that according to military records, their son was serving in the Philippines at the time of the surrender. The letter also stated that in the days before the surrender, there were casualties that were not reported to the War Department and that it "could not give you positive information" in that regard. However, the letter stated that the Japanese government had indicated its intention to comply with the provisions of the Geneva Convention on

American newspapers report the fall of Bataan. Courtesy of UC Berkeley, Bancroft Library. Photo taken by War Relocation Authority, an agency of the United States Government.

the exchange of information. That would include providing a list of prisoners. The letter expressed the War Department's intent to notify the Browns if his name was on such a list, but until then, he would be considered "missing in action."[9]

The uncertainty for the Browns was even more complicated. The May 16 letter referred to "Master Sergeant George R. Brown, 20,842,49." However, previous correspondence from the army had referred to "First Lieutenant George R. Brown, 0-890150." Given that both "George" and "Brown" are common names, there was another round of correspondence with the War Department to determine whether the letters were referring to the same person. In a letter dated July 29, 1942, the War Department explained the discrepancy and confirmed they were referring to the same person.[10]

Finally, on December 15, 1942, more than eight months after the surrender on April 9, the Browns received a telegram from the War Department:

> YOUR SON FIRST LIEUTENANT GEORGE R BROWN ARMY OF THE UNITED STATES REPORTED A PRISONER OF WAR OF THE JAPANESE GOVERNMENT IN THE PHILIPPINE ISLANDS.[11]

This news, coming shortly before Christmas, was received by the Browns as their most precious Christmas present. While Bobby was a POW, they now knew he was alive.[12]

A similar period of fearful apprehension was also playing out in the Davey family in Salt Lake City. Since the start of the war and throughout the Battle of Bataan, Captain Davey's sister, Hazel, and brothers, Lee and Ralph, had been on a constant vigil for information about their brother Bob. Hazel continued to write letters to her brother, even though they all came back labeled *Returned to sender; service suspended*. When Bataan fell, the Davey family feared their worst fears might have been realized. Indeed, on September 15, 1942, the Salt Lake County Chapter of the Service Star Legion sent Hazel an invitation to the Public Reception and Tea and a gold star. Hazel, however, returned the gold star and never displayed it, as she did not consider her brother dead.[13]

On November 11, 1942, the *Deseret News* published a list of those who had died or were reported missing in action in the Philippines. Captain Davey was on that list—not as one who had died, but as one who was "missing in action since May 1942." That wasn't exactly good news, but it was not the worst news either. Later, on December 13, Hazel received a telegram from the War Department:

> YOUR BROTHER CAPTAIN ROBERT GRAY DAVEY, FIELD ARTILLERY REPORTED A PRISONER OF WAR OF THE JAPANESE GOVERNMENT IN THE PHILIPPINE ISLANDS.[14]

His brothers and sister now knew he was alive. Just as with the Brown family, although it was not the best news, it was nevertheless good news.

Hazel also now had an address to use to write letters to her brother. During her brother's imprisonment, she conscientiously wrote him about four letters a week, even though there was really no assurance or even likelihood that the letters would ever reach him. Hazel was not the only one sending letters. Brothers Lee and Ralph also wrote, as well as aunts, uncles, nephews, and nieces. Davey's twelve-year old niece, Joanne, wrote in a very firm block print, "Dear Uncle Bobby, Hope you are well. We are praying for you. Keep your chin up. May God bless and protect you always. I miss you. Love, Joanne." Sadly, Captain Davey received only a few of these letters, and even those were not delivered until months after they had been written.[15] The fate of her brother Bob, however, was not the only concern weighing on Hazel's mind. Her own sons were sent to war in Europe, and her brother Ralph was serving in India.

For the rest of America, however, after the surrender of the Philippines, the abandoned boys of Bataan faded from public discourse and for a time were largely forgotten.[16] Perhaps recognizing that interest in the Bataan POWs was increasingly overshadowed by events in Europe and elsewhere, George Brown again wrote Congressman R. E. Thomason on June 20, 1943, urging him to make efforts to contact the POWs and to provide food and medical aid. George closed the letter with the following plea: "I fully realize the apparent impossibility in this situation but I sincerely believe that if strong enough effort is made by proper men and enough of them, we can still reach our boys with succor before it is too late. But Mr. Thomason, when everyone is busy in great problems the only way we can get attention in this matter is to keep insisting til we make our point, and please remember, 'The Lord helps those who help themselves' and we can't expect him to do it all."[17]

The Browns, the Daveys, and the other Latter-day Saint families of these POWs were people with great faith. With the public and government's attention largely elsewhere, this faith would now be tested with prolonged silence.

NOTES

1. Zundel, "Brown Family History," 3; Ruby Brown, "Personal History," 6.
2. Zundel, "Brown Family History," 2.
3. Ruby S. Brown, "Twenty Years Ago—1934–1954," vol. 4 (1954), item G, 13 (Ruby S. Spilsbury Collection), 2. The story of this infamous Nazi spy ring is recounted in Clint Richmond, *Fetch the Devil: The Sierra Diablo Murders and Nazi Espionage in America* (Lebanon, NH: ForeEdge, 2014).
4. Fern Brown Hyer, "Classy Grandmas All Come from Chupe" (unpublished personal history manuscript in possession of author), 8, 36–37 (Fern is the second youngest in the Brown family and the author's mother); Zundel, "Brown Family History," 7.
5. United States Air Force Statistical Digest of World War II, December 1945. Table 213, 309. Accessible at https://apps.dtic.mil/dtic/tr/fulltext/u2/a542518.pdf.
6. Zundel, "Brown Family History," 8. Rulon invented a number of the tools used to extract crewmen from the wreckage and obtained a pilot's license, enabling him to fly L-19 Bird Dog (Cessna Model 305) aircraft to look for downed planes. In one instance, he lowered himself down a cliff to rescue a downed pilot, but found only a burned torso, which he tied to his own and ascended the cliff. He smelled so bad that on the trip back the crew made him ride on the top of the fire truck. In a successful but more dangerous rescue, the pilot had to be cut out of the plane with a blowtorch while Rulon was standing in high-octane gas up to his knees. They recuperated together in the same hospital. Robin Brown (Rulon Brown's son), personal conversation with author.
7. Lukacs, *Escape from Davao*, 281–82; see Holmes, *Unjust Enrichment*, 2.
8. Article is in a newspaper clipping dated April 10, 1942, kept by Ruby Brown. The name of the newspaper is not indicated on the clipping.
9. Major General Ulio, The Adjutant General, War Department, to George A. Brown, dated May 16, 1942, NARA Records.
10. Major General Ulio, The Adjutant General, War Department, to Mrs. George A. Brown, dated July 29, 1942, NARA Records.
11. Telegram, Major General Ulio, The Adjutant General, War Department, to George A. Brown, dated December 15, 1942, NARA Records.
12. This sentiment was written on a Christmas card from the Browns and was saved by family members with other items related to Bobby.
13. Springgay, "Davey," 43–44. The gold star is the nation's way of honoring families with an immediate family member who died in combat in the service of their country.
14. Springgay, "Davey," 44.
15. Springgay, "Davey," 43–44.
16. Lukacs, *Escape from Davao*, 282–83.
17. George A. Brown to Honorable R. E. Thomason, June 20, 1943, NARA Records.

16

A PLACE WHERE A RANCH BOY MAY HAVE A CHANCE

Dearest children, God is near you,
Watching o'er you day and night,
And delights to own and bless you,
If you strive to do what's right.

—Charles L. Walker, "Dearest Children, God Is Near You"

Our story now returns to the POW camp at Cabanatuan on Luzon. The Japanese started distributing POWs, including these Latter-day Saint POWs, from Cabanatuan to other labor camps. Baclawski, Brown's tentmate from Fort Bliss, was sent to Las Piñas on Luzon and set to work building an airfield. East was sent to a work detail at Clark Field. It was a fortunate move, as the food and working conditions were better, and the officer in charge, whose wife had attended school in the United States, tried to help them where possible.[1]

In October 1942, Japanese commanders in Cabanatuan were looking for one thousand healthy, "literate laborers" to be transferred to another, undisclosed camp. It was the camp to which Hamblin had been sent earlier. Whether they volunteered or were ordered, Brown, Davey, and Allred were among this group.[2]

In late October 1942, this group of about one thousand men were led out of the camp, marched on foot to Cabanatuan City and then traveled by rail to Manila, where they spent the night on a concrete floor in the Bilibid Prison, a bleak and miserable concrete prison facility in Manila. The next day, the POWs marched down to the Manila Harbor and were loaded in the holds of the Erie Maru, a decrepit, coal-burning freighter. They sailed from Manila on October 28, 1942. While the POWs encountered conditions that could reasonably be described as miserable, this trip on the Erie Maru was by no means the "hell ship" experience they would later endure.

The POWs were crammed into a ship's hold intended for bulk cargo, not passengers. It was dark, hot, and infested with rats. However, the hatches were usually left open, and the air was fresh. The prisoners were allowed time on deck, and the food and the guards were better than in the camps. There was none of the wanton brutality of Camp O'Donnell, Cabanatuan, or the Bataan Death March. When one of the American officers became ill, the ship's doctor took care of him for several days, bringing him some pineapple juice and vitamins; interestingly, a shy Japanese sailor gave the ill American officer a small vase of flowers. For POWs, it was difficult to predict the Japanese, as these small incidents of kindness seemed randomly interspersed among the otherwise pervasive brutality and hate.[3]

After eleven days in the holds of the Erie Maru and with stops in Iloilo City, Panay, and Cebu City, the ship arrived on November 7, 1942, at a harbor near Lasang on the Davao Gulf of Mindanao, an island at the southern end of the string of Philippine islands.[4] From there the prisoners were marched about twenty miles deep into the interior jungle, finally arriving at Dapecol.[5] They arrived at the camp about two weeks after the Fifth Air Base POWs from Malaybalay. Dapecol now housed about twenty-one hundred POWs.[6]

To the prisoners already at Davao, including those from the Fifth Air Base group, or the "Foot Locker Fifth," these new arrivals from Cabanatuan looked like "walking skeletons."[7] Another description of the new arrivals, and an unintended indictment of their treatment by the Japanese, came from the Japanese Dapecol commander, Major Kazuo Maeda. As recounted by a prisoner, upon their arrival, Maeda "stormed about, declaring that he had asked for prisoners capable of doing hard labor, . . . and instead, he shouted, had been sent a batch of walking corpses." Maeda promised they would receive food to strengthen their bodies, but that "every prisoner will work until he is actually hospitalized. Punishment for malingerers will be severe."[8] He was true to his word, except for the part about food.

Unlike Camp O'Donnell and Cabanatuan, which were small military bases hastily converted to prison camps, Dapecol was a Philippine prison colony built in 1932. Located deep in the interior jungle, it was designed as a maximum-security prison along the lines of Alcatraz or the infamous French prison, Devil's Island, in French Guinea.[9] Dapecol was essentially an island within a large, impenetrable, mosquito-infested swamp, extending nearly twenty miles in all directions. Although tribes of headhunters reportedly frequented the area, little else but giant insects, poisonous snakes, and crocodiles lived in the swamp. The inhabitants of the fringe villages viewed the bog as an evil, supernatural entity. Inmates at Dapecol had included the Philippines' most violent criminals—most were serving life sentences for murder, and no one had escaped from Dapecol in its ten-year history. Before the arrival of these POWs, the Japanese had moved most of the civilian prisoners to Manila.

Dapecol was a clear improvement over Cabanatuan but was still much harsher than Camp Casisang. Wells provided plenty of water for drinking, bathing, and laundry. There were nine barnlike barracks allotted to the POWs based on rank. In each, 150–200 men were sardined into fifteen intervals of space known as bays. With its own hospital, railroad, and power plant, as well as living quarters for one thousand inmates and a staff of administrators and their families, it was essentially a self-contained city some 140 acres in size.

Although a prison camp, Dapecol functioned as a commercial enterprise powered by POW slave labor for the benefit of Japan's "Greater East Asia Co-Prosperity Sphere." It was largely an agricultural facility with a poultry farm; orchards with lemons, limes, papaya, bananas, coconuts, and apples; and fields (plowed with some ornery brahma steers) with cassava, camotes, corn, peanuts, and sugarcane. The camp also included a sand and gravel pit and various support and repair shops. The prisoners felled giant mahogany trees to supply logs to a Japanese sawmill down the river. Both officers and enlisted men were required to work.

Rice, however, was Dapecol's most important cash crop, with around six hundred rice paddies worked by 350 to 750 prisoners in an area known as Mactan. The rice detail was the most demanding and probably the most dangerous for prisoners. It was backbreaking, stooped labor in the hot, tropical sun. In addition to the hard labor and cruel guards, cobras and rice snakes filled the paddies. The snakes were, of course, a danger, but for the POWs they also presented an opportunity, as the POWs often tried to catch the snakes for food. Christensen recalled the prisoners in the rice paddies catching a python, which was later carved up and eaten.[10] Of greater concern, however, was the risk of contracting schistosomiasis from a parasitic flatworm that penetrated sores and caused debilitating rashes, headaches, cerebral hemorrhages, and nausea.[11] James Patterson contracted schistosomiasis at Davao and required treatment for years after the war.[12]

A prisoner's daily ration consisted of between 350 and 600 grams of rice, depending on his work assignments.[13] For perspective, a soldier's daily ration in the peacetime US Army at that time was four pounds seven ounces, or 2,013 grams.[14] The prisoners were sometimes also fed *kang kong*, a weed that grows in the swamps and drainage ditches, which the Japanese presented to the prisoners as "fresh vegetables."[15] Especially dispiriting was the fact that fields with a rich variety of fruits and vegetables surrounded the POWs, but those foods were never included in the POW rations, and attempts to steal them were severely punished.

In addition to the inadequate quantity and diversity of food, there was another problem with the rations. A prisoner's rations consisted for all practical purposes of only rice, but it was polished rice. A former POW at Dapecol described the effects of a diet of polished rice: "We soon found out that the rice has disadvantages other than general tastelessness. Polished rice contains no vitamins, and in a few weeks the effects begin to tell in badly aching feet (the first signs of beriberi), sores inside the mouth (the first signs of scurvy), and swollen ankles (edema)."[16]

The cause of beriberi is simply the lack of thiamine, or vitamin B1, which is found in the rice bran. The polished rice the prisoners received lacked this essential vitamin. But the Americans' pleas for unpolished rice were repeatedly denied. Eventually, someone broke the rice-polishing machine at Dapecol, and it never worked again. Whoever broke the machine likely saved many American lives as hundreds of beriberi sufferers' conditions subsequently improved.[17]

Both Hansen and Davey suffered from both dry and wet beriberi (dry beriberi affects the nervous system, and wet beriberi manifests in the accumulation of fluids and swelling). Their symptoms likely began in Dapecol. But beriberi was just one of the many maladies common among these POWs due to malnutrition. There were also scurvy, pellagra, and impaired vision, in addition to the ever-present malaria, dysentery, and open sores. The air corpsmen from the Fifth Air Base group came to the camp in better condition than many other POWs, but in time they too began to experience the effects of malnutrition. Referring to their time at Dapecol, Christensen wrote, "The men were now starting to get diseases. The lack of citrus with that essential ingredient of acid gave us scurvy. Malnutrition brought on many things such as beriberi, dysentery, diarrhea, stomach trouble, eye trouble, and just plain degeneration of body and soul."[18]

Many of these POWs, having entered the army in the midst of the Great Depression, were already resourceful and skilled at scrounging. The farm-based economy of Dapecol with its chickens, orchards, and vegetables provided an opportunity for prisoners to supplement their rations. Although the Japanese instituted searches to prevent prisoners from stealing and severely punished those who were caught, the prisoners became skilled in pilfering food and smuggling it back into camp. Doing so was essential to their survival.[19] Also, in the early days of captivity at Dapecol, the Japanese allowed POW barrack leaders to rotate work details, allowing them the flexibility to put a POW suffering from scurvy on an orchard plantation detail that would afford him the opportunity to steal a lime or lemon to cure the scurvy.[20]

Brown worked on the camp's chicken farm, a natural assignment with his boyhood ranch experience. It was also a very fortunate assignment. Sometimes for special occasions, such as a birthday or holiday, Brown stole some eggs, emptied them into his canteen, carefully buried the shells, shook it up, and later shared the "eggnog" back at camp.[21] On occasion, he was able to persuade a guard that an apparently healthy chicken was very sick and needed to be killed and buried in order to avoid infecting the rest of the flock. While killed, such a chicken was not buried; instead, it was dressed and cooked. These successes were more rare than common and always came at great risk, but they provided Brown and others with some meager amounts of needed protein in their diet.

There had also been changes in clothing. Many prisoners at Dapecol wore simply a "G-string" and perhaps a woven hat for clothing, and they typically were barefoot. The G-string was an eight-by-thirty-inch cotton panel with a cotton tie sewn across the top. The wearer tied the tie around his waist with the cloth panel hanging to the rear. He then bent over and pulled the panel to the front, tucked it in under the tie and allowed the remaining cloth to hang down in front. For Japanese soldiers, it was an undergarment. For a prisoner, it was his entire wardrobe.[22]

One POW observed that one "ever-present aspect of prison-camp life in the tropics which seemed to irritate many of us, was its partial similarity to a nudist camp. Nobody wore much clothing; many went around in G-strings. . . . I hardly realized before what a blessing clothes actually are, in that they serve, regardless of style, to cover up the brute."[23] This nearly naked approach to prisoner attire wasn't for the comfort of the prisoners in the tropical heat; it was to deter escapes. At Dapecol the prisoners were sometimes not that closely guarded, because there were few guards to patrol a large area, and the Japanese correctly concluded that without clothes and shoes, a prisoner would be less likely to try to escape.[24]

While prisoners at Dapecol were not dying from the level of violence and torture experienced in the Bataan Death March and at Camp O'Donnell and Cabanatuan, the guards—largely Taiwanese conscripts—were nonetheless mean, arbitrary, and unpredictable. The prisoners were still subjected to beatings and abuse almost daily; at times, they also suffered torture, shootings, and beheadings.[25] Nonetheless, during the early days at Dapecol and due to the influence of Japanese Lieutenant Youke, the guards tended to be less brutal. While the commander, Maeda, was an abusive, hateful man, Youke, who was in charge of the Americans, was generally amiable and often came into the camp at night to visit several officers with whom he had developed a friendship.[26] Brown learned some Japanese while imprisoned, and it might have been at this time that he started his effort to learn that language.[27] A knowledge of even a few rudimentary phrases would have been useful to better communicate with the guards and reduce the risk of misunderstandings.

Except for Davey and possibly Hansen, it appears that these Latter-day Saint POWs were in relatively good health given the circumstances. Murray Sneddon, author of *Zero Ward: A Survivor's Nightmare*, was among the POWs sent to Dapecol. When Brown enlisted, he weighed 148 pounds.[28] And Sneddon had a prewar weight of about 150 pounds.[29] While at Davao, Sneddon had a chance to weigh himself on a rice scale. The scale was set to ninety pounds, the minimum acceptable weight for a sack of rice. When Sneddon stepped on the scale, it failed to move—meaning his weight was less than ninety pounds; by how much was not known. Having been on reduced rations since the start of the war and on essentially a starvation diet in captivity, the typical "healthy" POW, such as Brown and some of the other Latter-day Saint POWs, may have weighed less than ninety pounds and been suffering from diseases related to nutritional deficiencies (such as scurvy and beriberi) and tropical diseases (such as malaria).

These POWs were likely able to supplement their diets with something beyond the meager allotment of rice, but it was unlikely that they would have been able to do so in the amounts needed to compensate for the insufficient and nutritionally deficient rations. The most well-fed prisoners were still doing hard labor with only a fraction of the necessary nutritional requirements. In short, although better fed than in Cabanatuan, these POWs were still slowly dying.[30]

The effect of this mistreatment on the body would be easy to see, but what about the effect on the mind and spirit? Christensen explained the situation this way: "The POW learns quickly that it does not pay to resist his captors and adapts himself to a docile life, aimed only [at] keeping alive. His attention is always centered on this one purpose. . . . Because working hard may mean death and cheating often means life, many POWs lost their character-stability. A whole camp is reduced to a very low moral level and nobody cares about much of anything except survival."[31]

One author asked these questions: "In a Japanese prison camp, under guards holding life-or-death power, what was it going to take to stay alive, stay sane, stay human? When a body is savagely beaten, what happens to the mind and to the spirit? Among starving men, can common human decency survive?"[32]

Just as disease, malnutrition, forced hard labor, and brutal beatings wear down a body, the hopelessness, the despair, the never-ending petty and malicious indignities of the Japanese guards, and the humiliation and shame of what a prisoner is compelled to do wear down a soul over time. In a place like Dapecol, could a prisoner find nourishment for the soul?

NOTES

1. East, "Army Life," 16.
2. Springgay, "Davey," 35; Brown and Zundel, "George Robin Brown . . . His Story," 16–17; see McCracken, *Very Soon Now*, 32; Lukacs, *Escape from Davao*, 108.
3. McCracken, *Very Soon Now*, 35–41; Gregory F. Michno, *Death on the Hellships: Prisoners at Sea in the Pacific War* (Annapolis, MD: Naval Institute Press 2001), 73–75.
4. Michno, *Death on the Hellships*, 75.
5. Sneddon, *Zero Ward*, 49; Lukacs, *Escape from Davao*, 116–17.
6. Michno, *Death on the Hellships*, 75.
7. Bolitho, "Japanese POW Story," part 3, 4; Lukacs, *Escape from Davao*, 119; see McCracken, *Very Soon Now*, 44–45.

8. Lukacs, *Escape from Davao*, 119; See Cave, *Beyond Courage*, 256; McCracken, *Very Soon Now*, 44.
9. Dapecol is generally described in Lukacs, *Escape from Davao*, 119–26; in McCracken, *Very Soon Now*, 43–44; and in Bolitho, "Japanese POW Story," part 3, 3–4.
10. Christensen, "My Life Story," 13.
11. Lukacs, *Escape from Davao*, 126–27; Patterson, "Interview," 21, 34–36; Bolitho, "A Japanese POW Story," part 3, 6; Bray, "War Memories," 17; Hamblin, "My Experience, 16.
12. Patterson, "Interview," 34–36.
13. The dipper used to serve the rice determined the size. Rice from the largest dipper contained about 600 grams and was known as the "Mactan Dipper" after the area where the rice paddies were located. Only those working the rice paddies received the ration from the Mactan Dipper. The second dipper, known as the "Workers Dipper," contained about 500 grams and was used to serve all other workers. The smallest scoop, reserved for non-workers and hospital patients, contained only 350 grams and was called the "Death Dipper." McCracken, *Very Soon Now*, 46–47.
14. Lukacs, *Escape from Davao*, 131.
15. McCracken, *Very Soon Now*, 45–46; Bolitho, "A Japanese POW Story," part 3, 4.
16. McCracken, *Very Soon Now*, 23–25. In East Asia countries, polished white rice had become a dietary staple generally, not just for POWs. Since the early twentieth century, the connection between beriberi and the nutritional deficiencies of polished rice had been understood. Since thiamine (vitamin B1), which is missing in polished rice, is also found in many other foods, a diet based on polished rice becomes a health a problem when, as was the case with these POWs, the diet is not balanced with a variety of other foods.
17. McCracken, 50; Springgay, "Davey," 34; see also Heimbuch, *Lucky Ones*, 60–61 (dry beriberi cured with eating ground rice hulls).
18. Christensen, "My Life Story," 14.
19. McCracken, *Very Soon Now*, 47–48; Lukacs, *Escape from Davao*, 127.
20. Bolitho, "A Japanese POW Story," part 3, 5.
21. Brown and Zundel, "George Robin Brown . . . His Story," 19; see also Lukacs, *Escape from Davao*, 127; Cave, *Beyond Courage*, 258.
22. Sneddon, *Zero Ward*, 56; see also Hamblin, "My Experience," 17.
23. McCracken, *Very Soon Now*, 98.
24. See Sneddon, *Zero Ward*, 58; Hamblin, "My Experience," 17.
25. Sneddon, *Zero Ward*, 42, 50–52; Lukacs, *Escape from Davao*, 129–30.
26. Lawton, *Some Survived*, 66.
27. Brown and Zundel, "George Robin Brown . . . His Story," 20.
28. Enlistment Record, National Guard of New Mexico, George Robin Brown, December 19, 1940, Physical Examination at Place of Enlistment, NARA Records.
29. Sneddon, *Zero Ward*, 3.
30. Lukacs, *Escape from Davao*, 131–32.

31. Christensen, "My Life Story," 30.
32. Daws, *Prisoners of the Japanese*, 19.

17
"WHERE TWO OR THREE ARE GATHERED TOGETHER"

> *My soul has often found relief,*
> *And oft escaped the tempter's snare,*
> *By thy return, sweet hour of prayer!*
>
> —William W. Walford, "Sweet Hour of Prayer"

Hamblin was among those who had arrived early from Cabanatuan to ready Dapecol for more prisoners. About ten days after his arrival, the Fifth Air Base squadron arrived from Camp Casisang. A couple of days later, Hamblin spotted a man lying on his back reading the Book of Mormon. Hamblin introduced himself and learned that he was Staff Sergeant Nels Hansen from Weiser, Idaho. From Hansen, Hamblin learned that approximately twenty other Latter-day Saint soldiers in that group were now at Dapecol.[1]

Under Hansen's leadership, those Latter-day Saint POWs in the Fifth Air Base squadron had been holding meetings—beginning on their voyage across the Pacific, continuing at Del Monte on Mindanao, and persisting in the more relaxed environment of Camp Casisang. That had not been the case at Camp O'Donnell or Cabanatuan. While a strong religious subtribe of Latter-day Saints formed in Cabanatuan, they were too few and too scattered to have organized any regular meetings or established any kind of organization.² When the approximately one thousand POWs from Cabanatuan later arrived, including Brown and Davey and a few other Latter-day Saints, there was now at Dapecol a critical mass of members and leadership for organized religious services.³

They also had the good fortune of having Japanese Lieutenant Youke as the officer in charge of the Americans. Youke, a Roman Catholic, allowed these Latter-day Saint POWs to hold their religious services on Sunday. A POW at this camp later observed that the few Japanese who showed compassion to prisoners were usually Christians.⁴

For Hansen and the other Latter-day Saint POWs of the Fifth Air Base squadron, this was more or less a continuation of what they had been doing since they left the United States. But for others—such as Brown, Hamblin, and Davey—it was the first time they were able to join with others of their faith in worship on a regular basis and to enjoy the blessing of their fellowship. Davey recalled the joy he experienced at finding "a group of LDS people and join[ing] with them and the strength that you can get from one another in church, meeting together.... It was one of the few things, you might say, that would give you the strength and courage to carry on."⁵ As the Gospel of Matthew teaches, "For where two or three are gathered together in my name, there am I in the midst of them."⁶

There is no surviving group membership list, but if there had been, it may have looked something like this:⁷

- Private First Class William Murle Allred from Artesia, Arizona
- Private David Weston Balfour from Salt Lake City, Utah
- Private Jack W. Bradley from Moroni, Utah
- Private First Class Rex D. Bray from Provo, Utah
- First Lieutenant George R. (Bobby) Brown from El Paso, Texas
- Private First Class Allen C. Christensen from Tremonton, Utah
- Captain Robert G. Davey from Salt Lake City, Utah
- Private Mack K. Davis from Lehi, Utah
- Private First Class Woodrow L. Dunkley from Franklin, Idaho
- Private First Class Charles L. Goodliffe from Park Valley, Utah
- Private Orland K. Hamblin from Farmington, New Mexico
- Staff Sergeant Peter (Nels) Hansen from Weiser, Idaho
- Second Lieutenant Richard E. Harris from Logan, Utah

- Private First Class Theodore Jackson Hippler from Bloomfield, New Mexico[8]
- Private First Class Ferrin C. Holjeson from Smithfield, Utah
- Private Russell Seymore Jensen from Centerfield, Utah
- Private First Class Ronald M. Landon from Kimball, Idaho
- Corporal Kenneth B. Larsen from Salt Lake City, Utah
- Private Harry O. Miller Jr. from Magrath, Alberta, Canada
- Staff Sergeant Ernest R. Parry from Salt Lake City, Utah
- Private First Class Lloyd Parry from Logan, Utah
- Private James Patterson from Sunnyside, Utah
- Private First Class Lamar V. Polve from Kenilworth, Utah
- Corporal Carl D. Rohlfing from Salt Lake City, Utah
- Private Jesse G. Smurthwaite from Baker, *Oregon*[9]
- First Lieutenant Gerald Clifton Stillman from Salt Lake City, Utah
- Private Frederick D. Thomas from St. Johns, Idaho
- Corporal Donald L. Vance from Fairview, Utah
- Corporal Ralf T. Wilson from Alta, Wyoming
- Corporal James Edmund Wilstead from Provo, Utah

Like the names on any group membership list, the list may not be complete, and those on this list likely varied in their participation and activity. Estimates of those in attendance at their regular Sunday services ranged between twenty-five and thirty, including a number who were not members of the Church. For example, Major Morris L. Shoss, a Jewish officer, frequently attended the meetings. In addition, there were others from Utah, such as First Lieutenant Dwayne W. Alder from Midvale, Utah, and Major Joseph R. Webb and First Lieutenant Carlyle Ricks from Salt Lake City, who, while not baptized members of the Church, had family ties to the Church and were likely friends with some of the members. They may have also attended some of the services.[10] Taking that into account, this listing, while not necessarily complete, seems a fairly close approximation.

This was, of course, an unofficial group of The Church of Jesus Christ of Latter-day Saints. The Church headquarters in Salt Lake City, Utah, would have had no way of even knowing of its existence, let alone providing any sort of official recognition or authorization. Nonetheless, drawing on their experiences as young men growing up in the Church, these POWs did what Church groups always do. They organized themselves. Hansen was the only high priest among them. Following ecclesiastical lines of authority rather than military rank, Hansen assumed leadership.[11] However, as is typical of Church organizations, there was a sharing of leadership responsibilities, with Brown taking on some of those responsibilities. It appears that Hansen and Brown were the driving organizational force in the group.[12]

In the more lenient circumstances of imprisonment in Camp Casisang, Hansen had been able to keep his copies of the Church's scriptures, along with five copies of the *Deseret Sunday School Song Book* and a copy of *Added Upon*, by Nephi Anderson.[13] Charles Goodliffe had with him a copy of *Unto the Hills*, by Richard L. Evans, a compilation of some of the short talks Evans had given in the *Music and the Spoken Word* programs with the Mormon Tabernacle Choir.[14] Goodliffe's father gave him the book before Goodliffe left for the Philippines.[15] These scriptures and Church materials, together with Brown's triple combination and hymnbook, provided a library of sacred materials at a time and place where such materials would have been both rare and priceless.

The group held Sunday services as regularly as possible.[16] The meetings were spiritual events, and testimony meetings were particularly moving.[17] They sang hymns, with Brown leading the singing. For these POWs, the hymns were like sermons and provided a source of great comfort. The group members reached out to others. Brown was something of a missionary for the group and appears to have taken a lead in encouraging others to attend.

They discussed gospel principles and had long conversations about points of doctrine and religion. They studied scriptures. Brown's triple combination and Hansen's scriptures circulated among them. Many prisoners took turns reading the Book of Mormon, the Doctrine and Covenants, and the Pearl of Great Price, and many wrote comments and testimonies in the margins.[18] Every blank space of Brown's triple combination was covered with notations signed by those readers, telling of their faith, their testimony, and their love of the gospel. It was the same with Brown's hymnbook.[19] Additionally, nearly all the Latter-day Saint POWs read Hansen's copy of *Added Upon*.[20]

Lieutenant Glenn L. Nordin, a former POW, took this photo in 1955 of the noncommissioned officer barracks at the Davao Penal Colony. The note on the back of the photo reads in part, "Protestant church services were sometimes held under these trees." After the war, Nels Hansen stated that some of the Latter-day Saint services were held under a "spreading mango tree," and James Patterson referred to meeting near some trees. Some of the Latter-day Saint services may have also been held at this site. BenHaven Archives. Courtesy of Walter J. Regehr.

They also got together during the week to tell stories or sing. They held a prayer circle almost every night when allowed by the Japanese guards.[21] They became very well acquainted with each other. They shared their past experiences with each other and, for want of things to talk about, retold them all again and again. Hamblin wrote of the happiness he felt "to have the association of men with whom I had so much in common," a sentiment likely shared by all.[22]

They also cared for each other. Major Morris L. Shoss, a Jewish officer who knew Brown well, often participated in the group services and was particularly interested in the songs and their poetry. At one time, he was asked by a superior to arrange help for an ailing prisoner. Shoss learned that the prisoner was a member of the group and contacted Brown as one of its leaders. Brown in turn asked Staff Sergeant Ernest R. Parry of Provo, one of his close friends, to help him, and together they took care of the ailing brother. There was no medicine to give, but it is evident from Shoss's description that Brown and Parry gave him a priesthood blessing. Shoss recalled that the soldier was soon feeling better.

Praising the character of the Latter-day Saint group, Shoss considered these POWs remarkable because, in spite of the horrible conditions in the prison camp, they tried to live according to the principles of their religion.[23] Two American majors who attended the services as visitors later joined the Church after the war. Others, through participation in the group, converted to the faith but were never baptized, as they did not survive the war.[24] Bray recalled that several of those converted to the gospel in the Davao camp sought baptism, but, lacking the required official authorization from Church authorities, the Latter-day Saint POWs could not perform the ordinance.[25]

That these POWs, scattered as they were among the two thousand prisoners in this camp, could come together and organize a group to comfort and care for each other in the midst of the horrific conditions of a WWII POW camp is a remarkable event in the history of the Church, but not an unexpected one. This was nothing more than what these young men had been taught and prepared to do. These POWs knew there was no need to wait for a priest, an ordained minister, or a commissioned chaplain to organize their religious worship. While Hansen was older than the others—forty years old at the time—a high priest, and had served a mission, others were relatively young, and most were without significant Church leadership experience or training. Nevertheless, these POWs drew on a reservoir of experiences and examples from growing up in Latter-day Saint homes and congregations.

For example, Brown had been an active member and participant in an established and fully functioning ward in El Paso that met in a beautiful meetinghouse. But as a young boy, he had also watched his father conduct church services in their home in Chuichupa, an isolated Latter-day Saint colony high in the Mexican Sierra. Later in Chihuahua City, Chihuahua, Mexico, where the family had briefly lived, Brown, as the only deacon, had passed the sacrament to the small group of Saints that had gathered together from that large city in a small home for that purpose. He had seen his father and mother go about performing their various church responsibilities, organizing and conducting church programs, leading the music, teaching gospel lessons, and ministering to and helping others in need, including the administration of priesthood blessings, and he had heard their faithful prayers. Although perhaps not appreciated at the time, such experiences had prepared them for such a time as this, "line upon line, precept upon precept."[26]

The Book of Mormon prophet Alma speaks of a people who "are willing to bear one another's burdens, that they may be light; . . . and to stand as witnesses of God . . . , that he may pour out his Spirit more abundantly upon [them]."[27] What the prophet Alma describes is perhaps the essence of a Christian life. It is also what these Latter-day Saint prisoners had organized themselves to do in the midst of a hellish POW camp.

NOTES

1. See Ashton, "Spirit of Love," 175.
2. Daws, *Prisoners of the Japanese*, 136; McCracken, *Very Soon Now*, 106. Although Hansen was never at Camp O'Donnell or Cabanatuan on Luzon, he later wrote, "I understand meetings were held at Cabanatuan and other camps on Luzon." Call, "Latter-day Saint Servicemen," 115 (quoting from a letter by Hansen to Call, August 14, 1954).
3. After the war, Hansen wrote "Five hundred officers and five hundred enlisted men were sent to our camp at Davao Penal Colony from Luzon and it was among these officers that we met Lt. Robin (Bobby) Brown. He had a very close friend among the enlisted men, . . . Orland K. Hamblin. He is a grandson of Jacob Hamblin." Call, "Latter-day Saint Servicemen," 115 (quoting from a letter by Hansen to Call, August 14, 1954); Brown and Zundel, "George Robin Brown . . . His Story," 17–18.
4. Lawton, *Some Survived,* 66; Call, "Latter-day Saint Servicemen," 115; see also Bray, "War Memories" (Bray notes that for a time at Dapecol the commander, who some thought may have been a Christian, did not require them to work on Sunday); Charles Goodliffe, interview with Sam Orwin,

undated, response to question 10, unpublished copy provided to author by Bonnie Goodliffe (Goodliffe recalled in an interview after the war that at that time they did not work on Sunday and so they could have Church services); see also Bolitho, "Japanese POW Story," part 3, 7.

5. Davey, "Last Talk," 3.
6. Matthew 18:20.
7. The author is not aware that any membership list was actually prepared by these POWs. Rather, the author created this list to illustrate the likely size and makeup of the group. The list was compiled using information from Clark and Kowallis in their article in *BYU Studies* and the author's additional research. Clark and Kowallis also identified eight men at Davao who, while there are no records indicating they were members of the Church, likely had a previous acquaintance with the Church (largely through parents or grandparents) and therefore may have attended or been involved with the group. Clark and Kowallis, "Fate of the Davao Penal Colony," 119. There is evidence that at least one of these eight, PFC Clay Lenno Rosenvall, attended some Church services with James Patterson. See chapter 8, note 3.
8. After the war, Hamblin wrote a letter to Hippler's sister, Herberta McDaniel, about Hippler and mentions his participation in the Church services at Davao and social activities with other members. A transcript of the letter was provided to the author by Marianne Loose. Hippler enlisted in the Army and was assigned to the 440 Ordnance group. That group was assigned to Mindanao, and Hippler likely surrendered along with the Fifth Air Base group and came to Davao by way of Camp Casisang.
9. Gary Dielman, a local Baker, Oregon, historian, authored a 2015 essay entitled "The WWII Sinking of the *Shinyo Maru*: A Story of Loss and Survival of Two Baker POWs," about two POWs from Baker—Smurthwaite, who did not survive, and William E. Hall, who survived the war. The essay includes a brief biography of Smurthwaite and a history of his time as a POW, including a few quotations from his diary. Dielman mentions Smurthwaite's Church membership and observes that because Smurthwaite and Hall became close friends and were usually together as POWs, Hall probably also attended Church services with Smurthwaite. Gary Dielman, "The WWII Sinking of the *Shinyo Maru*: A Story of Loss and Survival of Two Baker POWs" (2015), 20; accessible at Baker County Library District, https://www.bakerlib.org/photo-archive/dielman-local-history-files.html.
10. Major Morris L. Shoss was a survivor of the *Shinyo Maru* and returned to the United States a few weeks after his rescue. Wanting to know about the fate of their son, Ruby and George Brown contacted him, and a friend, Sadie O. Clark, interviewed Shoss on their behalf in Houston in November and December 1944. Although Jewish, Shoss had attended group meetings and is the source of much of what we know about Brown and this group. Shoss knew Brown well and identified him as one of the leaders of this group. Shoss estimated the size of the group at approximately twenty-five Latter-day Saint POWs. Shoss also specifically mentioned Staff Sergeant Ernest R. Parry, who had helped Brown provide what was likely a priesthood bless-

ing to another POW. "LDS Group in Jap Prison Described," *Deseret News*, January 20, 1945, 1, 11 (newspaper account interview by Sadie O. Clark of Major Morris L. Shoss); Clark and Kowallis, "Fate of the Davao Penal Colony," 117. Davey estimated the group size at about thirty. Davey, "Last Talk," 3. See also Ashton, "Spirit of Love," 175–76 (noting that nonmembers attended and some joined the Church after the war).

11. A *high priest* is an office in what is called the Melchizedek Priesthood, or higher priesthood, of the Church. If available, a high priest would normally preside in Church meetings. An *elder*, another office in the Melchizedek Priesthood, would preside only in the absence of a high priest. Brown was an elder in the Melchizedek Priesthood.
12. "LDS Group in Jap Prison Described," *Deseret News*, January 20, 1945, 1, 11; Clark and Kowallis, "Fate of the Davao Penal Colony," 117; Brown and Zundel, "George Robin Brown . . . His Story," 17. Major Shoss in interviews after the war identified Brown as the leader of this group. In a letter after the war, Davey referred to Brown as one of the "mainstays" of what Davey called their Sunday School at Davao. Robert G. Davey, letter to Dorothy Jacobs, December 1, 1945 (a copy of which was provided to the author by Davey's daughter Marilyn Springgay).
13. Ashton, "Spirit of Love," 175.
14. The choir is now known as the Tabernacle Choir at Temple Square.
15. Goodliffe managed to keep the book through his captivity and after returning home. He later gave his son the copy to take with him to Vietnam during that war. When he returned from Vietnam, he returned the book to Goodliffe, who still had it at the time of that interview. He said it was "ragged and torn and beat up and has lots of marks in it where I marked it while I was reading it." Goodliffe, "Recollections," 15.
16. Rohlfing, "Carl D. Rohlfing," 2; Hamblin, "My Experience," 15.
17. Davey, "Last Talk," 3; Clark and Kowallis, "Fate of the Davao Penal Colony," 117; Brown and Zundel, "George Robin Brown . . . His Story," 18.
18. Goodliffe also mentions that they had "some copies of the Book of Mormon and the Bible, and we did a lot reading in those when we had the chance." Goodliffe, "Recollections," 15–16.
19. Brown and Zundel, "George Robin Brown . . . His Story," 18.
20. Ashton, "Spirit of Love," 175.
21. Rohlfing, "Carl D. Rohlfing," 2.
22. Hamblin, "My Experience," 15.
23. "LDS Group," *Deseret News*, 1; Clark and Kowallis, "Fate of the Davao Penal Colony," 116–17.
24. Ashton, "Spirit of Love," 175–76.
25. Kurtis R. Bray, email message to author, February 22, 2017.
26. 2 Nephi 28:30.
27. Mosiah 18:8–10.

18

THE UNFORGETTABLE CHRISTMAS OF 1942

Then pealed the bells more loud and deep:
"God is not dead, nor doth he sleep;
The wrong shall fail, the right prevail,
With peace on earth, good will to men."

—Henry Wadsworth Longfellow,
"I Heard the Bells on Christmas Day"

For prisoners of war in the Philippines, all the days and nights became endlessly repeating copies of the last—each was just like the one before. In the words of a former POW at Davao, "The days of our years included hundreds upon hundreds that were characterized only by dreary, dragging emptiness, spiritual and mental, as well as physical."[1] However, December 24, 1942, in Davao was different. To everyone's surprise, Major Maeda, the camp commander, declared a rare holiday from work to celebrate Christmas; with it, he promised a little extra food and some entertainment. It all made for an unforgettable Dapecol Christmas of 1942.[2]

The Christmas show was something of a variety show involving the POWs and the Japanese as well as some local Filipinos. The first performance was a traditional harvest dance by some Filipino teenage boys and girls from local families. For the prisoners, it was mesmerizing; the graceful movements and colorful rainbow costumes were in stark contrast to their dreary khaki and dirty brown lives. That was followed by a musical interlude with harmonized singing of well-known Christmas songs. The prisoners and the local Filipinos managed to put together an orchestra that played some familiar pieces. For the Japanese part, the interpreter (who was especially despised by the POWs) surprised them all with a very skillful rendition of the Charleston. Some Japanese soldiers then performed a samurai sword dance that included what the prisoners thought was an unnervingly realistic depiction of hari-kari, the Japanese ritual suicide.

Then came the Americans. To a wave of communal laughter and applause, starting with the Japanese officers and guards seated in the front row, a Jewish private from the Bronx and an Italian corpsman from Philadelphia came jitterbugging across the stage accompanied by an accordion-playing officer. The program ended with wild applause for some prisoners from Brown's unit, the 200th and 515th, who donned face paint and feathers to provide a comical interpretation of a traditional Native American dance and an uproarious impersonation of Carmen Miranda. Miranda was a popular (and somewhat outrageous) singer and actress from Brazil known as the Brazilian bombshell who sang "Chica Chica Boom Chic." It's easy to see how some soldiers could have fun with that. We have no information on the specific identities of the participants from the New Mexico unit, but since this was Brown's unit—and we know of Brown's considerable choral and dramatic talents—this has his fingerprints all over it.

One Filipino, sympathetic to the prisoners, recalled that for a few moments the "difference between friend and foe [was] forgotten, and everybody in the audience united in a common feeling of enjoyment and laughter," an appropriate feeling for Christmas. Then just as the entire audience finished singing "Auld Lang Syne," a gong sounded, and the prisoners were abruptly ordered back to barracks. As the prisoners left the show, they did receive the promised extra food, but not from the Japanese. Each prisoner received a rice stick fried in coconut oil from generous and compassionate Filipinos.

THE SACRAMENT AND THE FLAG

The Christmas of 1942 was also special to these Latter-day Saint POWs for another reason. The afternoon prior to the show, about ten of them went over to some trees by the hospital and held a sacrament meeting. Corporal Carl D. Rohlfing from Salt Lake City had managed to find a cracker. With that cracker and water from a canteen, he prepared and blessed the sacramental bread and water, which were then passed among the men.[3]

There was also another event that made this Christmas especially memorable for these POWs. At the time of the surrender, a soldier had taken down an American flag and wrapped it around himself under his uniform. Once in captivity, he had hidden the flag in a regular GI blanket. The POWs were not allowed to own or display their flag, sing their national anthem, or wear any military badges or insignia. This flag, therefore, was a precious but dangerous thing to have; these American POWs would have been severely beaten and the flag confiscated if the Japanese had ever seen it.

Nonetheless, patriotism and a love of their country and its values were common among the POWs. The flag, the tangible symbol of those values, was a source of strength and pride, but that pride had to be expressed covertly.[4] On that Christmas Day, when the guards were not looking, the POW who had smuggled the flag unrolled the blanket, displaying the Stars and Stripes. According to Davey, "When the men saw the flag, . . . a ripple of wonder and amazement spread throughout the group. This was followed almost instantly by the deep silence that comes only when one's heart is too full to permit words to be spoken. With their eyes still gazing upon the colorful banner, the soldiers began to sing; softly, but with increasing depth of feeling, ['God Bless America']."[5]

Of this incident, Hamblin wrote, "A wave of emotion went through the crowd and tears were visible in many eyes. Just to get a glimpse of the Stars and Stripes, emblem of freedom, brought cherished memories to our hearts with gratitude for the land of America."[6]

We now live in a more secular society where religious symbols are not as meaningful to many and where the flag is sometimes seen as merely an ornamental decoration or symbol and is even debased as a sign of protest. Accordingly, for many today it may be difficult to fully appreciate the power of those symbols to those POWs—the partaking of the sacrament, the symbol of their Christianity and their hope and faith—and the display, though brief and clandestine, of the flag, the symbol of their country, freedom, democracy, and their families at home. These symbols, together with the singing of "God Bless America" on a Christmas Day, made for a deeply memorable event. Years later, James Patterson gave fireside talks about his experiences as a POW. That Christmas Day, with the sacrament and the flag, formed the core of his message.[7]

PRESENTS

The Red Cross had been sending packages to the prisoners, but the Japanese had kept the packages to themselves, sometimes with the starving prisoners looking on. But on January 29, 1943, Red Cross packages were for the first time delivered to the prisoners at Dapecol.[8] It was like Christmas. After so many false hopes and the lack of contact from the outside, the Red Cross boxes from the United States were something the prisoners would not believe had they not seen the packages with their own eyes. As one prisoner later wrote, "Hands trembled as they tore the boxes open. Eyes sparkled as edible treasures were pulled forth and held up to public view, while hard-bitten, battle-scarred soldiers and sailors, exactly like children on Christmas morning, shouted excitedly, 'Look what I've got!'"[9]

Each prisoner received two fifteen-pound boxes containing cans of corned beef and salmon, sardines, coffee, instant cocoa, jam, chocolate bars, butter, cheese, and powdered milk. There were also some clothing and toiletries and, importantly, vitamin tablets, sulfa drugs, anesthetics, and quinine.[10] But what was most emotionally moving for the prisoners were the labels on the products—familiar reminders of home, such as Kraft cheese and Welch's Grapeade.[11] Above all, the boxes were tangible evidence that they had not been forgotten.[12]

The resilience of the body and soul of man is not to be underestimated. The effect of this food on the prisoners was significant and almost immediate. Within days, bedridden men walked, ulcers and rashes disappeared, and spirits soared. When Davey arrived at Dapecol, he had been put in the hospital with malaria and beriberi. On December 1, 1942, he was discharged from the hospital but, still suffering from dry beriberi, was put in the sick barracks with others suffering from that disease. With the Red Cross packages, Davey finally received a B1 shot, a Christmas present for which he was most grateful. From then on, he gradually began to recover.[13] Not surprisingly, however, following receipt of the Red Cross packages, the Japanese reduced rations for the POWs.[14]

POSTCARDS HOME

Sometime after the Red Cross packages were received, the Japanese distributed a series of postcards—more accurately, comment cards—for the prisoners to send home. For most prisoners, this was their first opportunity to communicate with loved ones since the fall of the Philippines, although Japanese censors strictly limited the content of the messages. For example, the printed card stated, *My health is ____*, and provided four choices for the POW to select: *excellent, good, fair, poor*. There were also a few blank lines where the prisoner could write a short message. The prisoner prepared his message first in pencil, and then typed copies were made. Finally, the interpreter examined each man's card for seditious or otherwise objectionable material, and the prisoner signed the card. The Japanese, of course, censored the cards for any information of military significance and to assure that the Japanese and their treatment of the POWs were cast in a favorable light.[15]

While Brown was at Dapecol, his family received five such cards, all indicating that he was in good health and well treated. Although they were brief and impersonal and the families understood the limits on what the POW could actually write, each card was nevertheless signed by their loved one and each was gratefully received as evidence that their son or brother was alive.[16] Not all of these letters reached the families of the POWs, however. Most of Davey's cards, for example, were received by his sister five months after his liberation.[17]

So continued the seemingly endless days of the dreary, numbing captivity of these POWs at Davao, interspersed not only with the incidents of Japanese cruelty and torture, but also with Sunday worship services, the events of Christmas and reminders of their country, the Red Cross packages, and letters home, all of which gave substance to their hope that they had not been forgotten.

NOTES

1. McCracken, *Very Soon Now*, foreword.
2. This event is described in Lukacs, *Escape from Davao*, 141–42, based on that author's interview with a survivor of Dapecol, endnote 14, and in McCracken, *Very Soon Now*, 53–54, although without reference to the names of any prisoner participants. This Christmas program is also referred to in Hamblin's memoir and by Patterson in his interview and in one of Davey's letters published in the *Deseret News*. Hamblin, "My Experience," 16; Patterson, "Interview," 19; *Deseret News*, March 24, 1945, 7. See also, Springgay, "Davey," 35 (quoting letter). Goodliffe also recalled, "We had fun in Davao. We made skits and performed them." Goodliffe, "Interview with Sam Orwin," answer to question 10. For a description of other musical and dramatic productions put on by POWs at Cabanatuan, see Cave, *Beyond Courage*, 235–36.
3. Patterson, "Interview," 18–19. Patterson described himself as not having been particularly active in the Church. His friend Clay Rosenvall had never been baptized, although his parents were members. For the article in *BYU Studies*, the authors contacted Rosenvall's sister to determine whether she thought he might have nevertheless participated in the Davao group. She replied that she did not think her brother would have been part of that group. Clark and Kowallis, "Fate of the Davao Penal Colony," 119. Nonetheless, Patterson indicated that Rosenvall was there with the others on Christmas Day at this special sacrament meeting.
4. Daws, *Prisoners of the Japanese*, 135; Springgay, "Davey," 37–38.
5. Springgay, "Davey," 37–38 (quoting from an article by Davey published in the *Children's Friend*, June 1962). Although Davey refers to the anthem, Patterson indicates they were singing "God Bless America."
6. Hamblin, "My Experience," 17.

7. Richard Patterson, email message to author, dated October 12, 2016 (son of James Patterson). There was also another incident when the POWs returning from working in the rice fields broke into singing "God Bless America," with similar emotional effects on the POWs and recalled by several POWs. Patterson, "Interview," 21–22; McCracken, *Very Soon Now*, 49; Bolitho, "A Japanese POW Story," part 3, 8.
8. Lukacs, *Escape from Davao*, 79, 143–44.
9. McCracken, *Very Soon Now*, 63–64.
10. Shively, *Profiles in Survival*, 591n14.
11. Lukacs, *Escape from Davao*, 144.
12. After the war, a POW commented on how Red Cross packages not only provided needed nourishment, but also renewed morale and rekindled hope, offering a profound sense that these POWs had not been forgotten. Lawton, *Some Survived*, 69.
13. Springgay, "Davey," 36. Davey indicates that at Dapecol he spent most of his time in the hospital and was never well enough to work outside in the fields.
14. Springgay, "Davey," 36.
15. Lukacs, *Escape from Davao*, 144–45; McCracken, *Very Soon Now*, 66–67.
16. Brown and Zundel, "George Robin Brown . . . His Story," 16–17, 20.
17. Springgay, "Davey," 45.

19
ESCAPE AND ITS CONSEQUENCES

The Lord is my light; then why should I fear?
By day and by night his presence is near.

—James Nicholson, "The Lord Is My Light"

Among prisoners, escape was the most controversial topic. They rarely talked about it much, although every prisoner probably thought about it a lot. To deter escape attempts, the Japanese grouped the prisoners in "shooting squads" of ten men.[1] If any member of a group escaped or attempted to escape, the remaining nine men were to be executed. This directive was a violation of the Geneva Convention, but the Japanese had not ratified that convention and considered the squads an effective deterrent.

This directive was applicable to all camps but was not consistently applied or enforced. For example, while Hamblin was on a work detail from Camp O'Donnell, a soldier escaped with the aid of the local guerrilla forces. When the Japanese determined that the POW had escaped, they identified the five prisoners who had slept next to him the night before and summarily shot them in full view of the other POWs.[2] In contrast, Clarence Bramley, a Latter-day Saint POW from Long Beach, California, who had been at Cabanatuan, had also been on a work detail when a POW escaped. The other POWs were told that ten of them would be executed as punishment, but in that instance the executions were never actually carried out.[3] In any event, since any escape attempt would create risks well beyond the individuals involved, American camp administrators generally prohibited escapes and organized prisoners to prevent, not help, escape attempts by other prisoners.[4]

Apart from the execution squads, there were other practical impediments to any escape from a POW camp in the Philippines.[5] Outside the camp, the American prisoners' light skin brightly advertised their escaped POW status and prevented them from hiding among the masses of Filipino civilians. The prisoners also understood that in their weakened physical conditions, they likely would not survive in the jungle outside the camp. The Japanese view was that adequate feeding or caring for prisoners' health and medical needs might result in them growing strong enough to escape or challenge their guards. That was part of the reason for the poor care and treatment of the prisoners.[6]

Geography was also a problem. The Japanese POW camps were generally not too distant from major Japanese infantry units and nowhere near any Allied or neutral countries. Australia, the nearest Allied country, was some three thousand miles of ocean away. For those at Dapecol, the surrounding twenty miles of impassable swamp presented another unavoidable barrier. Those practical considerations largely deterred escape attempts.

Nonetheless, on April 4, 1943, ten prisoners escaped from Davao. The story of their miraculous escape, rescue, and eventual return to the United States is a fascinating one, well told in *Escape from Davao*, by John D. Lukacs. Those escapees were well aware of the risks to themselves and to other prisoners who remained, but in their view they were all dying a slow death anyway. They believed the only hope was to get back to the States and tell their stories to draw the world's attention to Japan's horrific treatment of these POWs.[7]

ESCAPE AND ITS CONSEQUENCES

For the prisoners at Dapecol, the days following the escape were ones of great uncertainty and peril. It had never been clear whether the "shooting squad" rule would be applied at Dapecol and, if so, to whom? The Japanese had never formally announced the shooting squads, and the escapees had so carefully and secretly planned and executed the escape that others in the camp were completely and innocently unaware of it.

In response to the escape, the Japanese cut the entire camp's rations and about 560 prisoners—about a quarter of the camp—were moved to a special compound where they were imprisoned in wood and wire mesh cages. Those included the twenty prisoners who had slept on either side of the escapees, the barracks leaders, the entire American camp leadership, and any men the Japanese believed had ever eaten with, conversed with, or even associated with the escaped POWs. Those in this special compound, confined like caged animals in a zoo, recognized that the Japanese would not let such a mass escape go unpunished and simply hoped the Japanese would shoot them as quickly as possible, without the torture.

A week later Major Maeda, the Japanese commander, addressed this group in the special compound. He first announced that this entire group was sentenced to confinement for a month. Then, in a very dramatic moment, he read off a list of names, consisting of the American camp commander, his assistants, and those who had slept next to the escapees; he ordered all to step forward twenty paces. Their sentences were then read. There is little doubt what those prisoners feared and expected to hear, but what they heard was not what they had expected. In an order that had likely come from Manila headquarters, those prisoners were simply "directed to reflect their faults, . . . to spend the number of days indicated in meditation of the past incident and [observe] modest and moral conduct at all times." There would be no summary executions.[8]

Life for the remaining American POWs at Davao, nevertheless, changed. The Japanese officer in charge of the American POWs, Lieutenant Youke, who had been somewhat friendly to the POWs, was removed and replaced. Guards became more hostile and quicker to beat the POWs for the slightest infractions. The hours working in the rice fields were increased, and the workload was made heavier. With important ramifications for the POWs' health, American details to the fruit orchards and vegetable gardens ceased, reducing the opportunities to steal much-needed food. Searches by guards for contraband food increased, as well as the severity of the beatings for those caught. And to complement those changes, there were cuts in rice and vegetable rations. There were also other changes with implications for the Latter-day Saint POWs and the Davao group: religious services and Sunday evening entertainment were abolished. Davao had suddenly reverted to a cruel slave labor camp.[9]

NOTES

1. Shively, *Profiles in Survival*, 227–28; Lukacs, *Escape from Davao*, 105, 196; McCracken, *Very Soon Now*, 19; Christensen, "My Life Story," 14.
2. Hamblin, "My Experiences," 12. In addition, as Hamblin was leaving Cabanatuan for Dapecol, he saw just outside the camp three POWs tied to posts along the road, stripped of all clothes except shorts. Anyone on the road was required to beat them before they would be allowed to pass. They had been caught trying to escape a few days earlier and by then had nearly been beaten to death. A few days later they were shot or beheaded. Hamblin, "My Experiences," 14.
3. Garner, *Unwavering Valor*, 85.
4. Lukacs, *Escape from Davao*, 106.
5. Lukacs, *Escape from Davao*, 149–59.
6. McCracken, *Very Soon Now*, 48.
7. Dyess, *Dyess Story*, 111.
8. Lukacs, *Escape from Davao*, 222–4; McCracken, *Very Soon Now*, 76–81; Bolitho, "A Japanese POW Story," part 4 (November 7, 2009), 3.
9. Lawton, *Some Survived*, 74; Bolitho, "A Japanese POW Story," part 4, 3, and part 5 (November 21, 2009), 1.

20

WHAT THE WORLD (AND GEORGE AND RUBY) NOW KNEW

As I have loved you,
Love one another.
This new commandment:
Love one another.

—Luacine Clark Fox, "Love One Another"

The escape of ten POWs from Dapecol in April 1943 affected not just the treatment of the remaining POWs at Dapecol but also events back in the United States. On July 24, 1943, three of the escapees from Dapecol arrived by submarine in Australia, where they were debriefed by General MacArthur and his staff. Their stories were "so horrifying that the stenographers could take them for only twenty minutes at a time."[1] They were flown to the United States and again debriefed. Much to their disappointment, they were quarantined and placed under a gag order with the risk of criminal prosecution and losing their commissions should they speak of their experiences to anyone but authorized personnel.[2] On September 9, 1943, President Roosevelt issued a secret order forbidding the disclosure of this information.[3] Their dangerous and miraculous escape had been motivated by a hope that, if the world knew what was happening, the care of

POWs back in the Philippines would improve. Their country had now put them under a gag order.

One of the three was Major William Edwin Dyess, US Army Air Forces, from Albany, Texas. Dyess, a skilled pilot and leader of a P-40 Warhawks squadron in the Philippines, was captured at Bataan. Dyess survived the Bataan Death March and ended up at Dapecol via Cabanatuan. Some journalists managed to get the Dyess story, but they were ordered by the government not to publish it.[4]

The official reason for the gag order was a concern that the publication of these Japanese atrocities might endanger a planned delivery by a neutral ship, the *Gripsholm*, of medical supplies for Allied prisoners in the Pacific.[5] However, some suspect the government may have also had other motives. The government had been heavily criticized for failures in the Philippines. While the government was still pursuing its Europe-first policy, some in the press and many civilians, especially the New Mexico based Bataan Relief Organization, were clamoring for action in the Pacific. Those at senior levels of the government may have feared that the Dyess story would draw more attention to the government's lack of action in the Pacific and more questioning of its Europe-first policy.[6]

While the press was far more compliant with government censors in WWII than now, even in those days, the press had its limits. The *Chicago Tribune*, which had the Dyess story, fully appreciated the journalistic significance of what it had and had been pressing the government for permission to publish.[7] Finally, on January 28, 1944, nine months after their escape and five months after the first telling of their story, the official army-navy statement on the atrocities committed by the Japanese military against American prisoners of war was released, and the press published the stories they had been holding for months.[8]

The stories rapidly spread, not only in the United States but also worldwide. The public, outraged and revolted, was riveted to the stories. George and Ruby Brown awakened to newspapers with headlines such as the one appearing on the front page of the *El Paso Herald-Post* that read "STORY OF BATAAN HORRORS REVEALED," or on the front page of *New York Times*: "5,200 AMERICANS, MANY MORE

The tragedy of Bataan was used by the government to promote the sale of war bonds. Created by the Office for Emergency Management, Office of War Information, Domestic Operations Branch, Bureau of Special Services. Courtesy of the National Archives and Records Administration.

FILIPINOS DIE OF STARVATION, TORTURE AFTER BATAAN." Some of the many subheads read "AMERICANS BURIED ALIVE" and "Men Worked to Death—All 'Boiled' in Sun—12,000 Kept Without Food 7 Days."[9]

The stories then repeated the "factual and official" testimony of Dyess and the other escapees, spanning the fall of Bataan to the murder of a Dapecol POW. A week later, a *Life* magazine issue contained an exclusive feature entitled "Death Was a Part of Our Life," authored by three of the escapees; the feature included photographs of all ten escapees and artists' conceptions of events related by the authors. The *Chicago Tribune* and its one hundred associated papers published a total of twenty-four installments, one appearing each day for almost the next month. New Mexicans, through the Bataan Relief Organization, were now even more outraged, and they demanded to know why their government had withheld this information.[10]

This was likely the first reliable and detailed information the prisoners' families would have received about the POWs in the Philippines since the surrender. We do not know the reaction of the families of these Latter-day Saint Pacific POWs to the release of the Dyess story or those of the other Davao escapees. In fact, these stories were notably absent from the stack of newspaper clippings that Ruby Brown had carefully clipped and saved. Nevertheless, after the publication of the atrocity stories, these families would have had a very graphic understanding of what may have happened or may yet happen to their captive son, brother, or husband.

George and Ruby Brown developed a deep and bitter hatred toward the Japanese that continued for many years.[11] An account of their efforts to forgive and shed that burden is included in President Spencer W. Kimball's book *The Miracle of Forgiveness*.[12] Even if the hatred did not start with the revelations by Dyess and the other escapees, those stories would have intensified and given substance to those feelings.

The hate-engendering effect of the stories of Japanese atrocities was perhaps anticipated. The US government funded the war effort in part by selling war bonds to the public. The government's release of the story appeared at the same time the government was launching a

$14 billion war bond drive.[13] Though the government denied it at the time, it would strain credulity to accept that this was purely a coincidence.[14] In a staggering change of policy, the escapees were suddenly released from their gag order and, to support the sale of war bonds, pushed onto the national stage to make appearances and give interviews on the Japanese brutality.[15]

With the release of the atrocity stories and its "appeal to hatred," war bond sales soared.[16] An El Paso newspaper quoted the chairman of the local war bond drive committee as saying, "The best answer to Japan's fiendish treatment of American war prisoners is to buy War Bonds. . . . These official revelations by our Army and Navy make our blood boil. We on the home front can do something about it. We can buy War Bonds and thus give our fighting men the tools of war with which to avenge their comrades of Bataan."[17] In appealing to vengeance and hatred to promote sales of war bonds, the government was building upon a prejudice already prevalent among many in the United States before the war.[18] After Pearl Harbor, the prejudice was particularly visible in the government-ordered incarceration of Japanese Americans in internment camps. Over 120,000 people of Japanese ancestry, mostly from the West Coast, were forcibly interned and relocated to the western interior of the country simply because of their Japanese ancestry.

Leonard J. Arrington, a noted historian and Latter-day Saint, studied the internment camps, including one located in central Utah, and the resettlement of Japanese Americans. Many fellow citizens made inflammatory and derogatory remarks against Japanese Americans. Although he found that Japanese Americans were generally more welcome in the Latter-day Saint–dominated Utah than in other states, there nonetheless was a strong sentiment against their presence, and they often faced blatant discrimination. Eventually, church authorities were compelled to publish a policy statement decrying this discrimination and pleading for the Saints to "banish these foolish prejudices from our natures."[19]

Over the course of the war, George and Ruby Brown developed a hatred of the Japanese. While the primary source of this hatred was the treatment by the Japanese Army of their son Bobby, George and Ruby were also simply absorbing a prejudice then prevalent among many in their country.

NOTES

1. Lukacs, *Escape from Davao*, 274.
2. Lukacs, *Escape from Davao*, 278.
3. Lukacs, *Escape from Davao*, 280.
4. Lukacs, *Escape from Davao*, 309.
5. Lukacs, *Escape from Davao*, 283; Daws, *Prisoners of the Japanese*, 274–75.
6. Lukacs, *Escape from Davao*, 282.
7. Lukacs, *Escape from Davao*, 309.
8. Lukacs, *Escape from Davao*, 319.
9. Lukacs, *Escape from Davao*, 319–23; "Story of Bataan Horrors Revealed: Japs Torture, Starve Murder Americans," *El Paso Herald-Post*, January 28, 1944 (accessible in archives of Ancestry.com).
10. Cave, *Beyond Courage*, 271–72.
11. Clark and Kowallis, "Fate of the Davao Penal Colony," 128.
12. Kimball, *Miracle of Forgiveness*, 287–93.
13. Lukacs, *Escape from Davao*, 324–25.
14. The release was also timed to occur shortly before a planned offensive action in the Pacific, suggesting that the release may have been deliberately timed such that the planned action would provide immediate proof of the retaliatory action that the American public would surely demand. Lukacs, *Escape from Davao,* 329. The timing of the release was not lost on the members of the Bataan Relief Organization, who claimed the government suppressed the information because it feared the public's demand for action in the Pacific and then only released it in time for the bond sale. Cave, *Beyond Courage*, 271.
15. Lukacs, *Escape from Davao*, 326.
16. Lukacs, *Escape from Davao*, 325.
17. "Answer Japan by Buying War Bonds, El Pasoans Urged," *El Paso Herald-Post*, January 28, 1944 (accessible in archives of Ancestry.com).
18. Beginning with the Chinese exclusion act in the late nineteenth century and culminating with the 1924 immigration act, the United States government overtly discriminated against Asians.
19. Leonard J. Arrington, "The Price of Prejudice" (Faculty Honor Lectures, paper 23, 1962), https://digitalcommons.usu.edu/honor_lectures/23, 41–42. Several United States presidents, as well as the United States Congress, have formally apologized for the treatment of Japanese Americans during the war. On August 10, 1988, President Ronald Reagan signed the Civil Liberties Act of 1988, which provided financial redress of $20,000 for each former internee who was still alive when the act was passed, totaling $1.2 billion.

21

THE SCATTERING

When life's perils thick confound you,
Put his arms unfailing round you.
God be with you till we meet again.

—Jeremiah E. Rankin, "God Be with You Till We Meet Again"

Major Stephen Mellnik was one of those who had escaped from Dapecol with Dyess and had reported on the atrocities in the Japanese POW camps. Mellnik later returned to Australia and served on General MacArthur's headquarters staff, where he coordinated espionage activities in the Philippines. He was, however, also obsessed with one thing: the rescue of the POWs at Dapecol.

While the Philippines was still under Japanese control, there was an active Filipino resistance organization with several groups of guerrilla forces operating on the islands. These Filipino guerillas were supported and largely directed by clandestine US officers stationed at secret locations in the Philippines. It was those forces that had found and protected these Davao escapees, including Mellnik, and had organized their escape from the Philippines. Mellnik's plan was to use these forces to rescue the rest of the POWs from Dapecol.

Mellnik had managed to secure approval to station an intelligence officer in the Philippines who could contact the guerillas and POWs and develop an escape plan. The agent, Captain Harold Rosenquist, was set to depart for the Philippines in February 1944. Unfortunately, there was mixed support for the mission, and, due to some internal discord within headquarters, his departure was delayed. It was not until June that Rosenquist was able to first meet up with the clandestine forces on Mindanao.

As Rosenquist made his way secretly across the island to the Dapecol site, Mellnik anxiously monitored his progress through infrequent and often-garbled radio messages. Finally, Mellnik was handed a transcript of the following radio message from Rosenquist: "Walked around penal colony. Found no, repeat no, PWs. Happy convicts say PWs evacuated ten days ago, probably to Manila." They were too late. A few days earlier, on June 6, 1944, Dapecol had been closed, and the remaining POWs were now gone. Mellnik writes that on reading that message he "sat down and cried."[1]

In this period between February 1944, when Rosenquist was scheduled to go to the Philippines to organize an escape, and mid-June 1944, when he actually reached the camp, the POWs were moved. With that move, the best (and likely only) opportunity for a rescue was lost. Whether Mellnik's rescue plan could have succeeded continued to be debated, but the loss of that chance caused deep regret.[2]

In February 1944, the Japanese camp commander at Dapecol had called for 650 healthy prisoners to work at another location. That was the beginning of the scattering of these Latter-day Saint POWs at Dapecol. Even though the camp then had about two thousand POWs, it was hard to come up with that many healthy prisoners.[3] The POWs were promised more food at the new camp and, as additional inducement, the return of their shoes. The POWs had received shoes in the last Red Cross packages, but the Japanese had confiscated them.[4] Even though conditions at Dapecol were on a steadily worsening course, and notwithstanding the promised food and shoes, only fifty volunteered. The rest were drafted.[5] With a superior Japanese officer looking on, a Japanese doctor selected those capable of hard labor for this detachment.[6]

Seventeen of the Latter-day Saint POWs from the Davao group, including Brown and his friend Ernest Parry, were among that group.[7] Hansen and Davey were not on the list, perhaps due to health conditions.[8] A healthy James Patterson was on the list but, due to what he later described as a miracle, he did not go. The day before the group was to leave, Patterson had returned a wallet he had found to its owner, another POW. The grateful owner had given him a banana that he had managed to steal earlier in the day. Patterson ate the banana that evening with his rice and awoke the next morning with a severely swollen face, hardly able to see. The Japanese doctor giving the POWs a final inspection looked at Patterson and sent him back to the hospital.[9]

Rex Bray, who had a few days earlier been senselessly hit in the face by a Japanese guard with a rifle butt, developed a problem with his wisdom teeth. They were removed without anesthesia, a painful ordeal but one that also left him unfit at the time for this detail.[10]

Hamblin was not on the list of those detailed, but he wanted to go to be with his friends who were members of the Church. He volunteered, and his name was put on a waiting list. He later wrote, "Two of the men were called sick and unable to go, so volunteers were called for. This was my opportunity, but at that moment I had a strong feeling that I should not go. In fact, I had suddenly lost all desire to go."[11] After the war, Hamblin told his family that when the time came for him to call out and volunteer, "he tried at least three times to answer, but he had no voice; it was simply not there."[12]

Fate had brought these Latter-day Saint POWs together at Dapecol, and fate would now begin to tear the group apart, starting with the separation of these seventeen Latter-day Saint POWs.

NOTES

1. Mellnik, *Philippine War Diary*, 315.
2. Lukacs, *Escape from Davao*, 344–45.

3. Bolitho, "A Japanese POW Story," part 5, 1; Sneddon, *Zero Ward*, 53. See also Lawton, *Some Survived*, 75.
4. Bolitho, "Japanese POW Story," part 5, 1.
5. Lawton, *Some Survived*, 138.
6. Nordin, *We Were Next to Nothing*, 121.
7. Clark and Kowallis, "Fate of the Davao Penal Colony," 118–20.
8. Davey was suffering from malaria, beriberi, and various infections while at Dapecol and spent most of his time in the hospital. *Deseret News*, March 24, 1945, 7 (Faith Sustains Interned Mormon Captain); Springgay, "Davey," 35–36. Hansen suffered seriously from beriberi later in captivity, although he may have suffered some symptoms as early as his captivity at Dapecol. Call, "Latter-day Saint Servicemen," 115–16.
9. Patterson, interview, 22–23.
10. Bray, "War Memories, 19.
11. Hamblin, "My Experience," 19.
12. Marianne Loose, email message to author, October 24, 2016.

22

HELL AND MAGIC

Let your heart be not faint
Now the journey's begun;
There is One who still beckons to you.

—Joseph Fielding Smith, "Does the Journey Seem Long?"

At this point in the story, it is helpful to note two developments in the war in the Pacific during 1943 and 1944 that had important consequences for POWs in the Philippines. From the beginning of the war in 1942, the Japanese had been transporting POWs to Japan to work in Japanese industries, but in 1944 there was an extraordinary increase in the movement of POWs from the Philippines.

By 1944, the war wasn't going well for the Japanese, and the Americans were preparing to launch their invasion of the Philippines. Not only did the Japanese continue to need the POWs in Japan due to the increasing labor shortages at important industrial facilities; they also wanted to avoid the liberation of these POWs by the advancing US forces.[1] They may have also wanted them as hostages in the event of an Allied invasion of Japan. In 1944 the Japanese began mass evacuations of POWs from the Philippines.[2] The Latter-day Saint POWs at Dapecol would be swept up in these mass evacuations.

To transport the POWs to camps in Japan or camps closer to Japan, such as in Korea or Taiwan, the Japanese herded the POWs by the hundreds into old merchant vessels, typically old bulk cargo vessels. In some of the ships, crude wooden ledges had been added in the cargo holds to increase the capacity for this human cargo.[3] These POW transport ships justifiably earned the epithet "hell ships."

Most of the Latter-day Saint POWs had endured voyages on Japanese transport ships previously, either on the route from Cabanatuan to Davao or for those from Camp Casisang along the Mindanao coast to Davao. While those voyages were clearly miserable, what these prisoners would now endure was truly horrific. POWs, including those who had endured the Bataan Death March and the deprivations of Camp O'Donnell, Cabanatuan, and Dapecol, described the ordeal in the hell ships as the worst experience of the war.[4]

POWs by the hundreds were squeezed into the holds of these ships, where they would remain for days with no food or water, crammed together in almost complete darkness with little air and in extreme heat. Not surprisingly, especially when deprived of water and oxygen, some began to go crazy. A survivor of a hell ship voyage later reported, "The prisoners had been so crowded in these other holds that they couldn't even get air to breathe. They went crazy, cut and bit each other through the arms and legs and sucked their blood. In order to keep from being murdered, many had to climb the ladders and were promptly shot by guards. Between twenty and thirty prisoners had died of suffocation or were murdered during the night."[5]

Sergeant Arthur Baclawski, Brown's former tent mate from Fort Bliss, described the scene in the hold of these hell ships: "Men were yelling and screaming. It was a seething mass of men moving around like Jell-O. Some climbed the walls and hung on the struts. One preached all night. In the morning, when they pulled the canvas off, a lot were unconscious. Eight were dead."[6]

Many, if not most, of the POWs were sick, often with dysentery, which further exacerbated the situation. Their only latrine was a five-gallon bucket sitting in the middle of the hold. When circumstances and the Japanese permitted, the prisoners pulled it up once a day to be emptied. For sick POWs with uncontrollable bowels, crawling over others crammed in the holds in order to try to reach the bucket, often unsuccessfully, was an especially difficult and degrading experience, in addition to the filth and discomfort of the disease.[7]

For perspective, about fifty thousand POWs were transported on those hell ships, and about twenty-one thousand of them died, a staggering death rate of more than 40 percent. In comparison, during the entire war in the Pacific, about twenty thousand US Marines died. As one author noted, "Clearly, it was deadlier to be a POW on a Japanese ship than to be a U.S. Marine fighting them."[8] The greatest danger to these POWs aboard these hell ships, however, was not the horrific conditions; the absence of adequate food, water, air, and basic sanitation; disease; or even the brutality of the Japanese guards. Rather, their greatest danger was the US Navy.

A major objective of the US war effort was the destruction of Japanese merchant shipping, the *marus*, as the Japanese merchant and transport ships were called. Over the sea, the *marus* carried Japanese men and weapons to the fighting front and brought back from the "Greater East Asia Co Prosperity Sphere" essential raw materials, making the marus Japan's essential life support system.[9] In the early years of the war, US attacks on Japanese shipping had been largely ineffective. Yet, by late 1943, US Navy submarines were then having extraordinary success in attacking the Japanese merchant fleet.[10] How could that be possible? What had changed?

While not diminishing the courage, skill, and heroism of the submarine crews or the importance of the improvements in tactics and the accuracy and reliability of the US torpedoes, it was actually quite easy. The United States simply listened while the Japanese unknowingly told them where the ships were and the routes they were going to take, along with the number of ships in a convoy, their names, cargo, and escorts.[11] In other words, in 1943 the United States had cracked the Japanese secret code used for the *marus*, and the Japanese were unaware of it.[12]

Intercepting the secret radio communications, decoding the messages, and managing all the information obtained about Japanese merchant ships and their convoys was part of a massive, but largely unseen, intelligence operation code-named Magic.[13] The intelligence operation and the information obtained in that operation were closely guarded secrets. Japanese messages were intercepted, translated, and transmitted to submarine commanders within minutes. However, historians combing through old submarine reports and logbooks find no indications of such. Captains had been ordered to remove any mention of such intelligence information in their diaries, reports, and logs.[14]

The ability to understand an enemy's secret coded communications is, of course, an advantage of inestimable importance, but only as long as the enemy does not know—and the United States and its allies were careful and discriminating in the use of this intelligence so as not to tip off the Japanese.[15] Nevertheless, by 1944, nearly every US submarine operation in the Pacific was conducted with aid of intelligence obtained from Operation Magic, and on some nights, every submarine was engaged in missions based on such information.

With a truly unfortunate convergence of events, the year 1944, the high point of this mass transfer of POWs in the hellish holds of these aging Japanese *marus*, coincided with the time when US submarine attacks on such Japanese merchant ships were at their peak. It was a time one author described as the "massacre of the marus."[16]

While immensely valuable to the Allies in defeating Japan, these intercepted messages, sadly, also spelled death for thousands of POWs. The Japanese military provided no identification of the POW ships, and the ships usually also held supplies, fuel, or ammunition, making them appear legitimate targets for US submarines and dive-bombers.[17] In addition to enduring the dark, sweltering, filthy, and claustrophobic conditions of these holds, these Latter-day Saint POWs from Dapecol would face the terror of their ship being attacked by Allied forces while helplessly trapped in those hellish holds.

NOTES

1. Michno, *Death on the Hellships*, 173.
2. As early as October 1942, the Japanese had begun shipping POWs north to Manchuria and Japan, but the mass evacuation from Philippines came later. Cave, *Beyond Courage*, 288, 291n5.
3. Michno, *Death on the Hellships*, 296–98.
4. Michno, *Death on the Hellships*, 305–6.
5. Lee A. Gladwin, "American POWs on Japanese Ships Take a Voyage into Hell," *Prologue Magazine* 35, no. 4 (Winter 2003). The US National Archives and Records Administration, http://www.archives.gov/publications/prologue/2003/winter/hell-ships-1.html (quoting John M. Jacobs). Such occurrences were reported on nearly every hell ship and were attributed to the lack of oxygen, causing the men to become crazed and unable to control their actions. Cave, *Beyond Courage*, 296n9.
6. Cave, *Beyond Courage*, 295.
7. Sneddon, *Zero Ward*, 81.
8. Michno, *Hellships*, 282–83.
9. W. J. Holmes, *Double-Edged Secret: U.S. Naval Intelligence Operations in the Pacific during World War II* (Annapolis, MD: United States Naval Institute, 1979), 129.
10. Daws, *Prisoners of the Japanese*, 275.
11. Ronald Lewin, *The American Magic: Codes, Ciphers and the Defeat of Japan* (New York City: Farrar, Straus and Giroux, 1982), 218–19.
12. The Japanese used three major coding systems for secret communications. One, called *Purple*, was used for diplomatic messages. A second, called *JN25*, was used for military communications, and a third, called the *maru code*, was the code used for merchant shipping. The US effort to break the Japanese codes was based in Hawaii and led by a group known as the Fleet Radio Unit, Pacific, or FRUPac. Before the war, the United States had cracked the Purple diplomatic code and by 1942 had cracked the important JN25 code for military communications, but it wasn't until early 1943 that they cracked the *maru* code. Holmes, *Double-Edged Secrets,* 126.
13. See Gladwin, "American POWs on Japanese Ships." For example, during January and February 1944, approximately 3,700 index cards were created in the ongoing effort to identify, describe, and locate the ships.
14. Lewin, *American Magic*, 220; Michno, *Hellships*, 295–96.
15. Holmes, *Double-Edged Secrets*, 128–29; Lewin, *American Magic*, 218; Daws, *Prisoners of the Japanese*, 285–86.
16. Lewin, *The American Magic*, 213, 224–25; see Clark and Kowallis, "Fate of the Davao Penal Colony," 111–12; Daws, *Prisoners of the Japanese*, 286.
17. Michno, *Hellships*, 292–95. At times the Japanese did mark a ship as a POW transport, but they did so to protect their own troops then loaded on the ship. Springgay, "Davey," 52. For its part, the United States had decided on unrestricted submarine warfare—attacking merchant ships without warning. Also, some argue that the United States did little through its spies on

the waterfront and among guerillas in the hills to track the movement of POWs or to identify the ships on which POWs were loaded. Daws, *Prisoners of the Japanese*, 296–97.

23

LEAVING THE PHILIPPINES

Brightly beams our Father's mercy
From his lighthouse evermore,
But to us he gives the keeping
Of the lights along the shore.

—Philip Paul Bliss, "Brightly Beams Our Father's Mercy"

The remaining POWs at Dapecol, including the Latter-day Saint POWs who had remained at the camp, began to suspect that the Japanese were worried about something and that change was coming. Hamblin observed, "We were kept in camp more and doing less work. The guards seemed nervous and kept a continual watch on the jungle."[1]

Their suspicions were correct. With an increase in local guerilla activity around Dapecol and the Americans closing in, the camp commander had been ordered to close the camp and deliver the POWs dockside for shipment north to Manila and then on to Japan. These POWs had been caught up in the mass evacuation of POWs to Japan.

YASHU MARU

On June 6, 1944—coincidentally the same day the Allies launched the D-Day assault at Normandy, France, and a few days before the arrival of Rosenquist, the intelligence officer working for Mellnik—the remaining 1,240 POWs at Dapecol (the ones who had not gone to Lasang) were loaded into trucks and the camp closed. Among those 1,240 POWs were the following Latter-day Saints, the last Church members at Dapecol:

- Private First Class Rex D. Bray from Provo, Utah
- Private First Class Allen C. Christensen from Tremonton, Utah
- Captain Robert G. Davey from Salt Lake City, Utah
- Private First Class Charles L. Goodliffe from Park Valley, Utah
- Private Orland K. Hamblin from Farmington, New Mexico
- Staff Sergeant Peter (Nels) Hansen from Weiser, Idaho
- Corporal Kenneth B. Larsen from Salt Lake City, Utah
- Private First Class Lloyd Parry from Logan, Utah
- Private James Patterson from Sunnyside, Utah
- Corporal Carl D. Rohlfing from Salt Lake City, Utah
- Corporal Donald L. Vance from Fairview, Utah
- Corporal Ralf T. Wilson from Alta, Wyoming
- Corporal James Edmond Wilstead from Provo, Utah[2]

The POWs, blindfolded and tied together with ropes, were crammed into trucks and taken to a dock near Lasang, where they were loaded into the holds of the *Yashu Maru*, a "small, greasy cargo freighter."[3]

This was the beginning of their "hell ship" experience. They were all placed in the forward holds, where, as one POW later wrote, "it was as bad as the proverbial slave ships. Included were the sick, the paralytics [likely those incapacitated by beriberi], and the insane. Water was limited, many men had diarrhea, and there were few toilets. We were terribly crowded [and] it was as hot as hell."[4] Davey wrote that they were so crowded "that only one man in three could lie down and we had to sleep in relays of sleeping four hours and staying up for eight hours."[5] Nonetheless, their conditions were not all bad. The POWs were allowed some time on deck, and they received another distribution of Red Cross packages that had been sent earlier.[6]

The ship remained in the harbor for six days until finally, on June 12, the ship left Davao, crossed the Moro Gulf, and anchored at Zamboanga on the southeast tip of Mindanao on June 14. While anchored at Zamboanga and in separate incidents, a couple of POWs managed to escape and swim to the coast, where they were rescued by guerilla forces. The Japanese were furious. Before the escapes, POWs had been allowed time on the deck, which allowed them to stretch in the fresh air and to reduce the crowding below; additionally, the hatches had been left open most of the time, allowing in light and fresh air. After the escapes, all POWs were forced into the hot, crowded holds below, and the hatches battened down, leaving them suffocating in darkness and fearing Japanese reprisals. Rations were also reduced.[7] Of that incident, Hamblin wrote:

> After much yelling, pushing and kicking, all men were forced into the burning hell of the two small holds. . . . We were cramped and crowded and suffering for air, there being only two small port holes. I think many would have become hysterical, but at that moment someone started a harmonica, and we all started singing. The tension was relieved, and we temporarily forget our troubles. . . . Under such conditions a day can seem like a year.
> Many days were spent with no relief from the sweltering heat except when it rained. Those who were sitting directly below the hatches would get wet and call for the hatches to be put on. When they were on, the men in the corners would smother for air and plead for them to be removed. Sometimes at night we would be suddenly awakened by someone having a nightmare and screaming. This torture went on for what seemed like months.[8]

On June 17, the POWs arrived at Cebu City, disembarked, and were marched to an old metal warehouse. About a thousand were crowded into the warehouse, and the rest—about three hundred—were left outside in the dirt in a wire stockade. Inside it was hot and suffocating; those outside endured the misery of the hot sun, flies, and mosquitos. It later rained, and all were forced inside. They were cramped and miserable, with many suffering from diarrhea and malaria. The food was inadequate and poorly prepared.

THE *SINGOTO MARU* AND BILIBID PRISON

After three days, the POWs were brought back to the dock to help load a ship. No one knew its name, but the POWs came to call it the *Singoto Maru* (Japanese *shigoto maru*, meaning "work ship"). After working as stevedores, the POWs were loaded into the holds of the ship. It was a smaller ship, and the crowded conditions were worse than before. To further add to the misery, the ship had last been used to haul coal—and, of course, it had not been cleaned. No one was allowed on deck, and the hatches were kept closed.

A POW described the conditions aboard that ship "as the worst you could possibly think about—filth of all kinds." The rice ration was cut. One man "went stark raving mad and had to be chained to a post. . . . Altogether . . . fifty-six men [were lost], and they were simply lifted up to the main deck with ropes and then thrown over the side."[9] On June 24, the ship docked at Pier Seven in Manila, and the POWs were marched to the Bilibid Prison. It had taken them nineteen miserable days to make an eight-hundred-mile trip that ordinarily would take only three days.[10] This, however, was only the beginning.

Bilibid was an ugly, inhospitable, old concrete civilian prison in Manila that the Japanese had converted to a POW camp. It was used as a hospital for the sickest POWs and as a transit camp to hold POWs until they could be shipped to other camps.[11] Those Davao prisoners who had previously been at Cabanatuan, such as Davey, were familiar with the camp, as they had stayed there briefly before being shipped to Davao. Bilibid was also used as a depository for mail and packages sent to the POWs from the United States. At Bilibid, both Davey and Hamblin received packages and letters from home, some that had been sent almost a year earlier. Hamblin wrote:

> I was lucky, for I received two packages, one from my sisters in Mesa, Arizona, and the other one had been ordered, packaged, and sent from Albuquerque through the Bataan Organization. Mother was in Farmington, New Mexico, and had not received a permit to send a package. Fearing she could not get one mailed from Farmington in time to go with the others from there, she solicited the aid of the Bataan Organization with the result as stated. This shows how cooperation worked in these trying times. Those packages sent by this organization all contained the same things and each contained a pipe and tobacco. I traded mine for food. It was nice to receive personal packages from home. There was a wool sweater, gloves and plenty of soap; an item that was really scarce in the prison camp.[12]

Three days after their arrival, about nine hundred POWs—a group of officers that included Davey—were moved to Cabanatuan. After a few days, those remaining at Bilibid were divided up among several hell ships and shipped to various camps in Japan. The sick POWs, however, remained at Bilibid.[13]

Hansen, Hamblin, and likely Patterson, Christensen, and other Latter-day Saint POWs, were among eleven hundred POWs loaded into the holds of the *Canadian Inventor*, a Japanese freighter ship that sailed from Manila for Japan on July 2, 1944.[14] Kenneth Larsen from Salt Lake City was among sixteen hundred POWs abroad the *Nissyo Maru* that sailed for Japan a few days later on July 17, 1944.[15] Rex Bray and Charles Goodliffe, along with more than thirteen hundred other POWs, were crammed into the holds of the *Noto Maru* and sailed to Japan on August 27, 1944.[16] While the voyage on each of these hell ships was horrific in its own unique way, in many respects the misery and terror were similar. The experience of those aboard the *Canadian Inventor* is likely representative, and we have several accounts of that voyage.

THE CANADIAN INVENTOR—THE MATI MATI MARU

The *Canadian Inventor* was an aging captured vessel one POW described as "an old freighter of dubious seaworthiness"; another called it "an ailing and miserable old tug."[17] The holds were about twelve feet deep, and crude wooden shelves had been built around the hold about halfway down. The POWs were placed in two layers, one layer being on the floor and the other being on this shelf. Each person had a space of about twenty inches by sixty inches. A POW on the ship described the living arrangements: "By sitting down, with our knees drawn up, we could all four sit down at the same time. In order to lie down, even in a curled-up position, we had to take turns. With only five feet it was impossible to ever lay down full length, unless the people in the next section made room for you in their section. Since they had no place to go, we never once during this entire time [sixty-two days] were able to lie down and stretch out."[18]

The ship sailed from Manila on July 4, but the next day boiler trouble occurred, and the ship returned to Manila. There it sat, with the POWs crammed in the oven-like hold, for another eleven days. With the boiler repaired, the ship again sailed on July 16. Outside the calm waters of Manila Bay, the ship encountered a typhoon. With the ship loaded with POWs instead of heavier bulk cargo, it rode high, "rolling like a cork in the waves." POWs became seasick, and their vomit and the overturning "honey buckets" resulted in an indescribable stench in the holds. There was, not surprisingly, an increase in the number of POWs becoming crazed and screaming out madly in the darkness. Then rain came, providing some respite with fresh water pouring in from the hatches. But that rain also brought colds and influenza.

The ship's engine kept breaking down, and the voyage was repeatedly delayed as the ship stopped at small islands for repairs. It crept slowly along protected coastlines where possible and waited for days, at times in small bays, to avoid Allied submarines. Two ships in its convoy were sunk by submarines. The POWs had now named the ship the "*Mati Mati Maru*" (Japanese *machi machi maru*), which means the "wait, wait ship." Some of the officers even discussed taking over the ship. The POWs outnumbered the guards, and some of the POWs could navigate. But they had little food and fuel, and the ship was too slow to get them to any Allied base before being overtaken. The idea was dropped.[19]

For Hamblin, however, it wasn't all uninterrupted misery in the hold. One of the Japanese officers had spent time in Hawaii before the war and had acquired a liking for American music. On some moonlit nights, when the ship was stalled with boiler trouble and not going anywhere, he gathered some of the prisoners on deck to enjoy a POW quartet singing American music. Hamblin was part of that quartet.[20]

On another occasion, after a POW died on the voyage from beriberi and malnutrition, Hansen was asked by the US commander to conduct the funeral. Hansen asked Hamblin to assist. Hansen opened the services with a prayer, and then a quartet, which included Hamblin, sang. Hansen spoke on the resurrection for about fifteen minutes and then Hamblin dedicated the body to a water grave. The quartet sang another song, and the body went overboard.

Of this burial at sea, Hamblin later wrote, "It wasn't a pleasant thought . . . , leaving one's fellow prisoner's body to be devoured by sharks, and I could not help thinking of his family and friends at home who would have wanted to give him a burial in the good earth. However, there is a promise that the sea will give up its dead at the appointed time. We felt this a great honor, in the absence of a Chaplain, to be selected from a group of hundreds present to render this service."[21]

On September 2, 1944, they finally arrived at the port of Moji in Fukuoka Prefecture. A POW later described the experience: "From the time we left Davao on June 6, we had spent ninety-two days traveling under horrendous conditions. One has no idea what a human being can endure until actually experiencing it. This was the end of the most horrible ninety-two days of my life."[22] Hamblin was more philosophical about the end of that voyage: "As we reached the shore and found ground under our feet, it was a wonderful feeling. However, we were so weak after being on the ship for three months that we could scarcely stand. But, to feel the good earth under our feet, and breathe the fresh air once again, was worth more to us than I can describe with words. I had learned that just the simple things of life, if we are deprived of them, become very valuable. I found the things that I had taken for granted before, now became very precious."[23]

Following their arrival in Moji, the POWs traveled by a regular passenger train. Even though the windows were blacked out, compared to the experiences aboard the ship it was pure bliss. The food was better, and they had all the water they could drink. Their destination was the Nagoya Branch #5 Yokkaichi POW camp, the next chapter in their imprisonment.[24]

NOTES

1. Hamblin, "My Experience," 19.
2. This list is simply those previously identified Latter-day Saint POWs at Dapecol less those who were aboard the *Shinyo Maru*.

3. Michno, *Death on the Hellships*, 173.
4. Michno, *Death on the Hellships*, 173 (quoting Carl Nordin).
5. *Deseret News*, March 24, 1945, 7 (quoting from a letter by Robert G. Davey).
6. Michno, *Hellships*, 174.
7. Michno, *Hellships*, 174; Hamblin, "My Experience," 20.
8. Hamblin, "My Experience," 20.
9. Michno, *Hellships*, 175–76.
10. Lawton, *Some Survived*, 104.
11. See Daws, *Prisoners of the Japanese*, 283; Lawton, *Some Survived*, 104; Heimbuch, Lucky Ones, 86–87; Michno, *Death on the Hellships*, 179.
12. Hamblin, "My Experience," 20–21.
13. Lawton, *Some Survived*, 104; Christensen, "My Life Story," 17. Michno put the number at five hundred and describes them as those in poor health—not the sickest, who remained at Bilibid, or the healthy, who were to be shipped to Japan. Michno, *Death on the Hellships*, 179.
14. Nordin, Hansen, and Hamblin were likely all on the same ship, as Nordin notes that "Hanson" acted as a chaplain in the burial at sea of Col. Weeks, and Hamblin notes that he assisted Hansen in a burial at sea. Nordin, *We Were Nothing*, 153; Hamblin, "My Experience," 21. Nordin was on the *Canadian Inventor*. Michno, *Hellships*, 179. In their accounts, neither Patterson nor Christensen indicate the name of the ship, but it is evident from their descriptions, in particular the ninety-day duration of the voyage, that it was the *Canadian Inventor*. Patterson, "Interview," 10–11; Christensen, "My Life Story," 17; Michno, *Death on the Hellships*, 315 (departure date and number of POWs).
15. Center for Research, Allied POWS under Japanese, "Pacific POW Roster," http://www.mansell.com/pow_resources/pacific_pow_roster.html; Michno, *Death on the Hellships*, 182–90, 315.
16. Center for Research, "Pacific POW Roster" (noting Bray and Goodliffe as having been on the *Noto Maru*); Michno, *Death on the Hellships*, 191–93, 315.
17. Michno, *Death on the Hellships*, 179.
18. Heimbuch, *Lucky Ones*, 88.
19. Michno, *Death on the Hellships*, 180–81; Heimbuch, *Lucky Ones*, 91; Hamblin, "My Experience," 21.
20. Hamblin, "My Experience," 21.
21. Hamblin "My Experience," 21. This death and burial is also mentioned in Nordin, *We Were Next to Nothing*, 153. (A diary entry notes that "Hanson" acted as chaplain.) Although neither Hansen nor Hamblin in their postwar accounts mention the name of the ship that took them to Japan; this note and Hamblin's account indicate that Hansen and Hamblin were on that voyage of the *Canadian Inventor*. Heimbuch, who also left Davao at the same time as Nordin, Hamblin, and Hansen, also identifies the *Canadian Inventor* as the hell ship that took them from Manila to Japan. Heimbuch, *Lucky Ones*, 91.
22. Heimbuch, *Lucky Ones*, 92.

23. Hamblin, "My Experience," 21.
24. Clark and Kowallis, "Fate of the Davao Penal Colony," note 29; Christensen, "My Life Story," 18; Ashton, "Spirit of Love," 176 (Hansen sent to a camp near Osaka); Heimbuch, *Lucky Ones*, 92–93 (Heimbuch, who was on the *Canadian Inventor*, refers to taking a train to Yokkaichi). Hansen, Larsen, Lloyd Parry, Patterson, Rohlfing, and Vance, all Latter-day Saint POWs from Davao, are listed on the roster of this camp in Japan. Hamblin is not, but the rosters were prepared at the end of the war at liberation, and Hamblin indicates in his history that he was later separated from Hansen and moved to a different camp. Center for Research, Allied POWS under Japanese, "Nagoya Branch #5 Yokkaichi American Rescue Roster (Nagoya #5 Yokkaichi Main)," http://www.mansell.com/pow_resources/camplists/Nagoya/nag_5_yokkaichi/nag_05_yanks.html.

24
LASANG AND THE HOPE OF AUGUST 17, 1944

O God, our help in ages past,
Our hope for years to come,
Our shelter from the stormy blast,
And our eternal home.

—Isaac Watts, "O God, Our Help in Ages Past"

Meanwhile, back on the island of Mindanao the 650 POWs selected from Dapecol, including Brown and sixteen other Latter-day Saints, had been taken to a new prison near an airfield at the village of Lasang. They had been told the Lasang camp would be an improvement with more food. It was not. The prison was small and tightly ringed by barbed wire, confining the prisoners to a much smaller area than at Dapecol. In addition, this was not an agricultural camp. Unlike at Dapecol, there would be no opportunities to surreptitiously supplement their inadequate diet with stolen food.

Instead of doing agricultural labor, the prisoners were put to work building an airfield.[1] It was hard, brutal work; the prisoners had to put crushed coral on the airstrip, which cut their bare feet to ribbons.[2]

Furious that they were forced to work for the clearly military purposes of the enemy, the prisoners engaged in a delicate balance of working at the slowest pace possible without attracting retribution by the guards. At times, they even deliberately sabotaged the work.³ The consequence of failing to convince the guards that they were trying to complete the work or of getting caught at sabotage was, if not death, a round of brutal torture.

After a while, their days at Lasang again became a monotonous, dreary, and dragging routine. They walked a mile or so from the camp to the airfield in bare feet on a gravel road with a knife-like layer of rocks. At the end of the day they walked back again, usually with bloodied feet, exhausted from the work in the heat. Throughout it all, they were constantly under the watch of brutal guards who were looking for the slightest provocation.⁴

This had been the daily routine for six months. They had now been prisoners for a long time. It was a time when a POW would be looking for some reason to have hope, and then that reason came.

On August 17, 1944, after the lights were out, the prisoners heard a sound in the darkness that initially seemed like the buzzing of a distant insect. Murray Sneddon, a prisoner at Lasang, recounts what he and the other POWs heard that evening. The reaction of the other POWs was likely similar to his:

> Once it disappeared completely, but soon emerged again sounding a little bit louder. I was certain the noise was increasing in volume and I began to feel more and more sure that it sounded like a distant airplane, and not just any airplane, . . . an American airplane. I knew Japanese engines had individual exhaust ports jutting from each cylinder; this gave the plane a rapid popping sound somewhat similar to a motorcycle. American planes, on the other hand, had collector rings around the engine, which received exhaust from each cylinder and fed the expended fuel out a single exhaust port. The resultant sound was a constant and continuous drone, just like the plane that was circling over our heads this very moment.
>
> I knew every man in the barrack was awake, despite the fact that not a sound could be heard from any of them. Their attention was riveted to the sound above us. . . . Our ears were suddenly attracted to a new sound—the rushing sound of heavy objects plunging down through the night air—and then the sharp staccato explosions as bombs slammed into the airfield that we had been working on only a few hours ago. This was the proof we had been waiting for. After an eternity of two and one-half years we now knew: Our forces were returning to take us home!

> Thank God! Thank God! Thank God! At last our most fervent prayer was being answered: life was taking on a new dimension. My eyes brimmed with tears of joy, and my thoughts flashed homeward. Maybe our long-hoped-for day of freedom was closer than we dared think.[5]

This was great news, but the hopeful expectation that the Allies might soon be coming also left the prisoners with a sobering thought—they were probably now in great danger. If the Allies were to invade, what would their Japanese captors do? Would their captors simply abandon them, take them to Japan as hostages, or kill them all before leaving?

The POWs had good reasons to be afraid, as evidenced by what the Japanese military did at another camp just a few months later. On December 14, 1944, more than 150 POWs at the Puerto Princesa Prison Camp in Palawan, an island near the Philippines, were ordered into trenches, purportedly to keep them safe from Allied bombers—that were, in fact, not coming. While the POWs were in the trenches, their Japanese captors poured aviation fuel over them and set them on fire while simultaneously raking them with gunfire and tossing grenades at the entrances to the trenches. All were murdered except for a few who managed to survive by appearing dead.[6]

This was the feared Japanese Army's way of closing a prison in advance of an Allied invasion: simply annihilating all the POWs en masse without leaving any traces.[7] While the POWs at Lasang would not have known of these incidents or this policy of POW annihilation, they were sufficiently familiar with the Japanese Army to suspect and fear such a plan.[8]

The level of anxiety among the POWs at Lasang was not lessened by what happened the following day—or rather what did not happen. In contradiction to everything they had previously experienced from the Japanese, when the POWs assembled for work at the front gate the next morning, they were told that it was a holiday and there would be no work. The prisoners were told to remain in camp. The same thing happened the next day. Something else roused the POWs' suspicion: there were fewer Japanese around, as many of the guards had left.[9] Clearly, things were about to change.

NOTES

1. Sneddon, *Zero Ward*, 53–63; Brown and Zundel, "George Robin Brown . . . His Story," 20–21.
2. Nordin, *We Were Next to Nothing,* 123–24.
3. Nordin, 122–23.
4. Sneddon, *Zero Ward*, 59.
5. Sneddon, *Zero Ward*, 66–67. Hayes Bolitho also makes references to this bombing, although his account differs slightly from Sneddon's account. Bolitho writes that work was discontinued on the airfield on August 4, which was after the bombing, but the POWs were not moved out of the camp until August 19, 1944. Bolitho, "Japanese POW Story," part 5, 3. See also Michno, *Hellships*, 225–26 (similar to Bolitho's account but states that the POWs left on August 20).
6. Sides, *Ghost Soldiers*, 7–12; Michno, *Hellships*, 272–73; Holmes, *Unjust Enrichment*, 116 (describes a similar incident at Wake Island).
7. Daws, *Prisoners of the Japanese*, 324–25. Documents discovered after the war indicate that the long-standing policy of the Japanese military was that if the commander of a POW camp believed his location might fall to the enemy, he was to kill all POWs first and leave no traces of them. Holmes, *Unjust Enrichment*, 114–16.
8. See, e.g., Parkinson and Benson, *Soldier Slaves*, 156 (comments of POW Harold Poole).
9. Sneddon, *Zero Ward*, 69.

25

SHINYO MARU

And should we die before our journey's through,
Happy day! All is well!
We then are free from toil and sorrow, too;
With the just we shall dwell!

—William Clayton, "Come, Come, Ye Saints"

On August 20, 1944, the 650 POWs from Lasang—including Brown, Ernest Parry, and fifteen other Latter-day Saints from the group in Davao—were roped together and marched shoeless a few miles to the Tibungco Pier, a small pier for a lumber mill near the Davao Gulf. There they were joined by one hundred prisoners from another camp.[1] Due to the increasing guerrilla activity in the area, they were heavily guarded. The POWs were first to be shipped to Cebu and then to Manila with Japan as the likely final destination.[2] Similar to the hell ship experience of other POWs, this group of prisoners would face the next three weeks living in the most miserable conditions.

At the Tibungco Pier, they were loaded aboard the old Japanese Army freighter *Tateishi Maru*, but it was marked only as "86"—a hell ship.[3] Many of the prisoners had been in a Japanese transport vessel before when they were taken to Davao, but this would be much worse. Suffocating heat, stagnant air, little food and water, the stench of sick and dying men, and darkness would now be their life. They were taken out to the side of the ship in small boats and then made to climb up a wide lattice rope to the deck. Four hundred were placed in one hold, and 350 in another. They climbed down ladders into the holds, where a Japanese soldier was waiting with his rifle and bayonet to crowd them tightly in the holds. They had to take turns standing and sitting because there was not enough room for all to sit, let alone lie down, at the same time.

In the intense heat in the holds, the POWs were soon drenched in sweat. In such heat, the sweat on dirty skin caused skin rashes that later became open sores. Toilet facilities consisted of three five-gallon cans dropped down through the hatch and placed in the middle of the hold for use in full view. The food was inadequate, but food was not the problem; many of the POWs had managed to bring with them food from Red Cross packages they had previously received in camp. Rather, the problem was the lack of water and fresh air.[4]

Two POWs had escaped during an earlier voyage of a hell ship in this area. For that reason, coupled with the increasing risk of Allied attacks, the Japanese now kept the hatches covered and opened them for only brief periods.[5] A POW provided this description of the conditions:

> Some got sick and many passed out for lack of oxygen. When the hatch covers were opened again, there wasn't a sound; we were all too weak to say anything. . . . Possibly as many as one hundred fifty to two hundred men passed out in both holds and two men simply went berserk and had to be tied down. . . .
>
> Many men were close to death by the time the hatch covers and tarp were removed. Revival was slow. Some thought they were dying and asked for last rites. . . . Many were desperate for water. . . . Some fought over who got the last drop from the canteen. All of us were terribly dehydrated. Those who had dysentery were in worse shape. Many were so weak they tried crawling to the latrine cans but just couldn't make it; they just wallowed in their own filth. We urinated only once in a great while and with excruciating pain![6]

While the conditions were indescribably horrible and the Japanese crew was merciless, the POWs understood that their greatest danger came from Allied planes and submarines. To the US Navy, their unmarked freighter was just another tempting enemy target.[7]

The ship arrived in Zamboanga Harbor on the southwest tip of Mindanao on the Moro Gulf late in the afternoon on August 24, 1944. There the prisoners remained, cramped and sweltering in the dark, hot, and filthy hold for ten days.[8] Finally, on September 4, the hatch cover was opened, and the prisoners were ordered up the ladder. The POWs climbed up the ladder and noticed another ship, the *Shinyo Maru*, a few feet away. They were then ordered across a narrow plank precariously stretched across the gap between the ships. Once on the *Shinyo Maru*, they climbed down a long narrow ladder into the darkness of the bottom of the ship.

Ships of this size were generally divided horizontally into two compartments: an upper compartment about one-third of the way down from the deck and a lower compartment below. On the first ship, the *Tateishi Maru*, the POWs occupied the upper compartment. On the *Shinyo Maru*, however, the prisoners were put in the lower compartment at the very bottom of the ship. The long metal ladder went all the way from the deck down through the upper compartment, which was loaded with bales of cargo, to a dark abyss. It was a death trap.[9]

The *Shinyo Maru* was an antiquated freighter built in Scotland in 1884 and captured by the Japanese in Shanghai in 1941. At 312 feet long by 40.2 feet wide and only 2,600 tons in weight, the *Shinyo Maru* was smaller than the 3,801-gross-ton *Tateishi Maru* they were leaving. While it had been crowded on the *Tateishi Maru*, the prisoners were absolutely sardined in the holds of the *Shinyo Maru*. As done on other ships, boards were put across the single hatch just above the end of the ladder, cutting off any possible air circulation and adding to the prisoners' terror and misery.

With information from the Magic intelligence operation, the United States already knew a lot about the *Shinyo Maru*, then at anchor at Zamboanga. On August 14, 1944, the US intelligence unit had first intercepted a Japanese naval message from Manila to Tokyo

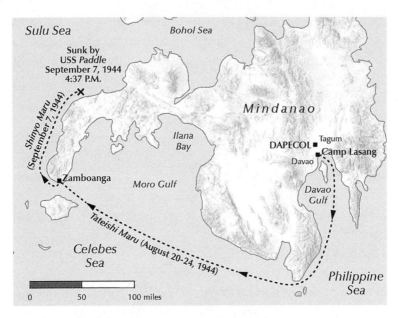

Map 3. Voyage of the *Shinyo Maru*. Map by Nat Case.

referring to the Japanese Navy's urgent need for the *Shinyo Maru*.[10] A few days later on August 18, 1944, US intelligence intercepted another message ordering the *Shinyo Maru* to proceed from Zamboanga to Cebu and then on to Manila. Finally, a message intercepted on September 6 stated that the "C-076 convoy" was to depart Zamboanga for Cebu on September 7 at 2 a.m. The message indicated that the *Shinyo Maru*, transporting "750 troops for Manila via Cebu," would be part of that convoy. Months later, British intelligence indicated that FRUPac, the US intelligence unit in Hawaii, may have erred in its interpretation of that message and that, correctly interpreted, the Japanese message stated that the *Shinyo Maru* was transporting 750 POWs, not 750 Japanese troops.[11]

Early in the morning of September 7, 1944, with the POWs crammed and suffocating in the hot, stale stench of its hold, the *Shinyo Maru* left for Cebu in a convoy.[12] It was not a coincidence that on that same day, a US submarine, the USS *Paddle*, was also in that part of the South China Sea looking for enemy ships to attack.[13]

USS *Paddle* (SS-263) underway 1944–45. Courtesy of United States Navy.

The *Paddle*'s report of September 7, 1944, states that while the submarine was in her patrol area, about ten miles north of Sindangan Point, Mindanao, she sighted a small convoy consisting of "a medium tanker, two medium AKs [AK refers to a cargo ship], two small AKs, two torpedo boats or DE-type escorts [DE refers to a destroyer escort] and one small coastal tanker type craft [and] the tanker was leading the medium AKs and very close to the coast." The submarine also observed two planes overhead.

To reduce the risk of being discovered, all periscope observations were very brief, and no effort was made to identify the actual names of the vessels spotted. The captain's report then states: "Fired four bow tubes at AO [the tanker]. Immediately shifted set-up to leading AK [the freighter] and fired two tubes. . . . All torpedoes were heard to run towards targets. . . . Escort on starboard beam seen to have turned directly toward, so order was given to go deep. Periscope went under . . . before extent of damage to AK and AO could be seen. Loud, characteristic, breaking up noises were heard almost immediately however, and continued for some time after depth charging began. It is believed that of those two ships at least the AK sank and possibly both."[14] The USS *Paddle* narrowly survived the forty-five Japanese depth charges and bombs aimed at it after the attack, and after a few hours it returned to its patrolling.

The "breaking up noises" that the USS *Paddle* crew heard came from the *Shinyo Maru*, which had been hit by a torpedo; trapped in its lower holds were 750 POWs, including the seventeen Latter-day Saints. For most of the POWs, death came quickly and violently from the explosion of the torpedoes. Others drowned as cargo bales and a bulwark from the upper compartment fell on them, trapping them at the bottom of the ship. Others were killed by Japanese guards firing machine guns into the hold and throwing down grenades. Some POWs, however, managed to escape through the hatch onto the deck or through the hole in the ship, only to face machine gun fire from Japanese guards as they emerged onto the deck or dived into the water.

The captain of the *Eiyo Maru*, the tanker also torpedoed, beached the ship near the shore to avoid sinking it. He then directed machine gun fire at the POWs who were swimming to shore. Lifeboats rescued the Japanese soldiers and crew from the *Shinyo Maru*, but the Japanese continued to shoot the escaping prisoners. Japanese patrol planes were also strafing POWs in the water.[15]

Despite the explosion, the sinking vessel, and the Japanese hand grenades and machine guns, eighty-three POWs managed to escape the sinking *Shinyo Maru* and reach the land, where they were gathered up by Filipino guerrillas and hidden from the Japanese in the jungle. In a remarkable rescue, all but two of them later escaped on the submarine USS *Narwhal*. One later died from injuries suffered in the attack on the ship, and another stayed in the Philippines to fight with the guerrilla forces. But none of the seventeen Latter-day Saint POWs was among those eighty-three survivors.[16]

For these Latter-day Saint POWs on the *Shinyo Maru*, the war was over, their respective missions on this earth complete. The seventeen Latter-day Saints who died in the sinking of the *Shinyo Maru* include the following:

- Private First Class William Murle Allred from Artesia, Arizona
- Private David Weston Balfour from Salt Lake City, Utah
- Private Jack W. Bradley from Moroni, Utah
- First Lieutenant George R. (Bobby) Brown from El Paso, Texas
- Private Mack K. Davis from Lehi, Utah
- Private First Class Woodrow L. Dunkley from Franklin, Idaho
- Second Lieutenant Richard E. Harris from Logan, Utah
- Private First Class Theodore Jackson Hippler from Bloomfield, New Mexico
- Private First Class Ferrin C. Holjeson from Smithfield, Utah
- Private Russell Seymore Jensen from Centerfield, Utah
- Private First Class Ronald M. Landon from Kimball, Idaho
- Private Harry O. Miller Jr. from Magrath, Alberta, Canada
- Staff Sergeant Ernest R. Parry from Salt Lake City, Utah
- Private First Class Lamar V. Polve from Kenilworth, Utah
- Private Jesse G. Smurthwaite from Baker, Oregon
- First Lieutenant Gerald Clifton Stillman from Salt Lake City, Utah
- Private Frederick D. Thomas from St. Johns, Idaho[17]

We know little of the particular circumstances of their deaths, although after the war, the Brown family learned from survivors more details about Brown's death. Over the course of his imprisonment, Brown learned some Japanese, and while on the *Shinyo Maru* he had become acquainted with one of the Japanese officers. Brown was either on the deck at the time of the attack or was able to make his way to the deck shortly after the attack, because after the attack, he was seen on the deck trying to persuade this Japanese officer to order the guards to stop firing into the hold. The officer ignored him. Brown and a friend, Lieutenant Colonel George T. Colvard, a doctor from Deming, New Mexico, then leaped into the water to help some wounded prisoners who were clinging to debris. When a volley of shots rang out in their direction, they both dove under the water, but neither surfaced.[18]

Having died in the attack, these seventeen Latter-day Saint POWs on the *Shinyo Maru* left us no personal histories or memoirs. We know them and their final years largely through inferences and educated speculation from military records and histories of others. But what we do know suggests that they were ordinary Latter-day Saints who endured extraordinary trials to the end.

We know a little more about Bobby Brown, however. His mother, Ruby, and his older sister, Nelle Zundel, conscientious family historians, wrote several personal histories about him. Family members have preserved those histories along with various photos and other reminders of his life. Although highly informative, family histories are not necessarily objective. These were written as tributes to a beloved son and brother, not dispassionate accounts memorializing his shortcomings. In perusing those histories, we see clues to an aspect of Bobby as a young man that, while not necessarily hidden in the histories, is not accentuated.

Before departing for the Philippines, Bobby received a blessing from a Church patriarch that included a promise that he would be "preserved to complete a mission on this earth." Family members regretted that Bobby was not able to serve that promised mission, and as people of faith in such blessings, I suppose they privately puzzled over why that blessing was not fulfilled.

When Bobby received that blessing, he was twenty-five years old. At that time, young men in the Church typically could serve missions as early as twenty or twenty-one years of age. A fair question would be why Bobby had not already served a mission. For example, although younger than Bobby, Orland Hamblin and Franklin East had each served missions before being drafted; East had even married shortly before leaving for the Philippines. Nels Hansen, although older than Bobby, had served two missions before being drafted—one at age nineteen, unusual for the time, and another at age twenty-one. Serving a mission for the Church is not required, and there are many acceptable reasons for not serving. Nevertheless, for those able to serve, missionary service is evidence of one's commitment to the gospel of Jesus Christ and the Church. Bobby's father, George, had served a mission in Mexico as a young man.

George sometimes made a personal list near the beginning of each year of things he needed to do or improve on, all with respect to the family. An item on one of those lists was to get "Bobby married or on a mission." While there would have been many good reasons for Bobby not having served a mission or married, his parents were concerned about what he was doing with his life—not an unusual worry for parents of a single twenty-five-year-old living at home.

All the family members worked to support the family, which was financially struggling in the Great Depression. Bobby's financial contributions to the family may have been especially important. He had a good job at the El Paso Electric Company, the local electrical utility, and had even provided some of the funds the family used to purchase their first home. A desire to continue this financial support may have been a reason for him not having yet served a mission. Even so, a perusal of old family photos reveals several with Bobby posing proudly by his new Ford, a car that incidentally was newer and nicer than his father's. In El Paso, he had also been active and successful in community theater, musical productions, and a radio show.

Bobby Brown was most assuredly a dyed-in-the-wool, true-blue Latter-day Saint as a product of his solid upbringing and culture. He was hardworking and industrious, with leadership and musical skills and talents, and deeply loved his family and his church. He may also have been a young man with a taste for the more worldly aspects of life—cars, money, and the excitement of public theater and performance. Perhaps at that particular time in the battle for Bobby's heart and mind, the lure of the world may have been winning over the call of his religion.

If so, Bobby changed. The war and his captivity purged him of any ambivalence about his commitment to his faith. While fragmentary, the evidence depicts a Bobby Brown who, with his leadership skills and musical talents, dedicated himself to bringing the blessing of gospel fellowship and hope to his fellow POWs. He became a leader, mainstay, and moving force in the group in Dapecol. Nonetheless, a challenge for his family is reconciling his fate with his patriarchal blessing.

NOTES

1. Sneddon, *Zero Ward*, 73–76; Bolitho, "A Japanese POW Story," part 6 (December 5, 2009), 1; Michno, *Hellships*, 225–26.
2. Clark and Kowallis, "Fate of the Davao Penal Colony," 123.
3. The ship was the 3,801-gross-ton Japanese Army transport No. 86 named the *Tateishi Maru*. West-Point.Org., "Hell Ship Information and Photographs," http://www.west-point.org/family/japanese-pow/photos.htm [*Tateishi Maru*]; Clark and Kowallis, "Fate of the Davao Penal Colony."
4. Bolitho, "A Japanese POW Story," part 6, 1–3.
5. Michno, *Hellships*, 173–74. The two POWs had escaped from the *Yashu Maru*, which coincidentally had been transporting the POWs who had remained at Dapecol.
6. Bolitho, "A Japanese POW Story," part 6, 2.
7. Lukacs, *Escape from Davao*, 111, 343.
8. Sneddon, *Zero Ward*, 88–89; Clark and Kowallis, "Fate of the Davao Penal Colony," 124.
9. Sneddon, *Zero Ward*, 90–94.
10. Gladwin, "American POWs on Japanese Ships."
11. On December 31, 1944, a note was added in pencil to FRUPac's translation of that September 6 message stating, "FRUEF [the British Fleet Radio Unit Eastern Fleet] (31 Dec '44) gets 750 Ps/W." Gladwin, "American POWs on Japanese Ships." Japanese ships were not well marked (names hardly visible) and, since the periscope of a submarine would reveal its presence and increase the risk being spotted, submarine commanders typically didn't take the time to specifically identify the name of each target ship. Notwithstanding the intelligence messages, *USS Paddle* probably did not know that it was targeting the *Shinyo Maru* but likely knew that the *Shinyo Maru* was among the ships in the convoy. See Michno, *Hellships*, 295.
12. Sneddon, *Zero Ward*, 94–95; Clark and Kowallis, "Fate of the Davao Penal Colony," 124; Gladwin, "American POWs on Japanese Ships;" West-Point. Org, "Hell Ship Information and Photographs."
13. Michno, *Hellships*, 295.
14. USS *Paddle* (SS263), Report of Fifth War Patrol, B. H. Nowell, Lt.-Cdr. USN, September 7, 1944, 7–10. (The report can be viewed at the "Submarine War Reports" page on pages 186–89 of the microfilm of the USS *Paddle* reports, accessible at the website for the Historical Naval Ships Association, at http://www.hnsa.org/resources/manuals-documents/submarine-war-reports/).
15. Lukacs, *Escape from Davao*, 344; Sneddon, *Zero Ward*, 99–107; Clark and Kowallis, "Fate of the Davao Penal Colony," 124–26.
16. Sneddon, *Zero Ward*, 99–107, Lukacs, *Escape from Davao*, 343–44; Clark and Kowallis, "Fate of the Davao Penal Colony," 124–27.
17. This list is simply the Latter-day Saint POWs at Davao whose names are also on the roster of the *Shinyo Maru*. "Roster of Allied Prisoners of War believed aboard *Shinyo Maru* when torpedoed and sunk September 7, 1944," http://www.west-point.org/family/japanese-pow/ShinyoMaruRosterJPW.html.

18. Brown and Zundel, "George Robin Brown ... His Story," 21; Nelle B. Zundel, "A Problem Solved" (unpublished manuscript, April 2, 1992). These accounts are similar, although with more detail, to the account in the Clark and Kowallis article, which was based on a nephew's recollection of the story as told him by Ruby. Clark and Kowallis, "Fate of the Davao Penal Colony," 124–26; see also Kimball, *Miracle of Forgiveness*, 288. In the family history account, Ruby and her daughter Nelle Zundel wrote that the story of Brown's death came from one of the survivors, but the name of the survivor was not mentioned. The family history account includes a specific reference to "a Doctor friend of Bob's, from Deming, N.M." Although the account does not name the doctor, he was likely Dr. George Colvard. The roster of those who died in the sinking of the *Shinyo Maru* includes Lt. Col. George T. Colvard, a surgeon in the 200th. *Shinyo Maru* Roster, http://www.west-point.org/family/japanese-pow/ShinyoMaruRosterJPW.html. Before the war, Dr. Colvard was a physician in Deming, New Mexico. Obituary of Patrick B. Colvard, http://obit.funeralchoices.com/obitdisplay.html?task=Print&id=1331007. In Cave's *Beyond Courage,* the author writes that Mike Pulice, one of the survivors, reported seeing "Doc" Colvard crawling on the deck to help wounded POWs and later saw him again in the water struggling to help others but was then lost in the waves. This account does not mention Brown. Cave, *Beyond Courage*, 301–2. See also Michno, *Death on the Hellships*, 229–30.

26

BILIBID

How gentle God's commands!
How kind his precepts are!
Come, cast your burdens on the Lord
And trust his constant care.

—Philip Doddridge, "How Gentle God's Commands"

Meanwhile, back in Manila, Captain Davey had been among the approximately one thousand POWs taken from Dapecol in June 1944 and shipped to the Bilibid Prison in Manila. Davey, however, was not sent to Japan with the other Latter-day Saint POWs but, after a few days at Bilibid, was sent with a group of other officers back to Cabanatuan. This group of officers included Dwayne Alder, Joseph Webb, and Carlyle Ricks from Utah who had been with Davey in Dapecol.

Davey had been at that camp earlier, but it was now a very different place. When Davey had been there shortly after the fall of Bataan, the camp held around ten thousand prisoners. Now there were about five hundred very sick POWs in the camp hospital, together with a few doctors and medics to care for them. Although Davey's stay in that camp could never be described as anything other than generally miserable, some good and encouraging things nevertheless began to happen. At Cabanatuan, Davey's health gradually improved. At one point early in his captivity, his weight had dropped to about 90 pounds, but after a couple of months at Cabanatuan, his weight was back up to 129 pounds.[1]

While working in the rice fields at Cabanatuan, Davey first saw American planes, a flight of more than one hundred planes, going on and returning from bombing raids on the Japanese. "They passed almost directly over us and it surely was a beautiful sight." They even watched a US fighter plane shoot down a Japanese bomber about a mile from their camp. They had been living on rumors about how the war was going for so long that "it was really a thrill to see an American plane after 2½ years of waiting for them."[2]

Optimism is what kept the POWs going, especially when fueled by sights such as that. Although there was always the fear that the Japanese would slaughter them first, the POWs grew increasingly optimistic that they soon would be rescued, as it was evident that the Japanese were on the run. That optimism, however, was dashed on October 7, 1944, when they were given orders to prepare to move. The news left them stunned and frightened. With the war not going well for the Japanese, the POWs' speculations on what the Japanese had planned for them now did not usually include happy endings.[3]

A detail of 950 POWs, including Davey, was scheduled to be sent to Manila by train on a Sunday night. That all changed, however, when a bombing raid on Manila destroyed the ship on which the Japanese had planned to transport them. Instead, they were moved to Manila in groups of two hundred by truck, forty men to a truck, with six guards.[4] Following an uncomfortable seven-hour ride in the trucks, the POWs arrived at the gates of the Bilibid Prison in Manila. Left behind at Cabanatuan were about five hundred sick POWs in the hospital and some medical officers caring for them. A few months later, in January 1945, these sick POWs and the medical officers left behind would be rescued by US Army Rangers in a stunning and famous behind-enemy-lines rescue.[5] For Davey and the others shipped out earlier in October 1944, however, their fate did not include a rescue.

Bilibid was a depressing sight. Having been there twice before, Davey was familiar with the walled-in isolation of the prison with

This photograph of the Bilibid Prison was taken shortly after the prison was liberated; US soldiers are seen searching for any Japanese. The garden to the right was planted by prisoners to supplement the inadequate rations provided by the Japanese. National Archives. Courtesy of John Tewell.

its ten-foot-tall brick walls, the discomfort of sleeping on concrete floors, and, most importantly, the scarcity of food. There were no work details—just boredom, isolation, anxiety about the future, and little food. Twice a day, they were fed a small canteen cup of "boiled rice, about the consistency of wallpaper paste."[6] Davey was receiving a ration of about 250 grams of rice and occasionally a small amount of coconut. He was beginning to lose weight again, although otherwise he seemed to have recovered from beriberi and the other diseases that had plagued him earlier. They were all losing weight and were continually hungry.

Isolated, bored, and starving, what would the men in this camp talk about? It wasn't about women or alcohol. Davey noted that he hadn't heard a "dirty story for months." They talked about food.[7] In fact, they created a dream world of food. Manny Lawton, one of the POWs, explained,

> The main pastime was swapping recipes. From that developed a daily lecture series. At ten o'clock each morning all hands assembled in a large second story room. Sitting in a semicircle on the floor with pencil and note paper, we listened entranced as some expert reviewed the tantalizing details of preparing, cooking and tasting a savory dish. We heard and made note of palate teasing delicacies from every land and every region of the United States: Italian, Polish, Greek, French, German, we eagerly heard them all. . . . Had the compound been divided into various places of amusement for the benefit of the prisoners, I am sure that not even a girlie show would have distracted anyone's attention from the dream world of food.[8]

Referring to tobacco, Davey observed, "Thank heavens I don't use it. It is really disgusting to me to see officers going around picking up butts, smoking leaves, trading off their food for cigarettes and tobacco. You can't realize what a hold it has on these men."[9] Tobacco was used like a currency in these camps, and other Latter-day Saint POWs also observed the benefit of not smoking—one could trade the cigarettes for something else, such as food and medicine.[10]

Although confined and isolated in the prison, the POWs were aware that the US bombings were devastating Manila and any Japanese ships that managed to get into the harbor. The windows were shuttered so the POWs could not see the damage done by the Allied bombers, but the POWs could hear the bombing, and they could get glimpses through window cracks of the bombers and the destruction. Davey wrote, "I guess that we are the only group in the world that cheer whenever we hear the sirens start."[11]

The POWs had figured out that the bombings, which had wreaked havoc on the Japanese ships in the Manila harbor, had delayed their shipment to POW camps in Japan. They also knew that the Allies had landed at Leyte, at the far southern end of the Philippines archipelago. There was by this time little doubt among the POWs (and the Japanese) that the Allies were winning the war and would recapture Manila; the key question was how soon. Specifically, for these POWs, would the Allied bombing of Manila prevent the Japanese from getting ships in to take them out before the Allies could retake Manila and rescue them? Several planned departures had already been canceled, keeping that hope alive.

During this period of anxious waiting at Bilibid, Davey wrote a series of letters home to his sister. They were written on scraps of paper and between the lines of letters he had received. They are particularly informative about his prison experience and are filled with poignant and tender wishes to his family. If he were rescued before the Japanese could ship him out, he did not intend to send the letters. Otherwise, he intended to leave the letters with a remaining POW at Bilibid to be delivered to the US Army when they arrived for ultimate delivery to his sister. Accordingly, he began the first letter, dated November 1, "This letter is one of the hardest ones I have ever had to write because if you receive it, it will mean my worst fears have come to pass."[12]

He recounted his experiences as a POW and provided assurances to his family that, although the food was inadequate and he was again losing weight, he was still relatively healthy and in good spirits. He also wrote lovingly about his family and his testimony of the gospel of Jesus Christ. After thanking them for their letters and packages, he wrote,

> Your faith and prayers in my behalf have given me strength and courage to carry on. I am truly thankful that I was born of such wonderful parents and for the teachings they have given me. I know that I have caused them much worry and sorrow and have truly repented of my thoughtlessness and waywardness that has caused them so much pain and heartaches. My only hope is that I can live a life based on what they have taught me and what I have learned from this war to in a small way redeem myself. I am thankful that I was born a member of the Church and for my testimony of the truth of the gospel. I have been protected many times only through the protecting care of my Heavenly Father.... I know that the gospel as taught by our Church is true and I am truly thankful for this knowledge.[13]

The regular bombings stopped in late November, either because the Allies had destroyed all the targets or due to a typhoon that had grounded the aircraft. With this pause, the Japanese decided to move the POWs to Japan. On December 12, 1944, Davey wrote,

It looks as though we are going somewhere. Our only hope is that we do not leave the island but move to another camp. Food conditions here are very bad and in the last two weeks ten men have died of starvation. . . . We haven't had any air raids since November 24, 1944, so maybe they have been able to get in a ship to take us out. It may be that we start from here but there is no assurance that we will get there. I am rather upset about having to leave because it means that much longer to be a prisoner of the Japanese. And at the rate I'm losing weight it doesn't look as though I will be able to make it. The only thing I can do is put my faith in the Lord and trust in his protecting care.[14]

The next day, December 13, Davey wrote in the dim light of the early morning that they were scheduled to leave at daylight for Japan. He again expressed gratitude for his parents and their teachings, his testimony of the gospel, and the blessing he had received. He also noted that "my health and spirit is good and I feel O.K."[15]

Later that morning he added to the letter:

10 a.m.
Just announced that the draft has been delayed several hours. I only hope that they can't get us out. There goes the bell so here we go again, Dammit.
Love,
Bob[16]

That bell marked the end of Davey's miserable time at Bilibid but also the beginning of one of the most horrendous POW experiences of the war.

NOTES

1. Davey, letter to family, November 2, 1944, reprinted in "Faith Sustains Interned Mormon Captain," *Deseret News*, March 24, 1945.
2. Davey, letter to family, November 2, 1944, reprinted in "Faith Sustains Interned Mormon Captain," *Deseret News*, March 24, 1945.
3. Lawton, *Some Survived*, 149–50; see Michno, *Death on the Hellships*, 273–76.
4. Davey, letter to family, November 2, 1944.
5. An account of the rescue is contained in Sides, *Ghost Soldiers*.
6. Davey, letter to family, November 2, 1944; see also Lawton, *Some Survived*, 151.
7. Davey, letter to family, November 14, 1944, reprinted in "Faith Sustains Interned Mormon Captain," *Deseret News*, March 24, 1945, 7, 16.

8. Lawton, *Some Survived*, 151. Christensen also wrote that POWs in the camps in Japan dealt with their constant hunger by creating books of elaborate recipes they planned to try out if they got back home. Christensen, "My Life Story," 20.
9. Davey, letter to family, November 23, 1944, reprinted in "Faith Sustains Interned Mormon Captain," *Deseret News*, March 24, 1945.
10. Jacobsen, *We Refused to Die*, 102–3.
11. Davey, letter to family, November 2, 1944.
12. Davey, letter to family, November 1, 1944.
13. Davey, letter to family, December 12, 1944.
14. Davey, letter to family, December 12, 1944.
15. Davey, letter to family, December 13, 1944.
16. Davey, letter to family, December 13, 1944.

27

THE SPECIAL HELL OF THE *ORYOKU MARU*

> *Though like the wanderer,*
> *The sun gone down,*
> *Darkness be over me,*
> *My rest a stone,*
> *Yet in my dreams I'd be*
> *Nearer, my God, to thee.*
>
> —Sarah F. Adams, "Nearer, My God, to Thee"

Davey had anticipated that if his letters were delivered, it meant his worst fears had been realized. But that was not quite true. Although Davey had experienced the Bataan Death March, the deprivations of several POW camps, and the brutality of his captors, as well as the miserable voyage on the *Yashu Maru* to Manila and starvation at Bilibid, this voyage would be worse. The Japanese hell ships are infamous among World War II historians and, when recounting the horrors of those ships, the voyage of the *Oryoku Maru* is considered the most horrific.[1]

Davey was among the 1,619 POWs that boarded that ship on December 13, 1944, for Japan.[2] Of those POWs, only about 425 would survive the voyage to Japan; of the survivors, 161 would arrive in such poor health that they would die within thirty days of their arrival. In other words, of the 1,619 POWs who boarded the ship in Manila, only 264 survived the ordeal with any chance of returning home.³ With faith and prayers, and as foreseen in a dream, Davey would be among those survivors.

VOYAGE OF THE ORYOKU MARU

Late in the morning of December 13, Davey and the other POWs, including Dapecol POWs Dwayne Alder, Joseph Webb, Carlyle Ricks, and James Wilstead from Utah, were marched about four kilometers through the bombed-out remains of Manila to Pier 7. As they looked out across the bay, they could see the results of the destruction they had only heard about in the walled prison—a ghostly scene of once-great warships and transports now just wrecked hulks littering the bay, listing and half submerged. There were doubtless more unseen below the surface.⁴

The Allied bombing had stopped for a few weeks, and the Japanese had been able to bring in a transport ship. At first glance, the ship they were to board was an encouraging sight. It was not the typical old, slow freighter; this ship, the *Oryoku Maru*, was a smaller and faster former luxury passenger ship. Although crowded, the ship could accommodate the 1,619 POWs in the first- and second-class passenger areas of the upper decks.⁵ That, however, was not where these POWs were headed.

The Japanese were also evacuating hundreds of civilians and diplomatic personnel and their families. These were loaded into the upper decks.⁶ The POWs were crammed thirty feet down into the cargo holds of the ship. Forced down a steep ladder, the POWs were met at the bottom by four guards, one with a sword and the others with brooms, who pushed the POWs back tighter and tighter into the hold. Ledges had been constructed out from the sides of the hull to increase capacity. With the ledges added, the hold could accommodate about 250 men, but with each barely having room to lie down simultaneously. The Japanese, however, were now stuffing about 800 men into that hold.⁷

Not only cramped and claustrophobic, the hold was also hot—about 120 degrees—and made worse by the body heat of the crowded, sweaty men. There was no ventilation other than the hatch at the top when it was open. They were enclosed on all sides by thick-plated steel, heated by the outside sun and creating for the POWs the sensation of being trapped in an oven. The POWs were also without food and, more importantly, water. Late that afternoon, the ship finally left the dock and headed cautiously out of the bay.

That night was, for Davey and likely every other POW on that ship, the worst night of their lives. The air in the hold was stagnant with insufficient oxygen. Vision was impossible in the absolute darkness. Sounds were amplified, and fights broke out. When men were deprived of water and then oxygen in these dark and claustrophobic conditions, they reacted in different ways. Some drank their own urine. Others passed out asleep, and others went insane. Throughout the night, men were crying out hysterically for water and air and at each other.[8]

In his official report, one colonel wrote of the hellish conditions aboard that ship, "Many men lost their minds and crawled about in the absolute darkness armed with knives, attempting to kill people in order to drink their blood or armed with canteens filled with urine and swinging them in the dark. The hold was so crowded and everyone so interlocked with one another that the only movement possible was over the heads and bodies of others."[9]

It wasn't until the dim light of the next morning that the POWs could fully appreciate what had happened that night. Fifty had died during the night, most from the heat and suffocation. Some died from being trampled. Some had been killed by fellow prisoners who in their oxygen- and water-deprived lunacy had decided to quench their thirst with someone else's blood. Some were killed by fellow POWs to keep them from killing others in their frenzy.[10]

Davey had a strong but not overly aggressive personality, which actually served him well on the ship. He managed to slip to the back of the hold, away from the hatch. Near the hatch, the only source of fresh air, was the favored place and where most of the commotion was occurring. But in the back of the hold, Davey avoided being caught up in the hysteria, and while away from the commotion, he was better able to stay calm, reducing his body's need for oxygen. In addition, at the back, he was able to lick condensation from the sides of the hold, providing little—but nonetheless precious—hydration.[11]

That next morning, as the Japanese convoy with the *Oryoku Maru* emerged from Manila Bay and cautiously sailed along the Bataan coast, the POWs heard a sound they had not heard for the last two weeks: the sound of attacking American planes.[12] Intelligence alerts from Operation Magic had gone out advising US ship commanders to watch for enemy ships coming out of Manila Bay.[13] Although the *Oryoku Maru* was not hit by American bombs, it was strafed and its antiaircraft guns were destroyed. It also lost a steering rudder. The ship took shelter in Subic Bay, on the west coast of Luzon, where it was run aground.

Down in the holds, the POWs could hear the chaos and confusion among the Japanese up on deck. The American doctors and medics were summoned up to care for wounded Japanese. There they saw a macabre scene of hundreds of Japanese soldiers and civilians dead; more were wounded. While the Allied bombs had missed the ship, the Allied planes had mercilessly strafed the ship. The POWs, crammed below in the bowels of the ship, were largely protected from the strafing fire. There was no such protection in the upper decks. Scores of Japanese civilians who had been lodged in the first-class section were found huddled together, dead.[14] The voyage had lasted less than twenty-four hours and had gone nowhere.

The Japanese civilians and troops were offloaded. The POWs were left on the ship and spent another harrowing night in the holds. As anticipated, the carrier planes attacked again the next morning. Hearing the sound of the approaching American planes, the Japanese ordered the POWs on deck to be seen by the American planes. Seeing the white Americans wearing only G-strings and waving frantically, the American pilots pulled out of their bombing dives, dipped the wings of their planes in recognition, and flew past without bombing the ship.[15]

The disabled ship had been run aground about a mile or so off the coast. Eventually, the Japanese told the POWs to disembark—mean-

THE SPECIAL HELL OF THE ORYOKU MARU

On December 15, 1944, aircraft from the USS *Hornet* attacked the *Oryoku Maru*. This is a US Navy photo taken from a reconnaissance plane shortly after the attack. The splashes in the water below the burning *Oryoku Maru* are surviving POWs swimming to shore. Courtesy of United States Navy.

ing they had to take a thirty-foot plunge off the deck to the water below and swim to shore. Davey was one of the last to climb out of the hold and onto the deck. Rather than immediately jumping off the ship, he took some time to look around for food. At that time, food was more important to Davey than quickly getting off the ship, even though the vessel was on fire and potentially about to explode.

While he didn't find much food, he found some extra canteens. The additional canteens would provide Davey the ability, when water was available, to get more to use later. He tied the canteens to a belt around his waist and swam to shore.[16]

Once on shore, those POWs who had managed to make it to land were herded onto a tennis court, which was used as a stockade to hold them. Again, they were crowded, and only through careful coordination and planning were all POWs able to lie down. They had little clothing. They suffered from the tropical heat and sunburns throughout the day on the hot concrete court and then suffered from the cold at night, when the hard concrete turned cold. The Japanese provided little food or water, and men continued to die one or two at a time from malnutrition, wounds suffered in the bombings, and disease. The Allies bombed the area several times, and the POWs watched in wonderment as the bombs fell from the sky, not knowing whether the bombs would land on them.

After five scorching days and freezing nights on the tennis court, the POWs were loaded into trucks and taken north to San Fernando, Pampanga, where some were put in a jail and the rest in a fenced-in yard. They received more food at San Fernando, and the condition of some started to improve. There were still many who were critically ill, however. The Americans pleaded with the Japanese to at least move them to a hospital. Finally, the Japanese relented and asked them to identify the fifteen sickest POWs. These fifteen were then taken, the POWs believed, to the hospital at Bilibid. However, in the war crimes trials after the war, it was shown that these sick POWs were not taken to a hospital but to a nearby cemetery, where they were beheaded and dumped into a mass grave.[17]

VOYAGES OF THE *ENOURA MARU* AND *BRAZIL MARU*

After three days in San Fernando, the POWs were marched through the town to a train station and loaded into small boxcars. For POWs like Davey, who had endured the Bataan Death March, this was a surreal moment. They knew this place. They had been here two and a half years before. They had walked here on that march and had been stuffed into those cars to be taken to Camp O'Donnell, where thousands had perished.

Despite their misery and an uncomfortable feeling of *déjà vu*, they were generally in good spirits. It was evident to all that the Allies were winning the war. The Allies had unchallenged control of the air, and all around them was evidence of the destruction of the once-powerful Japanese war machine. The POWs concluded that surely the Japanese would now give up on trying to transport them to Japan and instead leave them on Luzon, where the Allies would soon rescue them. Sadly, this hope, like so many others, was soon crushed.

While it seemed to make no sense to the POWs, they were not being taken back to Camp O'Donnell or anywhere else in the Philippines, but back to the coast to be loaded onto ships to Japan.[18] It was a dangerous train trip. American planes were patrolling, and it was unlikely that moving rail traffic would not be detected and bombed. The Japanese, therefore, put the sick and wounded POWs on the tops of the cars and told them to wave their bandages if American planes appeared. The trains took them north to the Lingayen Gulf, where they arrived on Christmas morning 1944. They were marched down to the beach and, two days later, were loaded onto two ships. Davey and about 1,070 others were loaded onto the *Enoura Maru*, and the remaining 236 were loaded onto the *Brazil Maru*.[19] They then set sail as part of a convoy for Taiwan.

Although the convoy was attacked, the *Brazil Maru* and the *Enoura Maru* managed to escape and arrived at the Takao (Kaohsiung) harbor in Taiwan on New Year's Day 1945. While they had avoided death from the American submarines and bombers, the POWs trapped in the holds of the ships had continued to die, a few each day, from sickness and starvation.[20] Earlier, the tropical heat in the Philippine camps and in the ship holds had been their enemy. Now the cold from the more northern climate was the source of their affliction. Still wearing little clothing, usually only a G-string, the POWs had little protection from the cold. Pneumonia, not some tropical disease, was now a primary killer.[21]

This photo taken by US Navy aircraft of the Takao Harbor area shows in the lower right two vessels targeted in the US attack: a Japanese tanker and the *Enoura Maru*. They were moored to the same buoy. Captain Davey was on board the *Enoura Maru* but survived the attack. Courtesy of United States Navy.

They remained at this harbor for several days, during which Davey experienced another small miracle. The POWs on the smaller *Brazil Maru* were transferred over to the *Enoura Maru* and, as a result, some POWs on the *Enoura Maru* were to be moved to a different hold. In preparation for this change, the Japanese asked for volunteers for a detail to clean one of the holds. Davey, now healthier than he had been at Dapecol, always volunteered for these details because it was a chance to get extra food and water. Once they had completed their task, they were to return to their original hold. However, the Japanese, perturbed about the time the POWs were taking to get back to their hold, ordered them back down into the hold they had been cleaning. As a result, Davey was not where he was supposed to be.

At this same time, General MacArthur's forces were preparing to land on Luzon at Lingayen Gulf—the place from which this group had left the Philippines about three weeks earlier. To prepare for that landing, General MacArthur had ordered air strikes on Japanese ships in southern Taiwan, as those Japanese ships could be used to attack the US ships during that landing. The ships at anchor at Takao, including the *Enoura Maru*, were among the primary targets of those air strikes. On January 9, 1945, bombers from the USS *Hornet* attacked the Takao Harbor. There were several hits on the *Enoura Maru*, and some bombs fell directly on the forward hold, killing more than four hundred prisoners. That was the hold Davey was supposed to have been in but was not.[22]

Hundreds of the POWs on the *Enoura Maru* died or were wounded in the attack. The surviving POWs remained trapped in the ship's holds without food or water for days. The Japanese did nothing. The wounded continued to die from shock, loss of blood, and infection. Bodies of the dead began to bloat and smell. Finally, on January 12, 1945, permission was given to remove the dead and assist the wounded. For weak and emaciated POWs, removing more than four hundred dead bodies from the lower holds of a ship that had been bombed was not an easy task. Using a large cargo net, fifteen to twenty bodies at a time were lifted out of the hold and, according to one author, "taken to shore on a barge where they were stacked with wood and set on fire."[23]

The surviving POWs, including Davey, were then all loaded onto the *Brazil Maru*, which joined a convoy for Japan. The convoy took a roundabout course, hugging the Chinese coastline to avoid US submarines operating in the open ocean. The POWs in the holds continued to suffer from the cold and lack of food, water, basic sanitation, and medicine. Getting weaker, sicker, and increasingly demoralized, prisoners were dying by the dozens.[24]

Dysentery broke out, and two of Davey's closest friends died of it. One was Dwayne Alder from Midvale, Utah, who had been with Davey at Dapecol. Alder died on the *Brazil Maru* around January 24, 1945, just a few days before the ship's arrival in Japan. Although not named by Davey, the other was likely Joseph Webb from Salt Lake City, another officer who had been with Davey in Dapecol. Webb died two days after the *Brazil Maru* arrived in Japan. Davey had managed to trade a fountain pen for some sulfa tablets, but it was not enough to save them. Davey later wrote to one of the widows, "It was really hard to have both your very best friends sick and not to be able to do more for them. Medicine, food and water were almost nonexistent at this time and the Japanese would not or did not have any to give us."[25]

The *Brazil Maru* finally arrived at Moji, Fukuoka Prefecture, on January 29, 1945.[26] On February 4, 1945, five days later, US forces arrived at Manila and liberated the Bilibid Prison. On arriving in Japan, Davey was at first placed in a prison camp in Fukuoka Prefecture. To Davey, Japan was a lovely place, with beautiful trees and land.[27] While he could not have known it at that time, the worst was finally behind him, and he had survived.

When Davey left Bilibid, he left his letters with Lieutenant William A. Montgomery, who was very sick and, therefore, not likely to be taken to Japan. As Davey had anticipated, Montgomery was not taken to Japan but remained at Bilibid until rescued by the Americans. Davey's letters were then passed on to the Red Cross, who saw to it that they were delivered to his family in Salt Lake City, where they were thankfully received by his sister and brothers. The letters were later published in the *Deseret News*.[28]

However, the family's joy was tempered by another item of news they received about the same time—that the ship Davey was on had been bombed by the Americans and that more than five hundred had died.[29] The faith and hope of his family remained resolute, but nonetheless they could not have avoided weighing the mathematical odds against their brother's survival.

NOTES

1. See, for example, Michno, *Death on the Hellships*, 260; 332n78. Judith Pearson provides a specific account of the horrific voyage of the *Oryoku Maru* in Judith L. Pearson, *Belly of the Beast: A POW's Inspiring True Story of Faith, Courage, and Survival Aboard the Infamous WWII Japanese Hell Ship Oryoku Maru* (New York City: New American Library, 2001).
2. James W. Erickson, "*Oryoku Maru* Roster," west-point.org. http://www.west-point.org/family/japanese-pow/Erickson_OM.htm (listing Davey among the POWs on the *Oryoku Maru*).
3. Lawton, *Some Survived*, 212, 214 (Lawton notes that others put the number of survivors at 435); see also Davey, "Last Talk," 5 (states that of the approximately 1,600 original POWs, less than 500 survived the voyage, and of those survivors, 153 later died in various camps before the others were transferred to Korea); Michno, *Death on the Hellships*, 265 (puts the number of survivors of the voyage at 450).
4. Lawton, *Some Survived*, 153–54.
5. Lawton, 154.
6. Michno, *Death on the Hellships*, 258.
7. Lawton, *Some Survived*, 155.
8. Lawton, *Some Survived*, 207–9; Michno, *Death on the Hellships*, 260–61; Davey, Talk Transcript, 4.
9. John Toland, *The Rising Sun: The Decline and Fall of the Japanese Empire, 1936–1945* (New York City: Random House, 1970), 601.
10. Lawton, *Some Survived*, 160; Michno, *Hellships*, 260–61.
11. Conversation by author with Marilyn Springgay, Davey's daughter, in November 2016.
12. Lawton, *Some Survived*, 160; Michno, *Death on the Hellships*, 260.
13. Michno, *Death on the Hellships*, 258.
14. Lawton, *Some Survived*, 162.
15. Lawton, *Some Survived*, 163.
16. Davey, "Last Talk," 5.
17. Lawton, *Some Survived*, 178.
18. Lawton, *Some Survived*, 178.
19. Michno, *Death on the Hellships*, 262. Davey, in his writings after the war, does not identify the name of the ship he boarded, but his description of the ship and a later bombing suggest it was *Enoura Maru*.
20. See Lawton, *Some Survived*, 188.
21. Lawton, *Some Survived*, 201, 207, 215.
22. Davey, "Last Talk," 6–7; Cave, *Beyond Courage*, 314–15; Lawton, *Some Survived*, 192–93; Michno, *Death on the Hellships*, 264.
23. Michno, *Death on the Hellships*, 264; see Lawton, *Some Survived*, 196.
24. Lawton, *Some Survived*, 200–2.
25. Springgay, "Davey," 52.
26. Michno, *Death on the Hellships*, 265; Lawton, *Some Survived*, 211.

27. Springgay, "Davey," 53. Carlyle Ricks and James Wilstead, two other Utah POWs from Dapecol, were also among the survivors.
28. "Faith Sustains Interned Mormon Captain," *Deseret News*, March 24, 1945.
29. "Faith Sustains Interned Mormon Captain," *Deseret News*, March 24, 1945, "Captain Davey Evacuated to Japan."

28

JAPAN

Be still, my soul: the Lord is on thy side;
With patience bear thy cross of grief or pain.
Leave to thy God to order and provide;
In ev'ry change he faithful will remain.

—Katharina von Schlegel, "Be Still, My Soul"

In early 1942 there was only one POW camp in Japan proper, but by 1944 around thirty-six thousand POWs were imprisoned in well over one hundred camps in Japan. Still others were in camps in Korea, China, and Manchuria. This handful of Latter-day Saint POWs from Dapecol were scattered among camps in Japan, though Davey ultimately ended up in a camp in Korea.

The camps in Japan were located in industrialized areas, and each camp was connected to a particular industrial site. The Japanese Imperial Army ran the prison camps and was responsible for guarding and feeding the prisoners. However, the POWs worked in factories, mines, smelters, or other industrial facilities owned by civilian Japanese companies. For example, Christensen, Hamblin, Hansen, Larsen, Lloyd Parry, Patterson, Rohlfing, and Vance were all held initially in the Nagoya #5B camp on the coast near Yokkaichi, Japan.[1] POWs from that camp worked in an adjacent copper smelter owned by a large Japanese chemical and mining company. They also worked in a related sulfuric acid plant. Hamblin, Rohlfing, and Christensen appear to have been later transferred to a small foundry near the city of Toyama, Japan, further splintering this group of Latter-day Saint POWs.[2]

Ralf Wilson ended up at Nagoya Branch Camp #11.[3] It was a relatively small camp, with about 150 POWs, the majority of whom were Dutch. The rest were American and British. The camp was adjacent to a chemical factory, the Nippon Soda Company.[4] Bray and Goodliffe were put in camps near steel mills in Yokohama. After the mills were closed due to Allied bombing, they were transferred to a copper mine north of Tokyo called Ashio.[5] Davey, who initially was imprisoned in a camp near Fukuoka, was shipped in late April 1945 to a light-duty POW camp in Incheon (Jinsen), Korea.[6]

When the POWs arrived at the camps in Japan, they were typically stripped to their underwear, and their clothes and other possessions were put in a large pile or placed in fifty-gallon drums of boiling water. Some were issued clothing, such as a poorly made shirt, pants, and a jacket.[7] Hamblin, however, reported that the prisoners in his camp initially received no new clothes. Rather, upon arrival at the camp, the POWs were stripped to their underwear, and all their clothes and other possessions were dumped in a pile. Hamblin had a sweater he had received at Bilibid in a package from home, a very appreciated gift in the colder climate of Japan. The sweater went into the pile. The prisoners were then marched into the camp dressed only in their G-strings and shoes while holding towels.

For the next week, they were marched around as the Japanese tried to teach them to march to Japanese commands. Not knowing the drills and unable to understand the Japanese commands, they mainly marched in circles. The frustrated guards yelled at them and beat them. Finally, the drills came to an end, and the clothing previously taken was redistributed to POWs, but not necessarily back to the original owner. A Dutch POW, for example, was issued Hamblin's sweater from home.[8] Christensen was required to toss all his belongings into a pile but was able to hide in his shorts a photo of his parents and a copy of his patriarchal blessing, two precious pieces he had managed to keep since his surrender.[9]

The quarters for the POWs were usually a large barn-like structure with a center hall running the length of the building and small partitioned rooms without doors. It resembled a barn, with rows of stalls on each side. Each room had an upper and lower bunk. In the middle of the isle was an open fire box. It was made of bricks, but without any flue. That was the only source of heat. The prisoner quarters were constructed of half-inch lumber, providing little protection from the cold.

The prisoners were given charcoal or wood each month, but it made a good fire for only a few hours. The POWs soon developed a number of ways of smuggling pieces of wood they picked up from the factories past the guards and into their barracks.[10] Also, the fires were not ventilated, so the smoke rose and hung in the air, creating a problem for the men in the upper bunks. In any event, it was simply impossible to heat the barracks; instead, the objective was merely to reduce the chill.[11]

To try to stay warm, the POWs wore their clothes both day and night. After a while, lice got into them, especially at the seams. Christensen wrote about feeling them moving around as he was trying to sleep at night.[12] The cold also made sleeping difficult. To combat the cold, the POWs snuggled together wearing every piece of clothing they had and covering themselves with all the blankets they could find. Such an arrangement sometimes helped them stay warm enough to sleep, but they were always cold that winter.[13]

Their diet consisted of inadequate amounts of rice, barley, and millet. They were always hungry. Their digestive systems had become so delicate that a small change of rice to barley could make them sick for days. When they had the chance, they sneaked out of the factory and went down to the beach to look for lettuce leaves, orange peelings, or any other food that may have washed ashore. In another camp, the POWs picked green weeds on the way to or from work to later mix in their rice.[14]

The POWs were required to perform heavy physical labor, frequently in unsafe working conditions.[15] The work directly or indirectly aided the Japanese war effort, and the POWs developed a variety of ways to sabotage their work while not getting caught. If caught in such sabotage, they likely would have been shot on the spot. Goodliffe recalled jamming steel scraps or wrenches in the cogs of a machine used to make steel plates for tanks while the machine was shut down due to frequent power outages. When the power came back on and the machines started up, the cogs broke, shutting down production. They also threw out the tar the Japanese used to lubricate the rollers, making them inoperable. There were also some Koreans working at the mill—and fortunately for Goodliffe and the other Americans, the Japanese always suspected the Koreans.[16]

Bray, who worked in a steel mill, spoke of POWs not repairing hooks on a crane properly, causing them to break and shutting down the crane. A repair took about two weeks. This had the additional benefit of giving the POWs working in front of the furnaces a break while the crane was repaired.[17] Hamblin wrote of rocks "accidentally" getting into a coal stoker, shutting it down. It would take six to eight hours to remove the rocks and start up again.[18]

Davey, who ended up at the POW camp in Korea, was assigned to work in a garment factory making Japanese uniforms. The Japanese were always complaining that the POWs were not sewing buttons on the garments fast enough, a skill at which none of these POWs were particularly adept. However, Davey developed a means of sewing them on more quickly by simply putting more thread around the button and using only a single strand to attach the button to the shirt. The Japanese were pleased with the higher production rate, and the POWs enjoyed fantasizing about Japanese soldiers "dashing out to formation with buttons popping off, or one of them standing at attention undergoing a severe slapping for not having his blouse buttoned."[19] While none of these acts were likely to have impeded the Japanese war effort in any significant way and the POWs would have been in great danger if caught, the sabotage was deeply satisfying to the POWs.

The most serious concern for these POWs, however, was the guards. Most of the guards, who the POWs derisively called the "stick guards," were civilians too young to serve in the military or were former soldiers who had been wounded or partially disabled in combat. "They'd take a pick handle and whittle it down and polish it off so it ended up looking like a sword. They like to wear a sword."[20] Although the guards were civilians, they were greatly feared by the POWs because they had disciplinary power as well as deep contempt for the POWs.[21]

The former soldiers especially seemed to have made it their purpose in life to exact vengeance on these POWs.[22] Many were disabled veterans of the Japanese occupation of China, including the infamous "Rape of Nanking." A POW speculated, "They must have been driven a little crazy because of what they had seen or done in China because their behavior was completely unpredictable."[23] As Goodliffe put it, "I think their main goal in life was to beat up an American every day that they could. They were bad. They would stand in the shadows, and when you walk by at night and didn't salute, they would come out and give you a beating for not saluting them."

Most POWs received frequent beatings from the guards, and many were tortured. Hamblin wrote of some POWs who, when returning to the camp from the factory, were caught with some salt that a civilian at the factory had given to them. "The men were stripped to their waists and beaten with a wide leather belt until their bodies were covered with welts. They were also beaten in the face. When anything like that happened, our blood would boil, but we were powerless to do anything to help them."[24]

Patterson described a common punishment for stealing. The Japanese hung a POW by his wrists from a tripod with a basket around his neck and bricks piled nearby. On each round the sentry would put another brick in the basket. As it got heavier, it would pull the POW's wrist from its socket, leaving the prisoner screaming in pain.[25] Hansen spoke of being made to walk with five-gallon buckets in each hand, with arms outstretched until he fainted.[26]

Goodliffe, returning from the latrine shortly after an Allied bombing raid, tiptoed up to a fence to look around and was caught by a Japanese guard. Preferring that the POWs not see the damage the bombings were wreaking on their country, the Japanese prohibited such gazing through the fence. The guard took Goodliffe to the middle of the compound and beat him with a two-by-two until he fell to the ground unconscious—all for looking through a fence. Goodliffe said that beating was "the worst beating I ever got from them, but there were many, many more."[27]

On another occasion, two English POWs were caught by a guard stealing food, and they killed the guard. Among the methods the Japanese then used to make the POWs confess the names of the perpetrators was to place little bamboo toothpicks under toenails. Goodliffe was among the POWs questioned and tortured about the incident. About this questioning, Goodliffe wrote, "Sitting across the table from me was one of the Englishmen that had killed the guard. You could just see the pain in his face, thinking that I might break down and tell who it was, but we endured it. Most of us lost our toenails, but after they had done that for a day and a night and another day, they finally decided that there was no American that could take that kind of punishment without breaking down. So it must have been the Koreans that did it, so they went after the Koreans."[28]

To coerce Bray into identifying someone who had been smoking during a raid, an act the Japanese prohibited, the guards made Bray hold a three-gallon wooden bucket above his head in front of the guardhouse in the freezing weather. As his arms tired, the bucket would slowly lower to his head. The guard, who watched through the guardhouse window, then came out, took the bucket, dumped the water on Bray, forced Bray to refill the bucket, and started the process over again. Bray went through about five buckets over the course of an hour and a half in freezing weather before he was allowed to return to his barrack. He went to work the next morning shivering in his still-wet clothes. He never identified the smoker to the Japanese.[29]

The POWs worked with, or were supervised by, Japanese civilians and, notwithstanding the guards, the POWs were often able to develop a friendship or working relationship with their civilian coworkers. Some of the civilians even shared food with the POWs when available.[30] For example, one day a kind civilian in the boiler room of the factory where Christensen was working gave him half a baked potato. Christensen said he "stuffed the whole thing into my mouth and tried to swallow it before the guard noticed." But the guard did notice and beat him with a stick.[31]

For Davey at the camp at Jinsen (now Inchon), Korea, life was better. However, the compound was enclosed by a ten-foot-high wall, blocking the POWs off entirely from the outside world and, like at Bilibid, creating a sense of lonely isolation.[32] While the food was still inadequate, it was not the starvation diet of Bilibid. There was a scarcity of rice, and the Japanese began substituting soybeans as part of the rations. The soybeans were tasteless and difficult to cook, but the POWs benefited from the substitution since the soybeans contained protein, the POWs' greatest dietary need.[33] The guards were largely Korean conscripts, who frankly hated the Japanese as much as the Americans and were looking forward to their defeat.[34]

In the prison camps in Japan, religious books were confiscated and religious meetings or activities were usually prohibited.[35] Hansen, who at the time was unable to walk due to the effects of beriberi, spoke of crawling across the ground to save his scriptures that had been confiscated and tossed by the Japanese into a fire.[36] There were, nevertheless, some religious moments. In the camp where East was imprisoned, the POWs received permission to have a Christmas program. East was asked to speak. He was introduced as an "Elder of the Church of Jesus Christ." He gave a talk, but soon forgot the substance of the talk, other than it was something about Christmas. A few years after the war, East received a Christmas card saying, "I remember you as the Elder of the Church of Jesus Christ. I have since joined the church and married a Mormon girl." It took East awhile, but he finally remembered who the writer was—the "nice clean cut fellow that worked in the kitchen in Japan" who had listened to that Christmas talk.[37]

While imprisoned, the POWs also endured natural disasters, such as a typhoon that flooded camps and caused waste from the toilets to wash up through the barracks. A major earthquake struck central Japan in December 1944, severely damaging the plants where the POWs were working and causing some of them to close.[38]

The prisoners also suffered through the man-made disaster of the Allied bombings of Japan. The objective of the Allied bombing campaign was to destroy the industrial, war-making capability of the Japanese, creating a danger for the POWs because the bombing targets often included the industrial facilities where the POWs were forced to work. Moreover, the facilities where the POWs were usually quartered had no markings to identify those quarters as POW camps. Nevertheless, for the POWs, the bombings were great morale boosters, evidence that the Allies were winning and that the war would soon be over.

By 1945, with the Allies enjoying almost complete control of the air, the bombing raids became more frequent and destructive, including the horrific firebombing raids. Goodliffe recalled watching a US bombing raid over Tokyo:

> The first bombing raid they had in Tokyo came right over the top of our steel mill [the Osaka Zosen Steel Mill]. First, they dropped flare bombs, and then they dropped firebombs. After those firebombs get started good, they came over and dropped high explosives and just blew the flames all over. Well, Tokyo was built of lots of little shacks, and that night they burned out an area about a mile wide and 10 or 15 miles long. They had over 150,000 casualties reported by the guards in the mill that night. They used the Osaka Zosen Steel Mill as a Red Cross after that raid.[39]

Hamblin wrote that by mid-June they saw more and more friendly planes each day and could hear the bombing of distant cities. Then, on August 8, 1945, they became the target:

> We were all out of the factory and inside the camp when the air raid siren sounded. The first bomb hit something near the center of the city and blew it sky high. From there the planes worked a systematic pattern until our camp was reached from the west. A barracks which looked the same as ours, but housed Korean workers, was bombed. According to the pattern, we should have been next, but they skipped

us and hit the factory where no prisoners were working at the time. Then they approached from the south, systematically bombing until they came to our camp. Again, we were spared, and the buildings to the north were hit. The raid had started about 8:00 p.m., and the last bombs dropped shortly after midnight.[40]

According to Hamblin, "there was [not] a man in that camp at that time, who didn't feel in his heart that we had been protected by 'Divine Providence.'"[41]

The POWs' hope for Allied victory and liberation was tempered, however; the Japanese Army intended to kill them all if the Americans invaded Japan. Patterson knew a friendly Christian guard who warned Patterson that if there were ever a siren signaling guards to move to the front, "You want to hide because the Japanese soldiers will kill you. They don't want to leave anybody alive here when they leave this camp."[42]

Similarly, Ralf Wilson—who was at a plant in Toyama, Japan, during the last days of the war—later recalled:

> Three months before the Japanese surrendered, we were called together by the camp commander. He was a graduate of Stanford University and spoke excellent English. He said, "You should prepare to die, because the Americans, being foolish, will probably try to invade Japan. The first time an American sets his foot on shore, my orders are to kill every one of you. We will fight to the last man. So why should we die, and you live? So you will die, and then maybe we will die." That was the most frightening news we had heard.[43]

NOTES

1. Patterson, "Interview," 11; Rohlfing, "Carl D. Rohlfing," 2; Center for Research, Allied POWs under Japanese, Nagoya Branch #5 Yokkaichi, American Rescue Roster, http://www.mansell.com/pow_resources/camplists/Nagoya/nag_5_yokkaichi/nag_05_yanks.html. The rosters generally reflect those in the camp at the end of the war. Hansen, Larsen, Lloyd Parry, Patterson, Rohlfing, and Vance are listed on the roster for this camp, although Hamblin and Christensen are not listed. Christensen wrote that he and one hundred other POWs were transferred in May 1945 to another camp in Tayoma. Christensen, "My Life Story," 22. Hamblin was likely transferred as well. He wrote that he was later separated from Hansen, suggesting that Hamblin was at this camp at least initially. Hamblin, "My Experience," 24.

Patterson refers to Christensen being with him at that camp. Patterson, "Interview," 38.
2. Patterson, "Interview," 38.
3. Center for Research, Allied POWS under Japanese, Nagoya 11B POW Camp American (48 men) roster, http://www.mansell.com/pow_resources/camplists/Nagoya/nag_11_nihon_soda_iwase/nag_11_yanks.html (listing Wilson on the roster).
4. Center for Research, Allied POWS under Japanese, Nagoya POW Camp No 11 (Iwase) Nihon Soda SCAP Investigation Report, 29 January 1946, http://www.mansell.com/pow_resources/camplists/Nagoya/nag_11_nihon_soda_iwase/nag_11_scap_investigation.html.
5. Bray, "War Memories," 23–25; Goodliffe, "Recollections," 11–14.
6. Center for Research, Allied POWS under Japanese, Roster, "Korea (Chosen) POW Camp: Jinsen "Inchon," http://mansell.com/pow_resources/camplists/other/korea-main.html (showing Davey on Jinsen camp roster); Lawton, *Some Survived*, 223, 227–28.
7. Heimbuch, "Lucky One," 94; see Jacobsen, *We Refused to Die*, 187–89.
8. Hamblin, "My Experience," 22; Jacobsen, *We Refused to Die*, 189 (also noting POWs were required to learn Japanese drills).
9. Christensen, "My Life Story," 19; Christensen, "Two Pieces of Paper Saved Me," *Ensign*, February 1991.
10. Christensen, "My Life Story,"19–20.
11. Heimbuch, "Lucky Ones," 93–94.
12. Christensen, "My Life Story," 20.
13. Hamblin, "My Experience," 22; East, "Army Life," 19; Heimbuch, "Lucky Ones," 94–95.
14. Christensen, "My Life Story," 20, 22.
15. See, for example, Jacobsen, *We Refused to Die*, 195 (dangerous conditions in coal mine); Hamblin, "My Experience," 22 (working with sulfuric acid); Holmes, *Unjust Enrichment*, chapters 5–7 (description of the dangerous conditions at various industrial facilities).
16. Goodliffe, "Recollections," 12.
17. Bray, "War Memories," 25.
18. Hamblin, "My Experiences," 24.
19. Lawton, *Some Survived*, 229; Springgay, "Davey," 34.
20. Patterson," Interview," 11.
21. Heimbuch, *Lucky Ones,* 97.
22. Heimbuch, *Lucky Ones,* 97; Goodliffe, "Recollections," 12; Jacobsen, *We Refused to Die,* 188–89.
23. Holmes, *Unjust Enrichment*, 48 (quoting Harold Feiner, a POW in Japan).
24. Hamblin, "My Experience," 24.
25. Patterson, "Interview," 37.
26. Thomas M. Fairbanks, email message to author, September 14, 2016.
27. Goodliffe, "Recollections," 13.

28. Goodliffe, "Recollections," 14. Hansen also spoke of having had bamboo driven under his fingernails. Thomas M. Fairbanks, email message to author, September 14, 2016.
29. Bray, "War Memories," 25–26. Jacobsen also wrote of being severely beaten and tortured by guards. Jacobsen, *We Refused to Die*, 199, 202–05.
30. Heimbuch, *Lucky Ones,* 97; Bray, "War Memories," 24 (friendship with female lathe operator in steel mill); Jacobsen, *We Refused to Die*, 195–97 (developed "respectful" relationship with civilian overseer but encountered another with a vicious temper); Patterson, "Interview," 11 ("those that hadn't been in the service were pretty good").
31. Christensen, "Two Pieces of Paper."
32. Lawton, *Some Survived*, 223.
33. Lawton, *Some Survived*, 227.
34. Lawton, *Some Survived*, 230.
35. Hamblin, "My Experience," 24; East, "Army Life,"19.
36. Thomas M. Fairbanks, email message to author, September 14, 2016. In relating this incident, Hansen did not mention the time or place. The author includes it here because it seems most likely to have occurred at this time when Hansen was likely unable to walk due to the effects of beriberi, and because others report that at this time books were being confiscated by the Japanese. See East, "Army Life," 19.
37. East, "Army Life," 20.
38. Hamblin, "My Experience," 23; Christensen, "My Life Story," 20; Wilson, in *Courage in a Season of War*, 326.
39. Goodliffe, "Recollections," 12–13.
40. Hamblin, "My Experience," 25.
41. Hamblin, "My Experience," 25.
42. Patterson, "Interview," 9.
43. Wilson, in *Courage in a Season of War*, 327.

29

LIBERATION

The day dawn is breaking, the world is awaking,
The clouds of night's darkness are fleeing away.

—Joseph L. Townsend, "The Day Dawn Is Breaking"

By mid-1945, events in Japan were accelerating toward a conclusion. The bombing raids were increasing, and more and more plants were closed due to the bombings. The POWs and the guards heard rumors about two incredibly large bombs and the devastation they had brought.[1] They were the atomic bombs the United States had dropped on Hiroshima and Nagasaki on August 6 and 9, 1945.

On August 15, 1945, just days after those bombings, the POWs were left in camp or isolated in small areas at work while the Japanese guards and camp commanders huddled around speakers to listen to a recorded broadcast from Emperor Hirohito. He informed them of the Japanese surrender. It would be a few days before most of the POWs were officially informed of the surrender, but with the Japanese uncharacteristically not requiring them to work, the prisoners suspected as much.[2]

The Japanese announced the surrender in different ways in the camps and in some camps it was not announced at all; the guards just left. At the camp in Incheon, Korea, where Davey was imprisoned, it was likely handled best:

> The Japanese camp commander lined up the American prisoners and lowered the Japanese flag. Japan had surrendered to the Allied forces. The Japanese commander of the prison camp went over to [Davey] and shook his hand, saying "The war is over, we are no longer enemies; we are friends." After three and one-half years of waiting, praying, and hoping, peace had come. . . . Pandemonium reigned. Men laughed, babbled, chattered, whistled; they did everything but sit still or sleep. They were free men again.[3]

While the war was over and they were free men again, the POWs were nevertheless instructed to remain in their camps for two weeks to allow the Allied forces to reach them and also for their own safety.[4] Japanese civilians, with tragic losses from the bombings, had become quite hostile to the POWs. Allied commanders believed they would not "pass up a chance to kill an American."[5]

Goodliffe explained that after the surrender, the Japanese guards patrolled outside the camp gates because they were "afraid that we were going to get out and take revenge for the atrocities that they had committed on us." The prisoners patrolled inside the camp because "we were afraid that they were going to try to get in at us because of the Americans dropping these atomic bombs and killing so many people."[6] Patterson recalled being advised not to eat or drink anything the Japanese gave him because it may have been poisoned since "they still have hatred for you."[7]

Nonetheless, with the surrender, the POWs had free access to the food supplies in the camps, including the Red Cross packages that the Japanese had been keeping from them.[8] The POWs were instructed to paint *PW* in large letters on the roofs of their camps. Soon planes came in low, seeking to locate the POW camps so supplies could be dropped. Hamblin wrote, "A day or two later (after the surrender) a friendly plane came in so low that we could see the pilot. He circled over our camp and waved his arms time after time. The men went wild with joy and excitement."[9]

A few days later, the air drops began. B-29 bombers flew in low over the camps, dropping from their bomb bay doors fifty-five-gallon drums full of goods and supplies, hanging from brightly colored red, blue, yellow, and green parachutes. Christensen later recalled that "seeing those large cans of supplies floating down from the sky on parachutes was better than Christmas, Thanksgiving, and the Fourth of July all rolled into one. We feasted. We gorged. Many of us, being unaccustomed to so much food, became sick."[10]

Clarence Bramley, the Latter-day Saint POW from Long Beach, California, concluded that they now needed a flag to fly; he fashioned an American flag from the parachute material. He brought it home with him, and in 2005 it was displayed at Brigham Young University as part of its "Remembering World War II: Pearl Harbor and Beyond" exhibit at the Harold B. Lee Library.[11] Davey brought some parachutes back home with him as well and, following a Latter-day Saint artistic tradition, his sister-in-law made a quilt of them in remembrance of that event.[12]

Unfortunately, some of the drums broke loose from the parachutes or the chutes never opened, creating a danger for the POWs below who were anxiously awaiting them. Davey recalled that his greatest danger from a bombing in the war was from these barrels falling unimpeded from the sky. The only safe place was outside the camp. Upon returning from outside the camp where the POWs had gone for safety, Davey found that "two items covered the camp from one end to the other, cocoa and pea soup."[13]

Hamblin wrote of a similar experience: "Some [of the barrels] came loose from the parachutes [and those that] hit that hard ground burst and splattered all over. The first one I came to was a fruit cocktail. I had my first taste of canned fruit in over three years. One load dropped [where it] was very rocky and the package was broken. When we arrived, we found Hershey bars and chewing gum scattered. . . . We sat down and ate chocolate until it melted and ran out our ears."[14]

In addition to food, the dropped supplies included medicine, clothes, and magazines. Among the magazines dropped was a copy of an issue of the *Improvement Era*, a Church publication. A POW found it and gave it to Hamblin, who "devoured everything in its pages." From it he first learned of the death of President Heber J. Grant. He also read a copy of an issue of *Life* magazine. From that issue, he first learned of the sinking of the *Shinyo Maru* and the fate of Brown, Ernest Parry, and the other Latter-day Saints from the group at Davao.[15]

Over the ensuing days, the POWs were taken to ships anchored off the Japanese coast or to airports to start their journey home. Rohlfing wrote, "We members of the Church gathered together for a prayer of thanksgiving that we had survived. On September 4, 1945, we marched out of camp waving flags some of the men had made, while U.S. and British planes buzzed overhead."[16]

On the ships they were stripped of their clothes, "deloused" with decontamination showers spraying DDT, and given hot showers and new clothes. Most importantly, they were fed. The ships' galleys were never closed to them. It was an eating marathon, and although their stomachs at first struggled to hold it, they began to put on weight.[17]

For the liberated prisoners, there were different routes back home, but most went to Okinawa and then to Manila. At Manila the POWs saw a ruined city but were nonetheless astonished at the sight of American supplies and equipment stacked up for miles in anticipation of the invasion of Japan. Warmly welcomed, they were placed in a rest camp at Nichols Field, where they were given food and treated to nightly movies. In Manila, Hamblin, Hansen, and Carl Rohlfing attended a Wednesday night meeting of Latter-day Saint servicemen. Hamblin noted, "We were all asked to talk but it was hard for me to say much. My heart was too full."[18]

The men continued to recuperate and gain weight in the Philippines, and then they made the voyage back to the United States. It was an emotional moment for these soldiers and former POWs as the outline of San Francisco's Golden Gate Bridge with its unmistakable shape and orange vermillion color slowly came into view. For them, the "Golden Gate" was "just as much a symbol of freedom as the Statute of Liberty had ever been to anyone."[19]

They received warm and enthusiastic welcomes. With family members having been advised of the POWs' expected arrivals, parents or other relatives living nearby were often there to greet their returning sons and relatives. Christensen met his father and brother in San Francisco. Of that meeting, Christensen wrote, "It was quite a reunion. No one could say a word. We just stood there with our arms around each other."[20]

In that era, telephone calls, especially long-distance calls, were still not common and were reserved for special occasions. The army arranged for the returning POWs to make calls home; every POW wanted to make a call, so each had to wait his turn. Family members were usually advised of approximately when they could expect the call. They often took turns sitting by the phone so they wouldn't miss the call.[21]

It was not the War Department telegram advising families that their son or brother was alive that most resonated with that truth, but that first phone call. It was the moment when the parent, brother, sister, or wife first heard the familiar voice that it became real. They were not long calls, but the important message was not delivered by the words of the conversation—it came with the hearing of a familiar voice, alive and coming home. Hamblin described his first call home: "Mother was too overcome with emotion to say very much, only to ask how I was. . . . Then my sister Sylvia took the phone with no better results, so I then talked a few minutes with my sister Helen. There was very little said, but just the sound of their voices was worth more than a million to me."[22]

Of the Latter-day Saint POWs identified as likely participants in the group at Dapecol in the Philippines, the following survived their captivity to return home:

- Private First Class Rex D. Bray from Provo, Utah
- Private First Class Allen C. Christensen from Tremonton, Utah
- Captain Robert G. Davey from Salt Lake City, Utah
- Private First Class Charles L. Goodliffe from Park Valley, Utah
- Private Orland K. Hamblin from Farmington, New Mexico
- Staff Sergeant Peter (Nels) Hansen from Weiser, Idaho
- Corporal Kenneth B. Larsen from Salt Lake City, Utah

- Private First Class Lloyd Parry from Logan, Utah
- Private James Patterson from Sunnyside, Utah
- Corporal Carl D. Rohlfing from Salt Lake City, Utah
- Corporal Donald L. Vance from Fairview, Utah
- Corporal Ralf T. Wilson from Alta, Wyoming
- Corporal James Edmund Wilstead from Provo, Utah

Although there would be more time recovering in hospitals from the various diseases that accompanied them to the US, these Latter-day Saint POWs had survived and were finally coming home.

NOTES

1. Goodliffe, "Recollections," 14; Springgay, "Davey," 55.
2. See, for example, Hamblin, "My Experience," 26; Christensen, "My Life Story," 23–24; Jacobsen, *We Refused to Die,* 210–13.
3. Springgay, "Davey," 55.
4. Springgay, "Davey," 55.
5. Bray, "War Memories," 27; Jacobsen, *We Refused to Die*, 214.
6. Goodliffe, "Recollections," 14.
7. Patterson, "Interview," 40.
8. Jacobsen, *We Refused to Die*, 212; see also Springgay, "Davey," 55.
9. Hamblin, "My Experience," 26; see also Bray, "War Memories," 27; Heimbuch, *Lucky Ones*, 104–5 (similar account of navy carrier planes locating camp followed by air drops from B-29 bombers).
10. Christensen, "Two Pieces of Paper."
11. Exhibit "Remembering World War II: Pearl Harbor and Beyond," L. Tom Perry Special Collections, Harold B. Lee Library, Brigham Young University. The exhibit ran from fall 2005 to spring 2006. A virtual exhibit can be viewed at http://exhibits.lib.byu.edu/wwii/index.html.
12. Springgay, "Davey," 58.
13. Davey, "Last Talk," 7; Springgay, "Davey," 56.
14. Hamblin, "My Experience," 26.
15. Hamblin, "My Experience," 26.
16. Rohlfing, "Carl D. Rohlfing," 2.
17. Goodliffe, "Recollections," 17; Bray, "War Memories," 27.
18. Hamblin, "My Experience," 27.
19. Jacobsen, *We Refused to Die*, 240.
20. Christensen, "My Life Story," 28.
21. Springgay, "Davey," 58.
22. Hamblin, "My Experience," 28.

30

SURVIVORS

Peace and plenty here abide,
Smiling sweet on ev'ry side.
Time doth softly, sweetly glide
When there's love at home.

—John Hugh McNaughton, "Love at Home"

Notwithstanding the warm welcomes from families, friends, and country back in the United States, life after the war was not always kind to many of the surviving Pacific POWs. There were the lingering effects of their illnesses and starvation as well as emotional scars from the horrors they witnessed and endured. Many returned home to begin their postwar life physically and emotionally devastated.

The average Pacific POW had lost sixty-one pounds in captivity, and these were men who were usually fairly lean to begin with. Roughly three-quarters of them had weighed less than 160 pounds upon enlistment. Tuberculosis, malaria, dysentery, malnutrition, anemia, eye ailments, wet and dry beriberi, and festering wounds were rampant. The hospitalization rates of former Pacific POWs for many diseases were between two and eight times higher than former European POWs.[1]

The emotional injuries, however, could be much more insidious, long-lasting, and destructive. A study of former Pacific POWs found that nearly forty years after the war, more than 85 percent suffered from post-traumatic stress disorder (PTSD) with flashbacks, anxiety, and nightmares in which they reexperienced traumas of their imprisonment in painful realism. In too many cases, these emotional injuries turned into tormented and sometimes ruined postwar lives, negatively affecting them and their families.[2]

There is no reason to believe that many of these Latter-day Saint POWs did not also suffer after the war from the effects of their imprisonment. They were not of a generation or culture that tended to write about such things, and those who wrote of their war experiences rarely made mention of these trials. Even so, many suffered.

Hamblin suffered from bouts of depression and died of cancer, determined to be service related, in 1983 at the age of sixty-six.[3] Patterson continued to be treated for schistosomiasis for most of his life.[4] Due to vitamin deficiencies, Christensen suffered atrophy of the optic nerve, resulting in degeneration in his eyesight. With proper diet and medication after the war, the deterioration stopped, but a small part of his vision was lost.[5] Hansen lost all feeling in his legs due to the effects of beriberi and was able to walk again only with great and courageous effort.[6] Late in life, Hansen also suffered from flashbacks—vividly reexperiencing the most horrible periods of his captivity.[7]

Although Rohlfing rarely spoke of his experiences as a POW, he also suffered from "night terrors," especially after reunions with former POW companions.[8] East suffered from periodic depression and nightmares and often awoke with chills.[9] Bray suffered recurrent bouts of a skin disease he had contracted in the Philippines. He wore dentures most of his life because he lost many of his teeth due to effects of his imprisonment. Family members also learned to wake him up by gently shaking a foot; otherwise, if awakened suddenly, he would likely bolt up with his fists swinging, a remnant of his POW experience.[10]

These Latter-day Saint POWs may have endured more pain after the war than can be appreciated. It would be a disservice to their postwar accomplishments to ignore the physical and emotional trials many continued to endure. Nevertheless, while many of these POWs brought back with them physical and emotional burdens of their captivity, with personal courage, supportive families and communities, and their religious faith, many went on to live full lives, blessing their families and their church and contributing to the nation they loved.

The geopolitics are far different today than they were in World War II, with former enemies now close allies and some former allies now perceived as threatening adversaries. With the passage of time, the events of that great war recede in our collective consciousness, pushed back by the force of current events. This is especially true of these Latter-day Saint POWs in the Philippines and their families, ordinary people caught up in a trial not of their making and that would in the end prove to be of no strategic significance in the war and without any widely celebrated war heroes. Yet through this ordeal we see the faith, courage, love of country, and resilience of seemingly ordinary people and the importance of those virtues individually and as a country. They earned their place among those who some consider America's "Greatest Generation."[11]

The following are some brief notes on postwar stories of a few from this group of Latter-day Saint POWs in the Philippines.

ROBERT G. DAVEY

Bob Davey finally made it back to his home ward, Salt Lake City's Cannon Ward, on October 24, 1945. His unexpected appearance at the Gleaner Jamboree turned the event into an unplanned celebration and welcome-home party. (The Gleaners was a young adult Church youth group at the time.) Not everyone in attendance appreciated this program change, however. Dorothy Jacobs, whose family had bought the Davey home during the war, had been looking forward to a different type of event. While she knew of the family, she did not know Bob Davey.

Nevertheless, Dorothy was intrigued by this new ward member. Although she thought he was good-looking, her real interest was more just student curiosity than romantic. Dorothy was then a nursing student at the University of Utah, and her professional interests

Lieutenant Colonel Robert G. Davey. Courtesy of Davey family.

were piqued by all the nutritional deficiency diseases he was known to have had. As for any possible romantic interests, she was then engaged to a sailor in the navy.

Davey, on the other hand, immediately recognized Dorothy as the girl of his dreams—quite literally—when he first saw her at the Gleaner Jamboree. At one of the lowest points in his captivity, this was the girl he had seen in his dream, walking in and out of his family house; it was the dream that had given him the courage and faith to know he would survive imprisonment and return home and marry her. To the dismay of the sailor fiancé, two months later Bob and Dorothy were married on December 26, 1945, in the Salt Lake Temple. Just as Davey had seen in that dream, they went on to have a beautiful family.

Davey stayed in the army with postings in California, the Pentagon, and Panama; he finally retired in Olympia, Washington, at the rank of Lieutenant Colonel. He and Dorothy enjoyed a fulfilling marriage and had four children. He remained active in the Church with callings as a branch president in Panama and in the Olympia Washington Stake presidency. In 1953, shortly after the birth of his youngest daughter, Davey became sick and was hospitalized with internal bleeding. He was not expected to live, but that was not his time to die. After receiving a priesthood blessing, he lived a healthy life for another fifteen years.

In 1967 he was diagnosed with cancer and told he would die within the next six months, a death he faced with faith and courage. His daughter commented that her father often said the refining fire of prison camp had given him a strong testimony of the truths of the gospel. He died on July 19, 1968. He was fifty-three years old.

Harold B. Lee, then a member of the Quorum of the Twelve Apostles, spoke at Davey's funeral. Referring to the scriptural passage that "he that hath faith in me to be healed, and is not appointed unto death, shall be healed" (Doctrine and Covenants 42:48), Elder Lee reassured the family that Davey was truly appointed unto death at this time.[12] As Davey had learned in a dream years earlier while sick and discouraged in a POW camp, his time to die was not in the Philippines in 1942 but in 1968, after having lived to fulfill that dream of returning home, marrying, and having a family.[13]

ORLAND HAMBLIN

After the war, Orland Hamblin returned to Arizona and went to work for the United States Post Office, where he continued to work until retirement. He married Iona Lucinda Bright in the Mesa Arizona Temple on June 30, 1948, and raised a family of three beautiful daughters. Indeed, his daughters and grandchildren still maintain a Facebook page dedicated to preserving the memory of this quiet but remarkable man.

Orland Hamblin following his release as a POW in 1945. Courtesy of Hamblin family.

In his history of his experiences as a POW, Hamblin concluded, "I have always recognized the hand of the Lord in protecting me from the dangers and diseases that were constantly around me.... Ten years from our liberation, over 2,000 of the 4,000 who were in the Death March and were liberated had died from the effects of the march and years of imprisonment. I have very good health considering the hardships and starvation diet I endured for three and one-half years. I have a wonderful wife and three beautiful little daughters. Yes, God has been very good to me."[14] Orland died in Arizona on November 4, 1983. He was sixty-six years old.

PETER NELSON HANSEN

Peter Nelson Hansen lost the use of his legs during imprisonment from the effects of beriberi. He spent the last one hundred days of captivity in a POW camp hospital. He was partially rehabilitated after the war, but without any feeling in his legs he always struggled to walk. A nephew recalled that on one occasion, a niece questioned whether Hansen genuinely could not feel anything in his legs. According to the nephew, "Pete [as he was known in the family] didn't argue, he just went over to my mom's sewing kit and took the longest straight pin he could find, about an inch long, and sat down and sunk it completely into his thigh without flinching, just to show us that he could not feel anything below the waist."[15]

Hansen was in one of the last camps in Japan to be liberated and was then detained in Manila as a witness in the war crimes trials of Generals Yamashita and Homma.[16] He was finally discharged from the army on November 7, 1946. One week later, he accepted a call to serve a mission to Japanese-Americans in Hawaii. Japan was not then open to Church missionaries, but when it was later opened for missionary work, Hansen, despite all he had suffered at the hands of the Japanese, was one of those missionaries. He went on to serve several missions to Japan. On April 13, 1952, he was set apart as the first counselor to President Vinal G. Mauss of the Japan Mission.[17]

Hansen was a remarkable Christian man. His faith and leadership proved to be a great blessing to many POWs. He never married, but he adopted two Japanese orphans, whom he supported. A nephew, with whom Hansen lived later in his life, offered the following assessment of his uncle: "The fact that he could walk was a miracle. He used that miracle to serve as a missionary for The Church of Jesus Christ of Latter-day Saints for over twenty years after the war and a few before."[18] He died on December 12, 1981, in Weiser, Idaho.

The presidency of the Japan Mission in 1952. From left to right: Peter Nelson "Nels" Hansen, first counselor; Vinal G. Mauss, president; and Dwayne N. Anderson, second counselor. Courtesy of familysearch.org. Used with permission.

ALLEN C. "ACE" CHRISTENSEN

Allen C. "Ace" Christensen returned home to Tremonton, Utah. In 1947 he married Doris Farnsworth in the Logan Utah Temple and went to work for the United States Post Office. He raised a family and was active in the community and the Church, holding various leadership positions. In particular, he was the chairman of the Box Elder County Veterans Memorial Committee, which was responsible for the funding and construction of the veterans memorial on Midland Square in Tremonton, Utah. The memorial was dedicated on August 18, 2001, by President Thomas S. Monson, also a WWII veteran and then first counselor in the First Presidency of the Church.[19]

Forty-five years after his liberation, Ace was called to return to Japan, this time with Doris to serve in the Osaka Japan Mission. Of that mission, Christensen wrote, "If my first visit to Japan as a POW had been characterized by hunger, my second visit to Japan as a missionary with my wife was quite the opposite. Generous neighbors and friends kept us supplied with rice, fruit, and vegetables; they fed us as honored guests. In turn, we kept those who were spiritually hungry supplied with 'spiritual food,' much as I had been fed by the kind man who had once given me half a potato."[20]

Doris passed away in 2013 at the age of ninety, survived by Ace as well as two children, seven grandchildren, seventeen great-grandchildren, and seven great-great-grandchildren.[21] Ace passed away on September 22, 2020, at the age of one hundred.

FRANKLIN T. EAST

Franklin T. East survived to return home to Pomerene, Arizona, to the wife he had married just days before he left for the Philippines and to resume his life as a chicken farmer and beekeeper. His new life, however, was not without personal tragedies. With changing market conditions, his poultry business failed. His wife died in 1976 from cancer. A son died in an automobile accident with a vehicle driven by a drunk driver.

In 1985 East was examined by a social worker for the Veterans Administration. The report noted, "The patient experiences periodic combat nightmares, especially after seeing a war movie. Sometimes, he has considerable difficulty falling asleep due to ruminating about his traumatic experiences. He states that over the years he has learned to 'put up with them' and focuses attention elsewhere. . . . He experiences periodic depression associated with these intrusive memories. He wakes with chills about every three months."[22]

Regarding his physical condition, the report stated that he suffered from hypertension, prostate cancer, and peripheral neuropathy with burning feet and swelling ankles. The prostate cancer and hypertension weren't particularly unusual for a man of his age; he was sixty-nine at that time. The neuropathy may have been related to beriberi and other diseases and malnutrition he suffered as a POW. The report also noted that East had returned home to a supportive wife and church. According to the report, East stated that he had gained "considerable satisfaction from community volunteer activities, and throughout the years, this work has overridden any preoccupation with his WWII traumatic experiences."[23]

The report noted that he had "post traumatic stress disorder which the patient effectively manages through positive activity" and that the patient "shows extraordinary personality strengths." Since the examination was made in 1985, East had likely been suffering from the effects of PTSD for nearly forty years.

Notwithstanding the PTSD and the postwar tragedies, East had managed to live an abundant and productive life. He raised a family of four children, served as bishop in the Pomerene Ward for five years, served on the Benson School Board for twenty-six years, and worked in the Scouting program for forty years. He remarried and served a mission at Temple Square in Salt Lake City. The social worker who interviewed East closed the report by noting that additional intervention by the clinic did not appear necessary and then wrote, "It has been my personal pleasure to interview/assess this outstanding individual."[24] East died four years later on August 1, 1989, at the age of seventy-three.

JAMES PATTERSON

James Patterson remained in the service and later served in the United States Air Force Strategic Air Command, the group responsible for the country's nuclear weapons. He married Cleolo Faye Richards of Magna, Utah, in the Salt Lake Temple on August 19, 1946.

After retiring from the air force, Patterson returned to the Philippines in 1986—this time not as a soldier or POW, but as a missionary to serve with his wife in the Manila Philippines Temple. He accepted with excitement this call to go back to the Philippines to serve the people where he had been imprisoned.[25]

He often spoke at firesides and other meetings about his experiences as a POW, always mentioning that special sacrament meeting and the unrolling of the flag in Dapecol on Christmas Day in 1942. He died on June 2, 2006. He was eighty-four years old. Previously, he had requested that at his funeral that scene of the sacrament meeting and the flag be reenacted. It was.[26]

CARL DENNIS ROHLFING

Carl D. Rohlfing was a faithful Church member during his captivity and a close friend to many other Latter-day Saint POWs. Hamblin described him as "a fine Mormon boy."[27] After liberation, Rohlfing arrived back in San Francisco, California, on October 15, 1945. After a few days of examination in the Letterman Hospital in San Francisco, he finally returned home to Salt Lake City on October 21, 1945, four years to the day after leaving.

In March 1946 he moved to Los Angeles to attend college; after graduation, he worked in several sales positions in California. Rohlfing had remained in the Air Force Reserve and was called up for the Korean War in August 1950. He was sent to Larsen Air Force Base in Moses Lake, Washington, where in December of that year, he contracted polio. He was in an iron lung for four months. He retired on April 1, 1951, and went to Wadsworth Veterans Administration Hospital in West Los Angeles for rehabilitation. He was there for two years. He recovered sufficiently to be able to walk with crutches and leg braces, although later in life he required a wheelchair.

In April 1953 he married Effie Cundick in the Salt Lake Temple. They had two children and seven grandchildren. Despite his imprisonment as a POW and his contraction of polio after the war, he was never a bitter man. Rather, he was known as a kind and gentle man who diligently and faithfully served his God, his church, and his fellow men his entire life until his death in 1999 at the age of eighty-one.[28]

RALF T. WILSON

Ralf T. Wilson was the young corporal from Alta, Wyoming, who on the eve of the US surrender to the Japanese, privately knelt in prayer in a small clearing in the jungle and opened his heart to the Lord in prayer. He was promised that "it's okay," and that he would be "all right." He remembered that experience and that promise throughout his captivity. He said, "Having assurance from the Lord gave me hope and confidence others did not have."[29] With that hope and confidence, Wilson survived Camp Casisang, Dapecol, Bilibid, the voyage in a hell ship, and imprisonment in Japan. After the war, he was sent to the Madigan General Hospital at Fort Lewis, Washington. There he met Second Lieutenant Janet Ross. They fell in love and married.

Wilson stayed in the air force. Janet was not then a member of the Church, and Wilson's church activity faded. However, while stationed in Alaska, Janet announced that she wanted to be baptized. Wilson was then challenged to get his life in order so he could perform the baptism, which he did. A little more than a year later, they were sealed in the Idaho Falls Idaho Temple. Wilson retired from the air force in 1961 while living in Redmond, Washington.

He continued as an active member of the Church, serving in various leadership positions and in the Scouting program. The Wilsons later moved to Rigby, Idaho. Ralf and Janet served a mission for the Church in New Mexico and served as ordinance workers in the Idaho Falls Idaho Temple for more than thirteen years.[30] He died in 2009 at the age of ninety-one and was buried in his birthplace of Alta, Wyoming. In addition to noting his military ranks, his obituary lists his occupation as "Scoutmaster."[31]

NOTES

1. Laura Hillenbrand, *Unbroken: A World War II Story of Survival, Resilience, and Redemption* (New York City: Random House, 2010), 346–47; Daws, *Prisoners of the Japanese*, 384–85.
2. Daws, *Prisoners of the Japanese*, 384–85.
3. Kendall Ingleby, comment on "Orland 'Sigh' Hamblin Bataan Memorial March," Facebook page, January 25, 2017.
4. Patterson, "Interview," 34–36.
5. Christensen, "My Life Story," 30.
6. Thomas M. Fairbanks, email message to author, September 14, 2016.
7. Thomas M. Fairbanks, email message to author, September 14, 2016.
8. Dennis Autry, email message to author, February 20, 2017.

9. Sam Atterbury, Social Worker, Veterans Administration, "Problem Oriented Initial Assessment and Plan for Franklin T. East," VAMC Tucson, Arizona, April 18, 1985 (a copy provided to author by Jacob Stewart, East's grandson).
10. Kurt Bray, email message to author, January 27, 2017.
11. Tom Brokaw, *The Greatest Generation* (New York City: Random House, 1998).
12. Doctrine and Covenants 42:48; Marilyn Springgay, email message to author, April 23, 2017.
13. Springgay, "Davey," 63–64; Marilyn Springgay, email message to author, February 20, 2017.
14. Hamblin, "My Experience," 29.
15. Thomas F. Fairbanks, email message to author, September 14, 2016.
16. Ashton, "Spirit of Love," 174.
17. Clark and Kowallis, "Fate of the Davao Penal Colony," endnote 29; Armand L. Mauss, email message to Thomas M. Fairbanks, September 14, 2016, forwarded to author that same day; B. L. Hinchman and Robert W. Wood, editors, *The Japan Christian Yearbook: A Survey of the Japan Christian Movement in Japan through 1952* (Tokyo: The Christian Literature Society of Japan, 1953), 272–74, accessible at http://www.archive.org/stream/thejapanchristia44unknuoft/thejapanchristia44unknuoft_djvu.txt. A copy of the relevant excerpt from this book is also available at familysearch.org under the stories section of the page for Peter Nelsen Hansen (KW86-JCJ).
18. Thomas F. Fairbanks, email message to author, September 14, 2016.
19. Program, Veteran's Memorial Dedication, Tremonton, Utah, August 18, 2001 (copy provided to author by Cody Christensen); "Memorial Dedication is Saturday," *Deseret News,* August 17, 2001.
20. Christensen, "Two Pieces of Paper." In addition to his personal history, accounts of Christensen's POW experiences are as found in Freeman and Wright, *Saints at War*, and Robert C. Freeman, ed., *Saints at War: Inspiring Stories of Courage and Valor* (Springville, UT: Cedar Fort, 2013), 252–53.
21. "Obituary, Doris Farnsworth Christensen," *Standard-Examiner* (Ogden, UT), 4A, March 16, 2013.
22. Atterbury, VAMC Report.
23. Atterbury, VAMC Report.
24. Atterbury, VAMC Report.
25. Patterson, "Interview," 25; Richard Patterson, email message to author, October 14, 2016.
26. Richard Patterson, email message to author, October 12, 2016.
27. Hamblin, "My Experience," 15, 24.
28. Rohlfing, "Carl Dennis Rohlfing," 1–5; Dennis Autry, email message to author, February 20, 2017.
29. Wilson, in *Courage in a Season of War*, 323.
30. Wilson, 328.
31. "Obituary, Ralf T. Wilson," *Post Register* (Idaho Falls, ID), March 24, 2009.

EPILOGUE
THOSE WHO DID NOT COME HOME

What is this thing that men call death,
This quiet passing in the night?
'Tis not the end, but genesis
Of better worlds and greater light.

O God, touch Thou my aching heart,
And calm my troubled, haunting fears.
Let hope and faith, transcendent, pure,
Give strength and peace beyond my tears.

There is no death, but only change,
With recompense for victory won;
The gift of Him who loved all men,
The Son of God, the Holy One.

—President Gordon B. Hinckley[1]

For the families of those Latter-day Saint POWs on the *Shinyo Maru*, there would be no War Department telegram advising that their loved one was alive and returning home, no hearing his voice in a long-distance phone call, and no warm welcome home by family and friends who had never lost hope. Instead, they, like so many others, received a series of terse War Department letters advising them of that which they had hoped and prayed never to be told.

These Latter-day Saint POWs had survived two and a half years of brutal imprisonment that included beatings, torture, sicknesses, and starvation at the hands of a brutal enemy—all while maintaining a faith and hope in God—only to be killed by an American torpedo. For many families, this was an incomprehensible tragedy. That none of the Latter-day Saint POWs were among the survivors of the *Shinyo Maru* was a crushing blow to their families' faith in God and their religion. Before receiving official confirmation of the POWs' deaths, one father wrote, "I believe that I have as much faith in my religion as any Latter-day Saint, but I will never be able to understand this. Certainly some of those boys were entitled to the blessings that are promised to those that obey the laws and keep the commandments of God. . . . I hope and pray that some of those boys are alive, otherwise I will have a hard time reconciling the fact they were all killed with what my faith has taught me to believe."[2]

How could these families find solace for such a heartbreaking loss? How could they reconcile their faith in God with the unfathomable injustice of the death of their sons?

Like other grieving families who lost loved ones in WWII, these Latter-day Saint families would find comfort and support from a nation that, while celebrating victory and the safe return of others, openly and genuinely acknowledged its gratitude for the sacrifices made. Sincere condolences were offered for their loss, as witnessed by the many memorials, monuments, ceremonies, and posthumous awards of medals and citations.[3]

The grieving families found comfort and support among caring family members, friends in their community and church, and sometimes from surviving POWs. It was not unusual for families to be visited by surviving POWs who had known their lost loved one, often to make good on an earlier promise made to him. The grieving families also found peace in their religious faith, and for the families of these lost Latter-day Saint POWs, their faith included particularly reassuring teachings about death.

A MOST COMFORTING DOCTRINE

As part of their faith, these Latter-day Saint families believed that families can be together throughout the eternities—that their son, brother, or husband was not lost to them forever. This belief is not merely a vague hope for the distant eternities, but their faith informs them, in considerable detail, of the state of their departed loved one now as well as in the eternities.[4]

From section 138 of the Doctrine and Covenants, which is President Joseph F. Smith's account of his 1918 vision of the spirit world, the faithful families of these POWs knew that there is a continuation of sociality among the spirits and that their loved one would be among friends and relatives who have died. In a passage that would certainly resonate with the families of these deceased young men, President Smith said that in his vision, "I beheld that the faithful elders of this dispensation, when they depart from mortal life, continue their labors in the preaching of the gospel of repentance and redemption, through the sacrifice of the Only Begotten Son of God, among those who are in darkness and under the bondage of sin in the great world of the spirits of the dead."[5]

The parents of these deceased Latter-day Saint POWs may have never adjusted completely to their tragic loss, and nothing can fill the empty place in the hearts and homes of these families or compensate for the dashing of all their hopes and dreams for their lost family member.[6] Nevertheless, for the faithful Latter-day Saint families, their understanding of death must have been an especially comforting source of solace and hope.

We now consider the families of two of these deceased POWs, Staff Sergeant Ernest R. Parry and First Lieutenant George R. Brown.

ERNEST R. PARRY

Staff Sergeant Ernest R. Parry was known to his family by his middle name, Reynolds. He was the only son of his widowed mother and was brother to two sisters. He was the caring companion who befriended

Private Franklin East at a difficult time on the voyage to the Philippines, earning East's eternal gratitude and respect, and was a mainstay of the group at Davao. His mother, Georgiana R. Parry, responded to the news of the death of her only son by writing a poem entitled "My Service Flag":

> *My service flag, so brilliant,*
> *With its silver, red, and blue,*
> *Tells of the service of my son,*
> *So young, so strong and true.*
> *He went away all smiling*
> *In his uniform so trim,*
> *With never a sign of sorrow*
> *But knowing war is grim.*
> *He wrote such cheerful letters!*
> *Wishing he could hear from home,*
> *Telling of islands far away,*
> *Of the ocean, blue, with its foam.*
> *"O Father," I prayed, "have mercy*
> *On all boys of tender age,*
> *Who answer the call of country*
> *To write across history's page."*
> *The story of war—its sorrows,*
> *Its shocking atrocities, too.*
> *How many died of starvation!*
> *How many the enemy slew!*
> *Today there came a letter.*
> *The gist of its message is old.*
> *As I looked up for solace, I saw*
>   *My blue star had turned to gold.*[7]

Reynolds has not been forgotten but continues to inspire his family. Although he was lost at sea, his family placed a grave marker for him in the Evergreen Cemetery in Springville, Utah. A family tradition that still continues is to place flowers on the grave marker on Memorial Day.[8] Suzanne Julian, the granddaughter of one of Parry's sisters, was honored to speak at a Devotional at Brigham Young University in 2014. Among those she offered as a source of inspiration for a righteous life was her great-uncle Staff Sergeant Ernest Reynolds Parry.[9]

GEORGE ROBIN "BOBBY" BROWN

Back in El Paso, the news of the death of First Lieutenant George Robin (Bobby) Brown came to his family as an emotional roller-coaster of tentative, incomplete, and in the end unfounded pieces of hope. The Browns received a letter from the War Department dated October 27, 1944:

> The War Department was recently notified of the destruction at sea of a Japanese freighter that was transporting American Prisoners of War from the Philippine Islands.
>
> A number of survivors were later returned to the military control of our forces. There were also a large number who did not survive or who were recaptured by the Japanese and about whose present status no positive information is available. It is with deep regret that I must inform you that your son, First Lieutenant George R. Brown, 0890150, was in this latter group. Because of the War Department's lack of definite information concerning First Lieutenant Brown, no change in his Prisoner of War classification is being made at this time.
>
> Please be assured that as soon as additional information becomes available you will be immediately notified.[10]

Ruby then began a series of anxious, but in the end fruitless, correspondence with her Congressman and the army, seeking additional information and confirmation of various rumors then circulating about the fate of those on *Shinyo Maru*.[11]

On February 14, 1945, the US War Department received from the Japanese an official list of the POWs aboard the *Shinyo Maru*, and Bobby was on that list. The War Department notified the Browns of Bobby's death in a letter dated February 19, 1945.[12] Similar letters were sent to families of all 688 who died in the sinking of the *Shinyo Maru*.[13]

However, since Japanese reports were not always considered accurate, there was still some hope that Bobby had not actually been on the *Shinyo Maru*. The family desperately contacted a number of men who had been POWs in the Philippines, desperately looking for some evidence to support that hope, but without success.[14] It slowly became clear and the facts unavoidable. The Japanese list had been correct.[15] Bobby had been on the *Shinyo Maru* and was dead. George acknowledged as much on February 27 by starting correspondence

IN GRATEFUL MEMORY OF

First Lieutenant George R. Brown, A.S.No. O-890150,

WHO DIED IN THE SERVICE OF HIS COUNTRY AT

in the Southwest Pacific Area, September 7, 1944.

HE STANDS IN THE UNBROKEN LINE OF PATRIOTS WHO HAVE DARED TO DIE

THAT FREEDOM MIGHT LIVE, AND GROW, AND INCREASE ITS BLESSINGS.

FREEDOM LIVES, AND THROUGH IT, HE LIVES—

IN A WAY THAT HUMBLES THE UNDERTAKINGS OF MOST MEN

Franklin D Roosevelt

PRESIDENT OF THE UNITED STATES OF AMERICA

Letter from President Franklin D. Roosevelt acknowledging the death of First Lieutenant George R. Brown. Courtesy of Robert C. Freeman.

with the government regarding the steps needed to "get Bobby's affairs with the government settled," as he wanted to "make it a closed book as soon as possible."[16]

For months during this period, Ruby was ill and bedridden with what her doctor had diagnosed as a heart ailment.[17] More likely she was simply overwhelmed, first with the fear and anxiety over the fate

Ruby Brown receiving a medal posthumously for Lt. George Robin (Bobby) Brown. Courtesy of Brown family collection.

of her son and then with the emotional shock of his death. As to her faith, she wrote, "You know very well that there have been thousands of prayers offered for Bobby, both by his family and friends, and I feel that he was worthy of the protection of the Priesthood, but it must be that his work was finished. . . . At least that is the most comforting thought to me and we had to have comfort from somewhere."[18]

A FINAL MATTER FOR ETERNITY

While Bobby Brown's mortal life ended on September 7, 1944, there remained a final matter of mortality to be attended to, one final gift to Bobby of eternal significance: the temple endowment. Ruby finally gathered herself up from her afflictions, and she and George went to take care of this final earthly ordinance for Bobby. On November 13, 1945—with his father, George, as proxy and his mother, Ruby, and sister Nelle in attendance—Bobby received the endowment ordinance in the Mesa Arizona Temple. It was a solemn but joyful day for the family.[19]

MEDALS AND CEREMONIES

After the war, George and Ruby, along with Bobby's older sister, Nelle, attended a special ceremony held in the office of Major General John L. Homer, the commander of Fort Bliss in El Paso, where Bobby was awarded a Bronze Star, a Purple Heart, and some other medals posthumously.[20] Friends and family attended, including Gregorio Villasenor, who had been Bobby's driver and who had been with him when they surrendered in Bataan. In presenting the medals, General Homer spoke to them of Bobby's heroism and offered thoughts of comfort.

Sadly, Homer had to conduct many such ceremonies and knew the medals and his words were little consolation for the grieving families. In that context, he said something else to the Brown family members that Ruby and Nelle were careful to record later in a family history. Nelle wrote,

> When he saw the attitude of the family, General Homer made a very profound statement, "On many occasions that have taken place in this office, I have had the privilege of honoring so many in ceremonies such as these, and there will be many more." Then he added, as he held both mother and father's hands, and looked into their faces, "Would that I could wrap into a package the feelings of acceptance of God's will, and the lack of bitterness that is in your hearts, that I might give it to those who are not so blessed with whatever it is that you have, that makes you so understanding. No greater gift, short of their loved one, could I give them."[21]

What General Homer was seeing but could not specifically identify in the Brown family was their religious faith—their belief that Bobby was not lost to them forever but that they would yet be reunited after death. As to the bitterness, perhaps their positive faith effectively hid it, but there was in the corner of the hearts of Ruby and George a gnawing bitterness and hatred toward the Japanese.

On December 7, 1946, five years after Pearl Harbor, George and Ruby, accompanied by Bobby's siblings Jane and Paul, attended a gathering held for surviving friends and families of those in the 200th Regiment who had not survived the war. It was held in Santa Fe, where the regiment had its origin. The venue was the old Seth Hall, a famous building with beautiful territorial-style architecture. To sad-faced parents, widows, and children of the men of Bataan—Anglo-Saxon, Native American, and Hispanic—was presented, along with other medals, the Bataan Medal, the highest honor from the State of New Mexico.

Army photo of Master Sergeant Nels Hansen, which was autographed by Hansen and given to Ruby Brown. Courtesy of Brown family collection.

VISITORS

During imprisonment, POWs spoke to each other of their homes and families and often promised, if they managed to make it home, to contact a fellow prisoner's family. They memorized fellow POWs' phone numbers and addresses. More than one hundred returning soldiers who knew Bobby visited the Brown family at their home in El Paso.[22] Many just walked up to the house unannounced, saying, "I was with your son in Mindanao." They would ask to see the fishpond and fountain in the backyard that Bobby must have spoken about, and they mentioned other personal recollections.[23]

Among those visitors was Major Robert G. Davey. He reenlisted and in 1946 was stationed briefly at Fort Bliss in El Paso. He had recently married, and he and his wife, Dorothy, lived in a small trailer parked in a vacant lot adjoining the Brown residence. He was a frequent guest in the Brown home; the Browns learned much from him about Bobby's experience as a POW and the group they had formed at Davao.[24]

Another visitor was Sergeant Peter Nelsen (Nels) Hansen, the high priest who served with Brown in the Davao group.[25] One of the first things Hansen did on arriving in the United States was telephone the Brown family. In that call, Hansen offered to be a proxy and to perform the temple ordinances for Bobby. That wasn't necessary, because by that time those ordinances had been done. However, to a devout Saint like Ruby, that simple offer conveyed a wealth of reassuring information about the nature of the Latter-day Saints her son had been with in captivity.[26] Among the pictures Ruby kept and treasured was an autographed army photo of Hansen.

Arthur M. Baclawski survived the Bataan Death March, Camp O'Donnell, and Cabanatuan camps in the Philippines, a hell ship voyage to Japan, and the cold and hardship of a POW work camp in Japan—one of the surviving New Mexico members of the 200th. He kept a diary of those he knew in the war who had died, and after the war he visited the families of many of them. Bobby Brown was on the list, and a couple of years after the war, Baclawski went to visit the Browns in El Paso.[27] While visiting with George and Ruby, he also met Bobby's younger sister Jane. There followed a courtship, romance, and marriage.

I knew him as my Uncle Art. While I assume he suffered some lingering effects of his captivity, I never noticed them, and whatever physical or emotional demons he may have carried home from his POW experience did not get the better of him. He went on to have a successful career as a landscape architect for the federal government. Uncle Art was not a member of the Church and did not join after the war or after his marriage. Even so, he encouraged Jane's and his children's activity in the Church, and his children were raised as active members of the Church. Finally, on November 28, 1991, he was baptized a member of The Church of Jesus Christ of Latter-day Saints. He died just over a week later on December 7, 1991.

AN EXTRAORDINARY EXPERIENCE

George and Ruby Brown understood and accepted the Church teachings on death and found solace in them. Nevertheless, they felt deeply the loss of their son Bobby and had yet to be emotionally reconciled to his death. Then, nearly five years after Bobby's death, they were unexpectedly blessed with their own personal, private "revelation" on death.

On July 31, 1949, a Sunday evening, George suffered a severe heart attack and was taken to the hospital. His prospects were not good. Ruby stayed in the hospital with him through Thursday.

Thursday evening, feeling lonely and worried, Ruby went home to get some sleep. But sleep did not come and she tried reading to get drowsy. Ruby later wrote that she had felt the unmistakable presence of Bobby in the house. His presence had entered through the front door and gone into the kitchen and other parts of the house, although not into her room. The strangeness of the experience left her unable to breathe. Nevertheless, Ruby described it as "the sweetest feeling in my soul that I have ever experienced." After a few minutes, it was gone.

Nothing was seen and no voices were heard, but Ruby later wrote that she knew then that Bobby's presence was real and knew it as certainly as she knew that she was "now writing this on my typewriter." She related that her first reaction had been panic, believing it was a sign that Bobby had come from the dead to take George from among the living, but that feeling was soon replaced by a "sweet, calm spirit," and she finally fell asleep.

The next morning, Ruby went to see George in the hospital and found him somewhat improved. George asked Ruby to close the door, as he wanted to tell her something. Speaking with difficulty because of his emotions, George explained that ever since the heart attack, he had had the feeling that he would die and had been desperately worried about the fate of the family. While he was in this state of worrying about his and the family's fate and drifting in and out of sleep and consciousness, he had had the following experience, which he related to Ruby:

> It seemed that [George] was in front of a large building, and a lot of people were there, and among them, his mother, and Dan Skousen, his brother-in-law, and they were talking and visiting, when a door opened, and Bobby came out, apparently by appointment. Very casually, he came over and greeted his father [George] and told him they were discussing and deciding just what they were going to do about him.
>
> It also seemed that there were some young people there, who were trying to get to speak to Bobby, but he told his father to tell them he had to go on an errand but would get back as soon as he could. . . . He soon returned and smilingly explained that he just had to go on, and then turning, he added that they had not yet reached a decision about [George].
>
> Bobby looked well and happy . . . and was well dressed. He had whispered to his father and told him to get ready for whatever was done with him, and to tell Nelle to get ready for she too had work to do.
>
> Bobby smiled, and walked quietly away, and then [George] heard the nurse tell [him] that he was better, and she was going to feed him some breakfast.[28]

Ruby then shared her experience of the prior evening. They wept together, "knowing that our prayers had been heard in the high heavens, and that Bobby was there . . . looking after us, and that at times he is not so very far away."[29]

George did not die but survived that heart attack and, according to Ruby, did "his level best . . . to make up for anything he might have failed to do, . . . trusting in the Lord for strength and courage" until his death eleven years later on August 20, 1960.[30] Ruby continued serving in the Church, doing genealogy and temple work, and, as a faithful family chronicler, writing family histories and stories.

In the misery of a World War II POW camp in the Philippines, Bobby had often found peace and comfort in singing the hymns of Zion, hymns he had first learned from his mother in Colonia Chuichupa high in Mexico's Sierra Madre. Late in Ruby's life, when the cumulative toll of infirmities and the effects of old age had left her troubled in mind and body, she too would find solace to her soul in that same source—the hymns of Zion. Ruby died in peace on May 3, 1981, at the age of ninety.

NOTES

1. Gordon B. Hinckley, "The Empty Tomb Bore Testimony," *Ensign,* May 1988. In 2007 the poem was put to music by Janice Kapp Perry and titled "What Is This Thing Man Calls Death?," *Ensign,* February 2010.
2. Clark and Kowallis, "Fate of the Davao Penal Colony," 128.
3. There are memorial markers for these POWs at the Manila American Cemetery and Memorial in Manila, Philippines. Brown's name, along with the other members of the New Mexico's 200th and 515th Coast Artillery, are engraved on twelve granite columns at Bataan Memorial Park in Albuquerque, New Mexico. In 1964, El Paso dedicated the El Paso County War Memorial. Inscribed on the wings of the monument are 657 names of those who sacrificed their lives in WWII and the Korean War, and Brown's name is among them.
4. In this spirit world, the spirits of the righteous are received into a state of happiness, which is called *paradise,* and the spirits of those who die without knowledge of the truth and those who are disobedient in mortality are received into a state called *spirit prison.* Spirits from paradise are able to teach the gospel of Jesus Christ to those in spirit prison. The Church of Jesus Christ of Latter-day Saints, Basic Doctrine, https://www.lds.org/manual/basic-doctrines/basic-doctrines?lang=eng.
5. Doctrine and Covenants 138:57.
6. Clark and Kowallis, "Fate of the Davao Penal Colony," 128. (Clark and Kowallis were able to interview some of the siblings of the deceased POWs who "reported that their parents probably never adjusted completely to the tragedy").
7. Julian, "Led by the Spirit" (quoting poem, which is used with permission). At that time families with a member serving in the war displayed a blue star in their window. Those who had lost a family member displayed a gold star.
8. Email from Suzanne Julian to author, April 20, 2017.
9. Julian, "Led by the Spirit."
10. J. A. Ulio, Major General, The Adjutant General, War Department, to Mr. George A. Brown, October 27, 1944, NARA Records.
11. Mrs. George A. Brown to Honorable R. E. Thomason, November 12, 1944, NARA Records; Honorable R. E. Thomason to J.A. Ulio, Major General, The Adjutant General, November 14, 1944, NARA Records (forwarding the Brown letter of November 12, 1944); Mr. and Mrs. George A. Brown to Major General J. A. Ulio, Adjutant General, November 17, 1944, NARA Records.
12. J. A. Ulio, Major General, The Advocate General, The Adjutant General's Office, War Department, to Mr. George A. Brown, February 19, 1945, NARA Records.
13. Clark and Kowallis, "Fate of the Davao Penal Colony," 127.
14. For example, Sergeant Calvin Graef from Carlsbad, New Mexico, a survivor from Bobby's unit, first told the Brown family that he had seen Bobby at Dapecol in October 1944 but later conceded that he had been mistaken about the date.
15. Clark and Kowallis, "Fate of the Davao Penal Colony," 127–28.

16. George A. Brown to Honorable R. E. Thomasson, February 27, 1945, NARA Records; Honorable R. E. Thomason to Major General J. A. Ulio, The Adjutant General, War Department, March 2, 1945, NARA Records (forwarding Brown's February 27, 1945 letter).
17. Brown and Zundel, "George Robin Brown . . . His Story," 17; Hyer, "Classy Grandmas," 9.
18. Clark and Kowallis, "Fate of the Davao Penal Colony," 128.
19. For members of the Church, the temple endowment ordinance prepares and qualifies a person to receive the fullness of God's blessings in heaven after death. For those who die without having received this ordinance, such as Bobby Brown, another person, a proxy, may receive this ordinance in the temple on their behalf. The realization of the blessings of the ordinance, however, depends on its acceptance and the faithfulness of the deceased. To provide this ordinance, through proxy, for a deceased family member is for Church members a sacred experience and offering. The temple endowment ordinances were also performed for Brown's close friend John Keeler, with Ivan Zundel as proxy, and for Ruby's cousin Acord Spilsbury with Ivan's father, Jacob E. Zundel, as proxy. Ivan was the husband of Bobby's older sister Nelle. Brown and Zundel, "George Robin Brown . . . His Story," 17. The Brown family histories refer to the ordinances as being performed on November 15, 1945. However, the Church records indicate those ordinances were performed on November 13, 1945.
20. Zundel, "Brown Family History," 5. Brown was posthumously awarded the following: Bronze Star Medal with Letter "V" Device, Purple Heart, Distinguished Unit Emblem with 2 Oak Clusters, American Defense Service Medal with Foreign Service Clasp, Asiatic-Pacific Campaign Medal with two Bronze Service Stars, World War II Victory Medal, Philippine Defense Ribbon with one Bronze Service Star, Philippine Liberation Ribbon with one Bronze Service Star, and Philippine Independence Ribbon. Official Statement of Military Service and Death of George R. Brown, 0 890 150 by Kenneth G. Wickham, Major General, USA, the Adjutant General, NARA Records. Brown was also posthumously awarded the "Bataan Medal" by the State of New Mexico.
21. Brown and Zundel, "George Robin Brown . . . His Story," 22–23.
22. Zundel, "Brown Family History," 5.
23. Brown and Zundel, "George Robin Brown . . . His Story," 20.
24. Brown and Zundel, "George Robin Brown . . . His Story," 17–18.
25. Brown and Zundel, "George Robin Brown . . . His Story," 17–18.
26. Brown and Zundel, "George Robin Brown . . . His Story," 17–18.
27. Based on emails and conversations with Paul and Robert Baclawski, two of Arthur Baclawski's sons.
28. Ruby S. Brown, "This Is a Very Sacred Story," December 16, 1953, El Paso, Texas, vol. 4, item H.4, Ruby S. Brown Collection, Church History Library, Salt Lake City, 1–2. See also Brent L. Top, "What Is This Thing That Men Call Death? Latter-day Saint Teachings About the Spirit World" (BYU Campus Education Week address, August 18, 2010), *BYU Speeches*, 12–13 (overview of Church teachings on living persons receiving help and comfort from a deceased family member in the spirit world).
29. Ruby S. Brown, "This Is a Very Sacred Story," 1–2.
30. Brown, "This Is a Very Sacred Story," 2.

AFTERWORD

HATE AND FORGIVENESS

> *Savior, may I love my brother*
> *As I know thou lovest me,*
> *Find in thee my strength, my beacon,*
> *For thy servant I would be.*
>
> —Susan Evans McCloud, "Lord, I Would Follow Thee"

After the war, these Latter-day Saint POWs would often say that it was their faith and love for their family at home that helped sustain them through their ordeal. Faith and love are, however, not the only powerful and sustaining emotions. Hate is also powerful and, in the view of some, even more powerful than love. One POW, referring to his time in the holds of a hell ship, concluded, "The ones that got out were the ones that hated. Love never kept anyone alive, . . . but if you hated, . . . it seems strange but those that did—I mean hated real hard—they lived."[1]

That many POWs would harbor a deep hatred for the Japanese, their tormentors in captivity, is not surprising, and for many that hatred carried over after the war. One POW said of the Japanese, "I will neither forgive nor forget. I will hate them until I die."[2] Another tersely wrote, "Americans have short memories and forgive too easily."[3]

In contrast, these Latter-day Saint POWs, or at least those who wrote of their Japanese POW experience, had a different reaction. In a talk to Church members after the war, Davey said, "I never had a feeling of hatred that so many others did and I think that this was a good thing for me, not to hate them."[4] Christensen, who later in life served a mission in Japan with his wife, wrote in an *Ensign* article, "I was grateful I had never harbored hard feelings toward my captors, but I knew I would never forget my experiences as a POW."[5] And it was clear to Rohlfing's children that he felt love toward the Japanese people and never held any animosity toward them during the remainder of his life.[6]

After the war, Hamblin wrote of an experience he had while a POW in Japan, shortly after one of the Allied bombings. Some sparks from the fires caused by the bombs had landed on the roof of their barracks, and Hamblin was sent up to the roof to put them out. From that roof he had a clear view of the damage from the bombing. He wrote,

> In every direction there was fire and confusion. Even the birds were stunned and confused. While sitting up there witnessing this awful destruction, a pigeon lit near me, and I reached over and picked him up. Here, at last, was the retribution that we had often wished to come to our captors, but somehow, the screams of terror I heard from women and children were no different than I would have heard if this had been an American city. Suddenly I realized that I didn't have it in my heart to be glad or feel vengeance. For this I was thankful.[7]

With remarkable prescience, these POWs recognized that the absence of hate was not a weakness, but a blessing and one for which they were thankful; it was a blessing that would allow them to go forward in life unencumbered by the burden and corrosive effect of hate.[8]

Some POWs went beyond forgiveness of the Japanese and found opportunities to serve and save. Staff Sergeant Nels Hansen, the man who had provided spiritual leadership to these POWs in captivity, had had his first experience with the Japanese in a Sunday School in Hawaii on his way to the Philippines before the war. That experience made a deep impression on him.[9]

Shortly after his discharge, and although he was able to walk only with great difficulty, Hansen accepted a call to serve a mission in Hawaii among the Japanese-Americans and later in Japan. In accepting this call, Hansen explained,

> Yes, I have seen the inhuman treatment by the Japanese in their prison camps. It was torturing all right. But, fundamentally, the Japanese people are not bad. . . . They need Christianity. They need the restored gospel of the Master as revealed to the Prophet Joseph Smith. Then they will be all right. A great work lies ahead. I have no hate in my heart toward the Japanese. My desire is to help them. I want to lift them up to the heights I found in that little Japanese Sunday School I visited in Hawaii before the war.[10]

Hansen's hope for a great gospel work among his former Japanese enemies was realized beyond what he could have foreseen, and the gospel has come to Japan in ways these POWs could not have imagined. Temples may be a useful indication of the number, strength, and faithfulness of Church members. There are three temples in Japan, and another temple in Okinawa was announced in April 2019. The Philippines has seven temples announced or completed, including a temple announced in Davao City.

Returning soldiers and POWs weren't the only ones to confront the problem of hate and the challenge of forgiveness. Before the war, an element of racial prejudice toward the Japanese prevailed among many Americans, and during the war that prejudice grew into a mean and enduring hatred for many. This hatred did not simply vanish with the end of the war but continued, and many Americans had to deal with a virulent hatred festering in their hearts. This included those who lost family members and loved ones in the war. Such was the case for George and Ruby Brown. As recounted in the book *Miracle of Forgiveness*, by President Spencer W. Kimball, George and Ruby carried the burden of a hatred toward the Japanese for many years. However, through the gospel of Jesus Christ and the wise counsel of a stake president, they were finally able to forgive and free themselves of that burden.[11]

The effect of Bobby's death was not limited to George and Ruby but rippled on to others in the family. Apart from George and Ruby,

Bobby's older sister, Nelle, had the clearest understanding of these events and the keenest view of the sadness and despair felt by her parents. She also was very close to her brother, missed him greatly, and deeply mourned his death.

Although hidden in the deepest corners of her heart, she had harbored for many years a repressed hatred toward the Japanese. While contained, this was nevertheless something that even after all these years still troubled her. In 1992 she wrote to her family of two events that caused her to confront what she termed her "problem." First, her daughter Dorothy and son-in-law Gene Furniss invited her to dinner with a Japanese couple. The couple was attending Brigham Young University in preparation for an assignment in Japan. She accepted the invitation. She found them to be delightful people.

Second, Sister Chieko Okazaki, of Japanese ancestry and then a member of the Church's Relief Society General Presidency, spoke at a general women's conference of the Church.[12] Nelle described her talk as an "excellent presentation" and wrote that she "was so impressed by her." She wrote of recalling the Japanese officer on the *Shinyo Maru* who Bobby begged to stop the shooting of the POWs following the torpedo attack. The officer rejected Bobby's pleas, and he was likely the officer responsible for giving the orders to shoot, including the shots that killed Bobby. Nelle then concluded her letter to her family with this: "And I got to thinking about Bobby and a thought came to me. I wonder if he might even have the privilege of teaching the gospel to that Japanese Officer. . . . Now I find great comfort in the assumption that he is doing just that."[13] Nelle passed away a few years later in December 2000.

There is a message in the lives of these POWs and their families. Humility, patience, an open mind, and the gospel of Jesus Christ is the antidote to hate and the prescription for personal peace.

NOTES

1. Michno, *Death on the Hellships*, 306 (quoting former POW Forrest Knox).
2. Michno, *Death on the Hellships*, 307 (quoting former POW Cliff Farlow).
3. Michno, *Death on the Hellships*, 307 (quoting former POW Bob Martindale).

4. Davey, "Last Talk," 8. Hamblin also wrote: "I have never felt any hatred or revenge for the Japanese people." Hamblin, "My Experience," 29.
5. Christensen, "Two Pieces of Paper."
6. Dennis Autry, email message to author, February 20, 2017.
7. Hamblin, "My Experience," 25; see also Cave, *Beyond Courage*, 365 (another account of this experience).
8. For example, Rex Bray's son wrote that his father "did not harbor any postwar ill will toward the Japanese as a people, preferring to blame the specific individuals for his suffering rather than to condemn an entire race or nationality." Kurtis R. Bray, email message to author, January 27, 2016.
9. Ashton, "Spirit of Love," 174.
10. Ashton, 176. This article in the *Instructor*, then an important publication of the Church, was published in April 1947, a time when the hateful emotions of the war toward the Japanese were still raw; it was a time when healing was needed. It was likely not coincidental that Hansen's story was selected to be featured at that time.
11. Kimball, *Miracle of Forgiveness*, 287–89.
12. Nelle Zundel was likely referring to the October 1991 general women's meeting where Sister Okazaki gave a talk entitled "Rejoice in Every Good Thing." Chieko N. Okazaki, "Rejoice in Every Good Thing," *Ensign*, November 1991.
13. Zundel, "Problem Solved," 2. Rachel, George and Ruby's fifth child, was born on March 15, 1922, but died shortly after birth. When Nelle wrote this, all her siblings except Bobby and Rachel were still living.

ACKNOWLEDGMENTS

Writing a book is not an easy thing to do, and this book was possible only with the help of a lot of different people. I am especially grateful to all who provided personal histories, memoirs, and other materials about these POWs. These include my cousins Dorothy Furniss, Ivan Brown Zundel, and Robin Brown for materials about Bobby Brown and my cousins Charles Baclawski, Paul Baclawski, and Robert Baclawski for information about Arthur Baclawski.

Marilyn Springgay not only provided a wealth of information about her father, Robert G. Davey, but she is also a talented writer and provided many helpful comments, suggestions, and corrections on draft manuscripts. Similarly, I appreciate the following for the personal history materials and information that were key to this book and for their comments and suggestions: Richard Patterson (James Patterson); Thomas M. Fairbanks (Nels Hansen); Kurt Bray and Heidi Campbell (Rex Bray); Kindall Ingleby and Marianne Loose (Orland Hamblin); Vauna Marie Kelley and Bonnie Goodliffe (Charles Goodliffe); Cristy Crawford, Crystal Grover, and Suzanne Julian (Ernest Reynolds Parry); Jacob Stewart (Franklin East); Cody Christensen (A. C. Christensen); and Dennis Autry (Carl D. Rohlfing).

I am also grateful for the efforts of Lieutenant Colonel Gregory D. Hammond and Alisa Hyer Hammond (his wife and my daughter) for their diligent efforts in securing the military records of Bobby Brown and for their review and comments on the book.

David L. Clark was a personal friend of my grandmother Ruby Spilsbury Brown and coauthored the *BYU Studies* article. His work in researching and recording the history of the Latter-day Saint POWs in Davao was both the springboard and foundation research for this book. In addition, he graciously reviewed the manuscript and provided important comments and suggestions, which were greatly appreciated.

I also have had the good fortune to receive superb substantive and editorial critiques from each of the following who carefully reviewed earlier versions of the manuscript: Lee Benson, Sydnee Hyer, James Wallmann, Gary Shumway, Ruby Lewis, Chelsea Jackson and Heidi Brockbank. I am grateful to Scott C. Esplin, Joany O. Pinegar, Cara L. P. Nickels, Brent Nordgren, and Carmen Cole of the Religious Studies Center at Brigham Young University for their encouragement and work in the publication of this book and, in particular, to the lead editor, Devan Jensen, for his skillful and meticulous editing.

Moreover, I am indebted to all the veterans, historians, families, and friends who through books, articles, and websites have recorded the experiences of the Pacific POWs and who have dedicated many hours in analyzing, organizing, and cataloging military records pertaining to these POWs. They have provided a great service to our country and to the friends and families of these POWs, and they have done much to assure that the service and sacrifice of each POW are not forgotten.

Lastly and most importantly, I thank my wife, Evie, for her help and support. She is an avid reader and first introduced to me two nonfiction books about POWs in the Philippines; together with the *BYU Studies* article, those books triggered my interest in the subject. As a careful reader, she also has a good eye for good and bad writing and carefully read draft manuscripts, pointing out much of the latter. It is not always easy being married to someone working on a book. I am grateful for her patience.

Michael H. Hyer

BIBLIOGRAPHY

PUBLISHED WORKS

"Answer Japan by Buying War Bonds, El Pasoans Urged." *El Paso Herald-Post*, January 28, 1944 (accessible in archives of Ancestry.com).

Arrington, Leonard J. *The Great Basin Kingdom: Economic History of the Latter-day Saints, 1830–1900*. Lincoln: University of Nebraska Press, 1966.

Arrington, Leonard J., "The Price of Prejudice." Faculty Honor Lectures, paper 23, 1962. https://digitalcommons.usu.edu/honor_lectures/23.

Ashton, Wendell J. "A Spirit of Love." *Instructor*, April 1947, 174–76.

Ballard, M. Russell. "The Vision of the Redemption of the Dead." *Ensign*, October 2018.

Benson, Lee. "About Utah: World War II Hero Harold Poole Showed U.S. How to Live." *Deseret News*, March 14, 2010.

Bolitho, Hayes. "The Hayes Bolitho Japanese Story, Parts 1–6," *Hawkins (Texas) Holly Lake Gazette*, a biweekly online newspaper, September 26, 2009–February 13, 2010, http://www.hlrgazette.com/2009-articles/85-september-26-2009/785-local-ww-ii-herojapanese-pow-1-of-6.html.

Burton, John. *Fortnight of Infamy: The Collapse of Allied Airpower West of Pearl Harbor.* Annapolis: Naval Institute Press, 2006, Google e-book.

Call, Lowell Eliason. "Latter-day Saint Servicemen in the Philippine Islands: A Historical Study of their Religious Activities and Influences Resulting in the official Organization of The Church of Jesus Christ of Latter-day Saints in the Philippines." Master's thesis, Brigham Young University, Provo, Utah, 1955. http://scholarsarchive.byu.edu/etd/4579/.

Cave, Dorothy. *Beyond Courage: One Regiment Against Japan, 1941–1945,* 2006 ed. Santa Fe, NM: Sunstone Press, 2006.

Center for Research, Allied POWS under Japanese. Roster. "Korea (Chosen) POW Camp: Jinsen 'Inchon.'" http://mansell.com/pow_resources/camplists/other/korea-main.html.

Center for Research, Allied POWS under Japanese. "Nagoya 11B POW Camp American (48 men) roster." http://www.mansell.com/pow_resources/camplists/Nagoya/nag_11_nihon_soda_iwase/nag_11_yanks.html.

Center for Research, Allied POWS under Japanese. "Nagoya POW Camp No 11 (Iwase) Nihon Soda SCAP Investigation Report, 29 January 1946." http://www.mansell.com/pow_resources/camplists/Nagoya/nag_11_nihon_soda_iwase/nag_11_scap_investigation.html.

Center for Research, Allied POWS under Japanese. "Nagoya #5-B Yokkaichi (formerly Osaka #17)" (main). http://www.mansell.com/pow_resources/camplists/Nagoya/nag_5_yokkaichi/nag_05_yokkaichi_main.html.

Center for Research, Allied POWS under Japanese. "Pacific POW Roster." http://www.mansell.com/pow_resources/pacific_pow_roster.html.

Center for Research, Allied POWS under Japanese. "Yokkaichi #5_b Nagoya Area."http://www.mansell.com/pow_resources/camplists/Nagoya/nag_5_yokkaichi/nag_05_yanks.html.

Christensen, Allen C. (as told to Renee Homer). "Two Pieces of Paper Saved Me," *Ensign,* February 1991.

BIBLIOGRAPHY

Christensen, Allen C. "The Pacific Theater." In *Saints at War: Experiences of Latter-day Saints in World War II*, edited by Robert G. Freeman and Dennis A. Wright, 300–301. American Fork, UT: Covenant Communications, 2001.

Christensen, Allen C. "Patriarchal and Priesthood Blessings." In *Saints at War: Inspiring Stories of Courage and Valor*, edited by Robert G. Freeman, 252–53. Springville, UT: Cedar Fort, 2013.

Christensen, Doris Farnsworth. Obituary, *Standard-Examiner* (Ogden, UT), March 16, 2013, 4A.

Clark, David L., and Bart J. Kowallis. "The Fate of the Davao Penal Colony #502 'Branch' of the LDS Church, 1944." *BYU Studies* 50, no. 4 (2011): 109–35.

Columbia University, Asia for Educators. "Japan's Quest for Power and WWII in Asia." 2009. http://afe.easia.columbia.edu/special/japan_1900_power.htm.

Colvard, Patrick B. "Obituary." http://obit.funeralchoices.com/obitdisplay.html?task=Print&id=1331007.

Davey, Robert G. Letters to family, November–December 1944, published in "Faith Sustains Interned Mormon Captain." *Deseret News*, March 24, 1945.

Davey, Charles Edmund. "Obituary." *Salt Lake Tribune*, September 1, 1941. Also accessible at familysearch.org under documents page for Charles Edmund Davey (KWCH-BQC).

Daws, Gavan. *Prisoners of the Japanese: POWs of World War II in the Pacific*. New York City: William Morrow and Company, 1994.

Dielman, Gary. "The WWII Sinking of the 'Shinyo Maru.'" 2015. Accessible at Baker County Library District, https://www.bakerlib.org/photo-archive/dielman-local-history-files.html.

Dyes, William E. *The Dyess Story: The Eye-Witness Account of the Death March from Bataan, Japanese Prison Camps and Escape*. New York City: G. P. Putnam's Sons, 1944.

Elsmore, Ray T. "Famed Aviator, Native Utahn, Dies on Coast." *Deseret News*, February 19, 1957, B-9, film #0164622.

Erickson, James W. "*Oryoku Maru* Roster. West-Point.Org. http://www.west-point.org/family/japanese-pow/Erickson_OM.htm.

Freeman, Robert C. *Saints at War: Inspiring Stories of Courage and Valor*. Springville, UT: Cedar Fort, 2013.

Freeman, Robert C., and Dennis A. Wright. *Saints at War: Experiences of Latter-day Saints in World War II*. American Fork, UT: Covenant Communications, 2001.

Garner, William T. *Unwavering Valor: A POW's Account of the Bataan Death March*, 2014 ed. Springville, UT: Plain Sight Publishing, 2014. Google e-book.

Gladwin, Lee A. "American POWs on Japanese Ships Take a Voyage into Hell." *Prologue Magazine* 35, no. 4 (Winter 2003). The U.S. National Archives and Records Administration. http://www.archives.gov/publications/prologue/2003/winter/hell-ships-1.html.

Goodliffe, Charles LaFount. "Obituary," *Standard Examiner*, March 17, 2012.

Heimbuch, Raymond C. *I'm One of the Lucky Ones: I Came Home Alive*. Crete, NE: Dageforde Printing, 2003.

Hillenbrand, Laura. *Unbroken: A World War II Story of Survival, Resilience, and Redemption*. New York City: Random House, 2010.

Hinchman, B. L., and Robert W. Wood, editors. *The Japan Christian Yearbook: A Survey of the Japan Christian Movement in Japan through 1952*. Tokyo: The Christian Literature Society of Japan, 1953. A copy of the relevant excerpt from this book is also available at familysearch.org under the stories section of the page for Peter Nelsen Hansen (KW86-JCJ).

Holmes, Linda Goetz. *Unjust Enrichment: How Japan's Companies Built Postwar Fortunes Using American POWs*. Lanham, MD: Stackpole Books, 2001.

Holmes, W. J. *Double-Edged Secrets: U.S. Naval Intelligence Operations in the Pacific during World War II*. Annapolis, MD: United States Naval Institute, 1979.

Hymns of The Church of Jesus Christ of Latter-day Saints. Salt Lake City: The Church of Jesus Christ of Latter-day Saints, 1985.

Jacobsen, Gene S. *We Refused to Die: My Time as a Prisoner of War in Bataan and Japan, 1942–1945*. Salt Lake City: University of Utah Press, 2004.

Julian, Suzanne. "Led by the Spirit." BYU devotional address, February 11, 2014. https://speeches.byu.edu/talks/suzanne-julian_led-spirit/.

Kimball, Spencer W. *The Miracle of Forgiveness*. Salt Lake City: Deseret Book, 1969.

Komatsu, Keiichiro. *Origins of the Pacific War and the Importance of "Magic."* New York City: St. Martin's Press, 1999.

Lawton, Manny. *Some Survived: An Eyewitness Account of the Bataan Death March and the Men Who Lived through It*. Chapel Hill, NC: Algonquin Books of Chapel Hill, 1984.

"LDS Group in Jap Prison Described." *Deseret News*, January 20, 1945.

Lewin, Ronald. *The American Magic: Codes, Ciphers and the Defeat of Japan*. New York City: Farrar, Straus and Giroux, 1982.

Lukacs, John D. *Escape from Davao: The Forgotten Story of the Most Daring Prison Break of the Pacific War*. New York City: Simon & Schuster, 2010.

McCracken, Alan. *Very Soon Now, Joe*. New York City: Hobson Book Press, 1947.

Mellnik, Stephen M. *Philippines War Diary, 1939–1945*, revised ed. New York City: Van Nostrand Reinhold Co., 1969.

Mellnik, Stephen M. "The Life and Death of the 200th Coast Artillery (AA)." *Coast Artillery Journal*, March–April 1947. http://www.angelfire.com/nm/bcmfofnm/history/mellnik_history.html.

Michno, Gregory F. *Death on the Hellships: Prisoners at Sea in the Pacific War*. Annapolis, MD: Naval Institute Press, 2001.

Morton, Louis. *The United States Army in WWII / The War in the Pacific / The Fall of the Philippines*, commemorative ed. Harrisburg, PA: National Historical Society, 1992.

Nordin, Carl S. *We Were Next to Nothing: An American POW's Account of Japanese Prison of War Camps and Deliverance in World War II*. Jefferson, NC: McFarland and Company, 1997.

Nuttall, James Arle. "Kamas Doctor Dies at 33 of Heart Ills." *Salt Lake Tribune*, December 25, 1952.

Okazaki, Chieko N. "Rejoice in Every Good Thing." *Ensign*, November 1991.

Parkinson, James W., and Lee Benson. *Soldier Slaves*. Annapolis, MD: Naval Institute Press, 2006.

Pearson, Judith L. *Belly of the Beast: A POW's Inspiring True Story of Faith, Courage, and Survival Aboard the Infamous WWII Japanese Hell Ship "Oryoku Maru."* New York City: New American Library, 2001.

Richmond, Clint. *Fetch the Devil: The Sierra Diablo Murders and Nazi Espionage in America*. Lebanon, NH: ForeEdge, imprint of University Press of New England, 2014.

Shively, John C. *Profiles in Survival: The Experiences of American POWs in the Philippines during World War II*. Indianapolis: Indiana Historical Society Press, 2012.

Sides, Hampton. *Ghost Soldiers: The Forgotten Epic Story of World War II's Most Dramatic Mission*. New York City: Doubleday/Random House, 2001.

Sneddon, Murray M. *Zero Ward: A Survivor's Nightmare*. San Jose, CA: Writers Club Press, 2000.

"Story of Bataan Horrors Revealed: Japs Torture, Starve, Murder Americans." *El Paso Herald-Post*, January 28, 1944. Accessible in archives of Ancestry.com.

"Three Utahans Missing in Army Action." *Salt Lake Tribune*, May 29, 1942.

Toland, John, *The Rising Sun: The Decline and Fall of the Japanese Empire, 1936–1945*. New York City: Random House, *1970*.

Top, Brent L. "What Is This Thing That Men Call Death? Latter-day Saint Teachings about the Spirit World." BYU Campus Education Week address, August 18, 2010.

United States Army. *A Brief History of the U.S. Army in World War II*. Washington, DC: Center of Military History, 1992.

U.S. Department of State, Office of Historian. "Milestones: 1899–1913, The Philippine-American War, 1899–1902. https://history.state.gov/milestones/1899-1913/war.

U.S. Department of State, Office of Historian. "Milestones: 1937–1945, Japan, China, the United States and the Road to Pearl Harbor, 1937–41. https://history.state.gov/milestones/1937-1945/pearl-harbor.

West-Point.org. "Hell Ship Information and Photographs." Updated January 17, 2005. http://www.west-point.org/family/japanese-pow/photos.htm.

West-Point.org. "Taikoku Maru Roster." Revised January 16, 2015. http://www.west-point.org/family/japanese-pow/TaikokuMaru/Taikoku-Index.htm.

West-Point.org. "Roster of Allied Prisoners of War Believed Aboard *Shinyo Maru* when Torpedoed and Sunk 7 September 1944." http://www.west-point.org/family/japanese-pow/ShinyoMaruRosterJPW.html.

Whitcomb, Edgar. "Introduction." *Profiles in Survival: The Experiences of American POWs in the Philippines during World War II*, by John C. Shively, 1–9. Indianapolis: Indiana Historical Society Press, 2012.

Whitney, Clarence B. "Graveside Service Announcement for Major Chauncey B. Whitney." *Salt Lake Telegram*, July 18, 1949.

Wilson, Ralf T. "Obituary." *Post Register* (Idaho Falls, ID), March 24, 2009.

Wilson, Ralf T. "Prisoners of War." In *Courage in a Season of War: Latter-day Saints Experience World War II*, edited by Paul H. Kelly and Lin H. Johnson, 322–28. Privately published, 2002.

MILITARY RECORDS

Army of the United States. "Oath of Office, (Temporary)," of George Robin Brown, January 20, 1942, National Archives and Records Administration, 1 Archives Drive, St. Louis, MO 63138 (hereinafter, "NARA Records").

Casualty Report, Form 52(b). Medical Department, U.S. Army, George, R. Brown 0-890150, January 27, 1942, NARA Records.

Clinical Record, Brief, Form 55a. Medical Department, U.S. Army, Bataan General Hospital, TWC, on George R. Brown 0-890150, NARA Records.

Enlistment Record, National Guard of New Mexico. George Robin Brown, December 19, 1940, Physical Examination at Place of Enlistment, NARA Records.

McBride, Allan C., Brigadier General, GSC, Chief of Staff, Headquarters, Philippine Department in the Field, United States Army, Special Orders No. 19, Extract, Paragraph 9, January 20, 1942, NARA Records.

National Guard of New Mexico. Enlistment Record of George Robin Brown, Serial Number 20,842,469, December 19, 1940, NARA Records.

Official Statement of Military Service and Death of George R. Brown, 0 890 150 by Major General Kenneth G. Wickham, The Adjutant General, NARA Records.

Report of Decorations Board. War Department, May 21, 1946, NARA Records.

USS *Paddle* (SS263). Report of Fifth War Patrol, B. H. Nowell, Lt.-Cdr. USN, September 7, 1944, 7–10.

Veterans Administration. "Problem Oriented Initial Assessment and Plan" for Franklin T. East, by Sam Atterbury, Social Worker, Veterans Administration Medical Clinic, Tucson, Arizona, April 18, 1985.

Wickham, Kenneth G., Major General, United States Army, The Adjutant General. Official Statement of Military Service and Death of George R. Brown, 0 890 150, NARA Records.

FAMILY HISTORY MANUSCRIPTS AND INTERVIEWS

Baclawski, Arthur M. "Personal History." Unpublished manuscript in family records, a copy of which was provided to author by Charles Baclawski.

BIBLIOGRAPHY

Bray, Rex D. "War Memories, 1941–1945." Unpublished manuscript, 1998.

Brown, Ruby S. "Personal History of Ruby Spilsbury Brown." Undated and unpublished personal history manuscript in possession of author.

Brown, Ruby S. "This Is a Very Sacred Story." Ruby S. Brown Collection, Church History Library, Vol. 4, Item H.4,. Salt Lake City: The Church of Jesus Christ of Latter-day Saints, December 16, 1953.

Brown, Ruby S., and Nelle B. Zundel. "George Robin Brown . . . His Story." Unpublished manuscript, July 27, 1977.

Christensen, Allen C., "My Life Story." Unpublished private manuscript, April 1961, copy provided to author by Cody Christensen.

Davey, Robert Gray. "Last Talk." Fireside talk given by Davey after the war, transcript provided to author by Marilyn Springgay.

East, Franklin T. "Army Life of Franklin T. East." Unpublished manuscript, November–December 1977.

Goodliffe, Charles LaFount. "Interview with Charles Goodliffe by Sam Orwin." Undated copy of interview transcript provided to author by Bonnie Goodliffe.

Goodliffe, Charles LaFount. "Recollections of Charles LaFount Goodliffe." Transcript of interview by David Morrell with Charles Goodliffe, October 23, 2003. Unpublished copy of transcript provided to author by Bonnie Goodliffe.

Hamblin, Orland K. "My Experience in the Service and as a Prisoner of War of the Japanese." Unpublished manuscript, June 1956.

Hyer, Fern Brown. "Classy Grandmas All Come from Chupe." Unpublished manuscript in possession of author.

Patterson, James. "Saving the Legacy: An Oral History of Utah's World War II Veterans." Interview by Luke Perry, Tape No. SL-283 & 284. Salt Lake City: Fort Douglas Museum and Marriott Library, Special Collections Department, University of Utah, August 15, 2001

Rohlfing, Carl Dennis. "Carl Dennis Rohlfing." Undated manuscript provided to author by Dennis Autry.

Springgay, Marilyn Beth Davey. "Lt. Col. Robert Gray Davey, 2 May 1915–19 July 1968." Unfinished life history of Davey written by his daughter, who provided a copy to author.

Wilson, Ralf T. "A POW Spiritual Experience." Talk given at a prayer meeting in the Idaho Falls Idaho Temple, November 13, 1998.

Zundel, Nelle B. "A Problem Solved." Unpublished manuscript, copy in possession of author, April 2, 1992.

Zundel, Nelle B. "George Robin 'Bobby' Brown." In *The Life and Posterity of Alma Platte Spilsbury*, compiled by Viva Skousen Brown, 297–98. Provo, UT: Privately published, 1983.

Zundel, Nelle B. "Story of the Family of George Andrew and Ruby Vilate Spilsbury Brown." Unpublished manuscript prepared for Brown family reunion, June 1961.

INDEX

A

afterlife, 233, 243n4
air drops, 215–16
Alder, Dwayne W., 119, 181, 190, 198
Allied bombing raids, 184–85, 208–9, 246
Allred, William Murle, 7, 16n11
American flag, 129–30, 215
Angel Island, 12, 17n24
anti-Japanese sentiment, 57–58, 142–44, 144n19, 245–48, 249n8
Arrington, Leonard J., 2, 143

B

Baclawski, Arthur M., 8, 150, 240
Baclawski, Jane Brown, 240
Baldonado, Jose M. (Pepe), 81
Baldonado, Juan T., 81
Bataan Death March, 63–67, 68n15, 140–42, 223
Bataan Peninsula
    abandonment of soldiers on, 46–48
    immediate threats on, 45–46
    retreat to, 37–39
    surrender of, 54–55, 57–61
beriberi, 110–11, 115n16, 131, 148n8, 224
Bilibid Prison, 158–59, 182–86, 198
Bloomfield, Don Charles, 7, 16n11
Bolitho, Hayes, 33n9, 168n5
Bramley, Clarence, 135–36, 215
Bray, Rex
    assignment at Del Monte Airfield, 84
    escapes work transfer, 147
    feelings of, toward Japanese, 249n8
    and Japanese invasion of Mindanao, 86
    on Latter-day Saint meetings at Dapecol, 122
    on MacArthur, 48
    postwar life of, 220
    as POW in Japan, 202, 204, 206
    surrender of, 59
Brazil Maru, 195–98
Briggs Field, 100–101

INDEX

Brown, Fern, 99
Brown, George, 46, 99, 104, 142, 143–44, 176–77, 235–39, 241–42, 247–48
Brown, George Robin (Bobby)
    assigned to 515th Coast Artillery, 37
    attends services in San Francisco, 10
    background of, 2, 3
    cares for ailing POW, 122
    death of, 175, 176–77, 179n18, 235–37, 248
    departure of, 9
    drives to Camp O'Donnell, 72n2
    enlistment of, 6–7
    experience as POW, 80–81
    given battlefield commission, 42
    Hansen on meeting, 123n3
    and Latter-day Saint meetings at Dapecol, 118, 120, 124–25n10, 125n12
    on Manila, 29
    miracles experienced by, 69–70
    posthumous recognition for, 238–39, 244n19
    procures food at Dapecol, 112
    promotion of, 8–9
    proxy endowment of, 237–38
    religious background of, 122–23
    reported as POW, 101–3
    separated from other Latter-day Saint POWs, 147
    visitors to family of, 239–40
    visits parents following death, 241–42
Brown, Jane, 240
Brown, Ruby, 3, 6, 72n2, 99, 101, 142, 143–44, 235–42, 247–48
Brown, Rulon, 100–101, 105n6
Bushido (Way of the Warrior), 59

C

Cabanatuan, 76, 80–81, 96, 107, 117–18, 135–36, 138n2, 181–82
Cabcaben Airfield, 43, 47, 51–55
Calumpit, 38–39
Camp Casisang, 91–95
Camp O'Donnell, 69–72, 72n2, 75–77, 135
Canadian Inventor (*Mati Mati Maru*), 159–61, 162n14, 162n21
care packages, 130–31, 133n12
censorship, 101
Christensen, Allen C. "Ace"
    assignment at Del Monte Airfield, 84
    on Camp Casisang, 92, 93
    on feelings toward Japanese, 246
    on food air drops, 215
    on hopelessness, 77–78
    on malnutrition, 111
    on mindset of POWs, 114
    postwar life of, 220, 225–26
    as POW in Japan, 202–3, 207, 209n1
    reunites with family, 217
Christensen, Doris Farnsworth, 225, 226
Christmas, 127–32, 207
Church meetings, held at Dapecol, 117–23, 124n7
cigarettes, 184
Civil Liberties Act (1988), 144n19
Clark Field, 28, 31, 35–37, 84
clothing, 112, 202
colonial order, 21–22
Colvard, George T., 175, 179n18
Corregidor, 63, 88–89
Culo River, 38–39

D

Davao Penal Colony (Dapecol)
  backgrounds of POWs at, 1–3
  Christmas at, 127–32
  closing of, 155, 156
  conditions at, 109–14, 139–40
  Davey transferred to, xiii–xiv
  escaped POWs report on, 139–40
  escape from, 136–38
  Fifth Air Base Squadron transferred to, 95–96
  Latter-day Saint meetings held in, 117–23, 124n7
  Latter-day Saint POWs at, xv
  plan to save POWs at, 145–46
  POWs moved from, 146–47
  prisoners arrive at, 108–9
  prisoners transported to, 107–8
  surviving Latter-day Saint POWs from, 217–18
Davey, Hazel, 103, 104
Davey, Lee, 104
Davey, Ralph, 104
Davey, Robert G.
  aboard *Brazil Maru*, 198–99
  aboard *Oryoku Maru*, 189–90, 191–92, 193–94
  on American flag at Dapecol, 129
  avoids attack on *Enoura Maru*, 196–97
  background of, 1–2, 15
  on Bataan Death March, 65
  contracts beriberi, 111
  on despair, 77, 78–79
  enlistment of, 6, 15
  on feelings toward Japanese, 246
  on food air drops, 215
  heeds prompting, 42
  horrors faced by, 80
  illness of, 131, 133n13, 148n8

  and Japanese attack on Philippines, 41–42
  and Japanese surrender, 214
  and Latter-day Saint meetings at Dapecol, 118
  letters from Bilibid, 185–86, 198
  miraculously survives death march, 71–72
  postwar life of, 221–23
  as POW in Japan, 202, 204, 207
  reported as POW, 103–4
  revelation received by, 79–80, 222
  souvenirs of, 215
  on tobacco, 184
  transferred to Bilibid Prison, 182–83
  transferred to Cabanatuan, 181–82
  transferred to Davao Penal Colony, xiii–xiv
  visits Brown family, 239–40
Del Monte Airfield, 31–33, 83–89
despair, 77–79
Dielman, Gary, 124n9
disease, 45, 71–72, 76, 110–11, 115n16, 131, 148n8, 150–51, 198, 219, 224
draft, 5–15
dream, of Robert G. Davey, 79–80, 222
Dunkley, Woodrow, 84
Dyess, William Edwin, 61, 82n10, 140, 142
dysentery, 76, 150–51, 198

E

East, Franklin
  befriended by Ernest Parry, 234
  on Cabanatuan, 77
  on cruelty of Japanese guards, 61

East, Franklin (*continued*)
  experiences of, in Hawaii, 13–14
  give Christmas talk in POW camp, 207
  on Manila, 29
  miraculously saved from bombing, 70–71
  mission served by, 176
  postwar life of, 220, 226–27
Eiyo Maru, 174
Elsmore, Ray, 14, 18n36
endowment, 237–38, 244n18
Enoura Maru, 195–97
Erie Maru, 107
escape, 135–38, 139–40, 156–57
eternal families, doctrine on, 233

F

family, doctrine on eternal, 233
Fifth Air Base Squadron of the Army Air Corps, 12–14
  at Camp Casisang, 92–95
  at Davao Penal Colony, 95–96
  at Del Monte Airfield, 83–89
  Latter-day Saint air corpsmen in, 17–18n29
  Latter-day Saint meetings held by, 117–18
  on Mindanao, 31–32
  surrender of, 91–92
515th Coast Artillery, 37, 38–39, 43, 47, 51
flight training accidents, 100–101, 105n6
food, 45–46, 81, 84, 93–94, 110–12, 115n16, 131, 183–84, 203, 215–16
forgiveness, 245–48
Fort Stotsenburg, 28

G

Goodliffe, Charles L.
  on entertainment in Dapecol, 132n2
  on Japanese surrender, 214
  and Latter-day Saint meetings at Dapecol, 120
  obtains food, 84, 92
  as POW in Japan, 202, 204, 206
  on stick guards, 205
  Unto the Hills owned by, 120, 125n15
Graef, Calvin, 243n14
Gripsholm, 140

H

Hall, William E., 124n9
Hamblin, Don Carlos, 29–30
Hamblin, Jacob, 2
Hamblin, Orland K.
  on Allied bombing raid, 209
  on American flag at Dapecol, 129
  on arriving in Philippines, 28
  background of, 2
  on Bataan Death March, 65, 66
  on Bilibid Prison, 158
  on Camp O'Donnell, 76–77
  on *Canadian Inventor*, 160–61, 162n21
  on closing of Dapecol, 155
  death of father of, 29–30
  defends Cabcaben Airfield, 52–53
  drafting of, 7
  on feelings toward Japanese, 246
  on food air drops, 215–16
  on Japanese surrender, 214
  and Latter-day Saint meetings at Dapecol, 117, 118, 121
  on liberation, 216, 217
  on MacArthur, 48

INDEX

mission served by, 176
postwar life of, 220, 223–24
as POW in Japan, 209n1
prays for strength, 70
on punishment for escape attempts, 138n2
restrained from volunteering for work detail, 147
on *Yashu Maru*, 157
Hansen, James, 4n1
Hansen, Peder Niels, 1, 4n1
Hansen, Peter Nelsen (Nels), 224
background of, 3
on *Canadian Inventor*, 160–61, 162n21
contracts beriberi, 111
and Del Monte Sunday School, 32–33
experiences of, in Hawaii, 14
on feelings toward Japanese, 246–47
illness of, 148n8
and Latter-day Saint meetings at POW camps, 117, 119–20, 123n2
on meeting Brown, 123n3
missions served by, 176
postwar life of, 220, 246–47
as POW in Japan, 205
visits Brown family, 240
hatred, xv, 57–58, 142–44, 144n19, 245–48
Hawaii, 13–14
Heimbuch, Raymond C., 33n9, 162n21
hell ships. See *marus*
Hippler, Theodore, 32, 124n8
Holy Ghost, heeded by Davey, 42
Homer, John L., 238
Homma, Masuharu, 54, 64, 67n4, 224
hopelessness, 77–79

Hornet, 197
Hugh L. Scott, 12
hymns, 120, 242

I

Immigration Act (1924), 57

J

Jacobs, Dorothy Elizabeth, 79–80, 221–22
Jacobsen, Gene, 29, 33n5, 48, 58–59
Japan and Japanese
Allied bombings of, 208–9
attack on, from Philippines, 35–36
attacks Cabcaben Airfield, 43
attacks Clark Field, 35–37
attacks Philippines, 41–42
coding systems for secret communications of, 153n12
Fifth Air Base Squadron surrenders to, 91–92
hatred of, 57–58, 142–44, 144n19, 245–48, 249n8
invades Mindanao, 86–87
liberation of POWs in, 213–18
oil embargo on, 22–23
POW camps in, 201–9
POWs annihilated by, 167, 168n7, 209
POWs transported to, 149–51, 185–86, 189–98
reinforces hold in Philippines, 51
surrenders to Allies, 213–14
surrender to, 54–55, 57–61, 62n10
US intercepts radio communications of, 151–52, 153n12
and War Plan Orange, 23–26
Japanese Troop Ship #760, 95
Julian, Suzanne, 234

INDEX

K

Keeler, John A. (Jack), 6–7, 37, 70, 244n18
King, Edward, 53–55, 88

L

Larsen, Kenneth, 159
Lasang, 95–96, 165–68
Lawton, Manny, 184
Layac Junction, 38–39, 40n10
Lee, Harold B., 223
Luzon, 31

M

MacArthur, Douglas, 24, 31, 40n14, 47, 48, 53, 197
Maeda, Kazuo, 108–9, 113, 127, 137
malaria, 45, 71–72
Malaybalay, 91–95
malnutrition, 76, 80, 110–12, 115n16, 131, 148n8, 183–84, 203, 216
Manila. *See also* Bilibid Prison
    Allied bombing of, 184–85, 190, 193–94
    antiaircraft defense in, 37
    excursions into, 29
    liberated POWs pass through, 216
    retreat from, 37–38
Manila Bay, geography of, 63
Maramag Forest, 85–86
marus, 150–52
    Brazil Maru, 195–98
    Canadian Inventor (*Mati Mati Maru*), 159–61, 162n14, 162n21
    Eiyo Maru, 174
    Enoura Maru, 195–97
    Erie Maru, 107
    Nissyo Maru, 159
    Noto Maru, 159
    Oryoku Maru, 189–94
    Shinyo Maru, 171–77, 178n11, 216, 231–32, 235, 248
    Singoto Maru, 157–58
    Tateishi Maru, 169–71
    Yashu Maru, 155–57
Mellnik, Stephen, 145–46
Mindanao, 31–32, 83, 86–87. *See also* Del Monte Airfield
miracles, 69–72
monkeys, eating, 45–46
Montgomery, William A., 198
Moros, 84, 90n4
"My Service Flag" (Parry), 234

N

Nagoya Branch #5 Yokkaichi POW camp, 161, 163n24, 201–2
Nagoya Branch Camp #11, 202
natural disasters, 208
news media, 101, 140–44
Nichols Field, 216
Nissyo Maru, 159
Nordin, Carl, 33n9, 162n14
Noto Maru, 159
Nuttall, James Arlo, 82n4

O

oil embargo, 22–23
Okazaki, Chieko, 248
Operation Magic, 152, 192
Oryoku Maru, 189–94

P

Paddle, 172–74, 178n11
Pampanga River, 38–39
Parry, Ernest R., 13–14, 122, 124–25n10, 147, 233–34

INDEX

Parry, Georgiana R., 234
Patterson, James
   contracts schistosomiasis, 110
   enlistment of, 5
   escapes work transfer, 147
   on Japanese surrender, 214
   on MacArthur's departure, 53
   participates in sacrament meeting, 132n3
   postwar life of, 220, 227–28
   warned about murder of POWs, 209
   watch stolen by soldier, 92
Pearl Harbor, 35
Peck, Harry M., 37, 80
Philippines
   abandonment of soldiers in, 46–48
   attack on Japan from, 35–36
   colonial order in, 21–22
   criticism over failures in, 140
   evacuation of POWs from, 149–51, 155–61, 169–77, 185–86, 189–98
   Filipino resistance on, 145
   Japanese attack on, 41–42
   Japan reinforces hold in, 51
   news revealing mistreatment of POWs in, 140–44
   and oil embargo on Japan, 22–23
   soldiers arrive in, 27–29
   soldiers' lives in, 29
   strategic position of, 24–26
   Wainwright assumes command of, 53–54
polished rice, 110–11
postcards home, 131–32
post-traumatic stress disorder (PTSD), 219–21, 226, 227
prayer
   comfort through, 91–92
   for strength, 70
President Coolidge, 11–12

press coverage, 101, 140–44
prisoners of war (POWs)
   backgrounds of, 1–3
   deceased, 231–42
   drafting and enlistment of, 5–15
   escape of, 135–38, 139–40
   evacuated from Philippines, 64, 149–51, 155–61, 169–77, 185–86, 189–98
   faith and endurance of, xiv–xv
   hatred as survival mechanism for, 245
   held in Japan, 201–9
   interpersonal relationships of, 62n12
   Japanese annihilation of, 167, 168n7, 209
   liberation of, 213–18
   lives of families of, 99–104
   memorials to, 232, 243n3
   mindset of, 77–79, 114
   miracles experienced by, 69–72
   news revealing mistreatment of, 140–44
   postwar lives of, 219–29
   religious lives of, xv
prompting, heeded by Davey, 42
PTSD (post-traumatic stress disorder), 219–21, 226, 227
Puerto Princesa Prison Camp, 167
Pulice, Mike, 179n18

R

racism, 57–58, 142–44, 144n19, 245–48, 249n8
Rainbow plan, 46, 48n5
Red Cross packages, 130–31, 133n12
rice, 110–11, 115n13, 115n16
Ricks, Carlyle, 119, 181, 190
Rohlfing, Carl D., 5–6, 87, 129, 216, 220, 228, 246

Roosevelt, Franklin D., 46, 47
Rosenquist, Harold, 146
Rosenvall, Clay, 132n3
Russell, Isaac, 1–2

S

sabotage, 166, 204
sacrament meeting, 129, 132n3
scriptures
    and Latter-day Saint meetings at Dapecol, 120
    rescued by Christensen, 207
    retained by Brown, 69–70
Selective Service Act (1940), 5
Sharp, William F., 87, 88–89
Shinyo Maru, 171–77, 178n11, 216, 231–32, 235, 248
Shoss, Morris L., 119, 121–22, 124–25n10, 125n12
Singoto Maru, 157–58
small miracles, 69–72
Smith, Joseph F., 233
Smurthwaite, Jesse G., 124n9
snakes, 110
Sneddon, Murray, 113, 166–67
Sparks, Russell, 72, 78–79
spirit world, 233, 243n4
stick guards, 205
Stimson, Henry, 47
submarine warfare, 151–52, 153–54n17, 172–74
support groups, 81

T

Taiwan, bombing run on, 35–36
Takao Harbor, 195–97
Tateishi Maru, 169–71
Thomason, R. E., 46, 104
tobacco, 158, 184
torture, 65, 76, 112–13, 205–6. *See also* Bataan Death March; *marus*

Traywick, Colonel, 89
Tsuneyoshi, Captain, 75–76
20th Pursuit Squadron of the Army Air Corps, 18–19n38
200th Coast Artillery Regiment of the New Mexico National Guard, 6–12, 36–39, 47, 51–53

U

United States Army Forces in the Far East (USAFFE), 24
United States Army Infantry, 15

W

Wainwright, Jonathan, 53–54, 88–89
war bonds, 142–43
war effort, in United States, 99–104
War Plan Orange (WPO), 23–26, 37–39
Webb, Joseph R., 119, 181, 190, 198
Whitney, Chauncey B., 85
Wilson, Janet Ross, 229
Wilson, Ralf T., 89, 91–92, 202, 209, 228–29
Wilstead, James, 190
Word of Wisdom, 70, 72–73n5, 78

Y

Yashu Maru, 155–57
Youke, Lieutenant, 113, 118, 137–38

Z

Zero Wards, 76–77
Zundel, Nelle, 3, 72n2, 80, 176, 179n18, 238, 242, 247–48

ABOUT THE AUTHOR

Michael H. Hyer is the author of several articles published in law journals and is the nephew of First Lieutenant George Robin (Bobby) Brown, one of the Latter-day Saint POWs who died in the sinking of the Japanese ship *Shinyo Maru*. He is a corporate attorney and retired vice president and general counsel of the North American arm of one of the world's largest multinational aggregates, cement, and concrete companies. Most recently, he served in the Church's Office of General Counsel as the associate area legal counsel in Lima, Peru. He is a graduate of the J. Reuben Clark Law School and of Brigham Young University with a degree in political science. He resides in Park City, Utah.